Betty Crocker
vegetarian
cooking

WILEY
JOHN WILEY & SONS, INC.

GENERAL MILLS

Editorial Director: Jeff Nowak

Publishing Manager: Christine Gray

Senior Editor: Diane Carlson

Food Editors: Andrea Bidwell and Catherine Swanson

Recipe Development and Testing: Betty Crocker Kitchens

Photography: General Mills Photography Studios and Image Library

Photographer: Val Bourassa, Patrick Kelley

Food Stylists: Carol Grones, Nancy Johnson, Patty Gabbert

JOHN WILEY & SONS, INC.

Publisher: Natalie Chapman

Associate Publisher: Jessica Goodman

Executive Editor: Anne Ficklen

Editorial Assistant: Heather Dabah

Senior Production Editor: Amy Zarkos

Cover Design: Suzanne Sunwoo

Art Director: Tai Blanche

Interior Design and Layout: Holly Wittenberg

Manufacturing Manager: Kevin Watt

Published by John Wiley & Sons, Inc., Hoboken, New Jersey

Published simultaneously in Canada

Library of Congress Cataloging-in-Publication Data:

Crocker, Betty.
  Betty Crocker vegetarian cooking.—3rd ed.
    p. cm.
  Includes index.
  ISBN 978-1-118-14608-8 (pbk); ISBN 978-1-118-19909-1 (ebk); ISBN 978-1-118-19974-9 (ebk); ISBN 978-1-118-19976-3 (ebk)
  1. Vegetarian cooking. 2. Cookbooks. I. Title. II. Title: Vegetarian cooking.
  TX837.C8 2012
  641.5'636—dc23

                    2011048948

Manufactured in the United States of America

10 9 8 7 6 5 4 3 2 1

Cover photos (clockwise): Quinoa and Corn Salad (page 61), Black Bean Sliders (page 39), Bell Pepper Mac and Cheese with Fondue Cheese Sauce (page 132), Pesto, Mozzarella and Tomato Panini (page 165) and Mexican Potato Tacos (page 171)

Dear Friends,

Eating meatless isn't just for vegetarians! More and more people are enjoying meatless meals without committing to a vegetarian lifestyle. And why not? Vegetarian meals are delicious, they're good for you and they can also take the strain off your food budget!

If you're new to the meatless trend, try eating vegetarian once or twice a week. California Black Bean Burgers or Mexican Potato Tacos are easy enough to make any night—and you won't miss the meat! Lasagna Cupcakes or Sweet Potato–Cauliflower Curry are also perfect for weeknights—or great company fare.

Eating vegetarian is easy, with this variety of taste-tempting recipes the entire family will love. You'll also find loads of information—everything you'd want to know about meatless cooking! Vegetarian menus will help you entertain—whether you want a meatless dish or an entirely meatless meal. With recipes this good, your family will be asking you to make them again and again. So go ahead and dig in!

Warmly,
Betty Crocker

Contents

The Icons

quick   Ready to eat in 30 minutes or less

easy   Prep time of 15 minutes or less

lowfat   Main dishes with 10g of fat or less; all other 3g of fat or less

The Everyday Vegetarian

Welcome to the colorful, nutrition-packed, tasty world of vegetarian cooking! There are many reasons to go meatless: whether you're looking for healthier, vegetarian options that increase the amounts of grains, legumes, vegetables and fruits your family eats or you have health, ethical, environmental or economical reasons for being vegetarian—grab a fork. You'll find something for everyone here.

You may be enjoying vegetarian dishes already and don't really think about the fact they're missing the meat. Pasta with marinara sauce, cheese enchiladas and vegetable pizza are all meatless choices that taste great. But that's just for starters. Be prepared for your taste buds to take a flavorful ride, with the yummy recipes in this book.

If you're new at eating meatless, try it one or two days a week. Use protein-rich foods containing beans and legumes, tofu, soy or cheese. You'll find the wide variety of delicious recipes here range from familiar and comforting to flavor-sparked and imaginative combinations. All are easy enough for everyday cooking!

Vegetarians Defined

Many people call themselves vegetarians, yet each can eat very differently. How vegetarians choose to eat is a matter of individual preference, and there are many ways to enjoy a wide variety of meatless meals! Here are some popular types of vegetarianism:

Ovo-Lacto Vegetarian

This diet includes eggs (ovo) and dairy products (lacto), but eliminates meat, poultry, fish and seafood.

DIET INCLUDES: Vegetables, fruits, grains, legumes, nuts, seeds, eggs and dairy products like milk and milk-based foods, and tofu and soy.

DIET DOESN'T INCLUDE: Meat, poultry, fish or seafood. May not eat animal-based broths like beef, chicken, fish or seafood.

Lacto-Vegetarian

This type of vegetarianism is popular for those trying to avoid egg and milk-containing foods. Some people following a subcategory of this diet may also eliminate milk and milk products in addition to eggs.

DIET INCLUDES: Vegetables, fruits, grains, legumes, nuts, seeds and dairy products like milk and milk-based foods, and tofu and soy.

DIET DOESN'T INCLUDE: Eggs, meat, poultry, fish or seafood. May not eat animal-based broths like beef, chicken, fish or seafood.

Vegans

This is the strictest kind of vegetarianism because the diet includes no animal products or by-products. It can be more challenging to get enough iron, calcium, vitamin B_{12} and zinc with this form of vegetarianism.

DIET INCLUDES: Vegetables, fruits, grains, legumes, nuts and seeds, and tofu and soy.

DIET DOESN'T INCLUDE: Meat, poultry, fish, seafood, eggs, dairy products like milk and milk-based foods or foods containing animal products like beef, chicken, fish or seafood broth, lard or gelatin. Vegans may not use animal products or animal by-products like honey, leather, fur, silk, wool, and cosmetics and soaps that contain animal by-products.

Semi-Vegetarian (Also Known as "Flexitarian")

This kind of eating continues to grow in popularity, and is sometimes defined as "vegetarians who occasionally eat meat." It can refer to people who eat meatless meals some of the time but occasionally eat fish, seafood, poultry and meat. Or it may define those who eat fish, seafood and poultry but no red meat. "Meatless Mondays" are an example of this growing trend. Folks choose to enjoy a meatless meal one or two days a week, as a way to cut calories and eat healthier or as a way to save on their food budget. People who eat this way include more grains, legumes, soy and tofu, vegetables and fruits in their diet, which contributes to a healthy lifestyle.

> **DIET INCLUDES: Vegetables, fruits, grains, legumes, nuts, seeds, eggs and dairy products like milk and milk-based foods. May include poultry, fish and seafood but usually limits these foods to occasional use.**

> **DIET DOESN'T INCLUDE: Usually avoid red meat.**

Vegetarian Is Healthy!

What we eat can either lead to a healthier lifestyle or contribute to health problems down the road. Plant-based diets, which emphasize fruits, vegetables, grains, soy, beans, legumes and nuts, are rich in fiber, vitamins and other important nutrients. Embracing a vegetarian way of eating—which can be lower in fat and saturated fat—has been shown to provide health and nutrition benefits.

Research data support that vegetarians are at less risk for the following disorders: high blood pressure, heart disease and Type II (adult-onset) diabetes. Studies also show that some vegetarians have a lower body mass index, a measure of height and weight appropriateness. Some data support a reduced risk of diverticular disease and colon cancer.

A reduced risk of certain diseases may be due to a combination of both lifestyle and the foods we choose to eat. More studies are necessary to determine the true benefits for vegetarians and whether they can translate to a larger population.

The "Meat" of Vegetarian Nutrition

You can get all the nutrients you need while going meatless, if you follow these nutrition guidelines to ensure a healthy vegetarian diet:

Protein

Protein is important for the growth and maintenance of body tissues. You can get enough protein on a vegetarian diet. Eliminating or cutting back significantly on animal protein will decrease protein intake, but vegetarian diets usually meet or even exceed the Recommended Dietary Allowance (RDA) when a variety of foods are consumed daily.

Proteins are made of building blocks called *amino acids*. Some of these amino acids we can make in our bodies. Those we can't produce, called *essential amino acids*, must come from the foods we eat.

Proteins that contain all our essential amino acids, called *complete* or *high-quality proteins*, come from animal sources like meat, eggs, chicken, fish and dairy products. Nonanimal protein sources, like legumes, grains, pastas, soy, cereals, breads, nuts and seeds, are *incomplete* or *lower-quality proteins* because the protein they provide is missing at least one of the essential amino-acid building blocks. But they can be eaten in combination throughout the day to make complete proteins.

THE RECOMMENDED DAILY AMOUNTS OF PROTEIN BY AGE ARE:

Girls 15-18:	Boys 15-18:	Adult Women:	Adult Men:
46 grams	52 grams	46 grams	56 grams

Recent studies confirm that as long as you eat a variety of foods each day, you'll most likely get enough protein to meet your needs. Vegetarians not eating protein from animal sources rely on protein found in combinations of soy, legumes, grains, pastas, cereals, breads, nuts and seeds.

Vitamin B$_{12}$

Vitamin B$_{12}$ is necessary for all body cells to function properly. It occurs naturally only in animal foods but can be found in supplements and foods fortified with vitamin B_{12}. Vegans are the only vegetarians who need to supplement their diets with B_{12}. A B_{12} deficiency can lead to anemia and nerve damage.

Calcium and Vitamin D

Calcium is important for building bones and healthy teeth and vitamin D can help. Teenage girls, and women in general, even nonvegetarians, have difficulty getting enough calcium and vitamin D in their diets.

THE RECOMMENDED DIETARY ALLOWANCES (RDA) OF CALCIUM AND VITAMIN D FOR WOMEN BY AGE ARE:

	Ages 9–18:	19–50:	51–70:
Calcium	1,300 mg	1,000 mg	1,200 mg
Vitamin D	400 IU	400 IU	400 IU

If you take a supplement, follow these guidelines to get the most out of it:

- Limit doses of calcium to 600 milligrams at one time and take it with meals to help with absorption.

- If not taking multivitamins, look for calcium tablets containing vitamin D, which helps with absorption.

Iron

Teenage girls, and women in general, even nonvegetarians, have some difficulty getting enough iron in their diets. The RDA for iron for women ages 19 to 50 is 18 milligrams. Taking an iron supplement is the best way to get the iron you need if you're not eating animal-based foods. Iron supplements, either alone or in a multivitamin, are absorbed more easily when taken with vitamin C, so take them with an orange or orange juice, for example.

Zinc

Some vegetarians don't get enough zinc, which helps repair body cells and is important in energy production. The zinc found in plant foods isn't absorbed by the body as well as zinc from animal foods. Whole grains, legumes, tofu, seeds and nuts provide zinc. Vitamin supplements also are an option.

Vegetarian Kids

Often teens desire the vegetarian lifestyle for ethical or environmental reasons—or to follow what their peers are doing. Fear not! The majority of vegetarian diets are healthy and incorporate the principles of the U.S. Department of Agriculture (USDA) and U.S. Department of Health & Human Services food guidelines that emphasize eating plenty of grains, legumes, vegetables and fruit.

With some minor alterations, a portion of the family meal can be tweaked to meet your vegetarian teen's needs, so that separate meals aren't necessary! For example, if you're making spaghetti and all but one person wants meat in their sauce, take out a portion of the sauce for that person before adding cooking meat or sausage to the remaining sauce. The key to a healthy, successful vegetarian diet is variety.

Encourage your kids to generate ideas for their own recipe creations, and let them shop for the ingredients and make meals for the family. If your kids are very strict about what they eat, they may want to help make their own part of the family meal. Letting that type of initiative and creativity shine through makes the transition to vegetarianism easier for everyone.

Choosing Meatless While Dining Out

Many restaurants are getting on the vegetarian bandwagon by offering a selection of vegetarian options or meatless versions of their dishes. Asian, Indian, Mexican, Middle Eastern and other ethnic restaurants have vegetarian options because these dishes are part of their traditional diet. The appetizer section often offers meatless choices that you can make into a meal by ordering several—think dim sum, meze and tapas! Or combine an appetizer with a few vegetable side dishes.

If there aren't these kinds of offerings, look for choices where the meat in a dish could easily be left out; such as pasta choices or salads. Don't be shy about asking for the meat to be left out of a dish, so that you can stick to your healthy eating plan! Also, if you don't see anything that you can eat, ask your server if he or she can make a suggestion for you.

15 Top Calcium Sources for Vegetarians

FOOD	AMOUNT	CALCIUM (MILLIGRAMS)
Firm tofu (raw) prepared with calcium sulfate	½ cup	430–860
Parmesan cheese (grated)	1 oz	310
Orange juice (calcium-fortified)	1 cup	300–500
Soymilk (low-fat) with added calcium, vitamins A & D	1 cup	300
Romano cheese	1 oz	300
Milk (skim) with vitamins A & D	1 cup	300
Spinach (frozen)	1 cup cooked	290
Turnip greens, frozen	1 cup cooked	250
Yogurt (low-fat)	6 oz	200–500
Mozzarella cheese (part skim)	1 oz	200
Kale, frozen	1 cup cooked	180
Canned pink salmon with bones	3 oz	180
Mustard greens, frozen	1 cup cooked	150
Cottage cheese (1% milk fat)	1 cup	140
Ready-to-eat cereals (calcium-fortified)	1 cup	100–900

10 Top Iron Sources for Vegetarians

FOOD	AMOUNT	IRON (MILLIGRAMS)
Hot wheat farina cereal, original	1 cup cooked	9.0–13.7
Lentils	1 cup cooked	6.5
Ready-to-eat cereals (fortified)	1 cup	4.5–8.1
Lima beans	1 cup cooked	4.4
Navy beans	1 cup cooked	4.3
Kidney beans	1 cup cooked	3.9
Swiss chard	1 cup cooked	3.9
Spinach	1 cup cooked	3.7
Black beans	1 cup cooked	3.6
Firm tofu (raw) prepared with calcium sulfate	½ cup	3.3
Quinoa	1 cup cooked	2.7

Vegetarian Myth Busters

Myth: Going vegetarian means eating weird foods!

FACT: You've probably been eating meatless or vegetarian for a long time but just didn't think of it that way. Take a look at the vegetarian foods most of us eat regularly! Cheese or vegetable pizza, grilled cheese sandwiches, spaghetti with pasta sauce, vegetable omelets, macaroni and cheese, peanut butter and jelly sandwiches, cheese quesadillas, cheese enchiladas and pasta primavera. They all qualify as a kind of vegetarian eating.

Myth: I can't get enough protein if I go meatless.

FACT: Protein can be found in many nonmeat foods including legumes (dry beans and peas), tofu, eggs, nuts and seeds, grains and whole-grain products (such as breads and pastas), milk and milk products. Read more about protein in "The 'Meat' of Vegetarian Nutrition," page 7.

Myth: I have to combine proteins at every meal to get the essential amino acids I need.

FACT: You don't have to combine protein foods at the same meal to reap the benefits of complete protein. Recent studies show that as long as you eat a variety of foods every day, you'll get enough complete protein to meet your needs. If you want to combine proteins, however, you certainly can. Combining lower-quality protein foods can complement or complete the amino acids missing from one another to create complete protein equaling the quality of animal protein.

Here's the "scoop" on what to pair to get complete proteins: Grain foods complement legumes; legumes complement nuts and seeds. The pairings are almost endless. Familiar examples of combinations that create high-quality protein include peanut butter on whole wheat bread, macaroni and cheese, beans and rice or a bean and cheese enchilada.

Myth: I will have to eat mushy, bland meals.

FACT: Variety is what helps you stick to a diet—offering different tastes, textures and colors to your meals. Sprinkle toasted nuts or seeds on a salad or casserole for added pizzazz and protein. Go on an adventure by adding herbs and spices, flavored vinegars, condiments and fresh citrus juice or peel to your meatless dishes. A dash of vinegar or lemon juice added just before serving a legume soup provides a kick of flavor. Cook vegetables just until they are tender or crisp-tender for texture. Sprinkle them with chopped fresh herbs or serve a few brightly-colored vegetables together, for an enticing pop of color on your plate.

Myth: Being vegetarian takes more time and will cost more.

FACT: Anything new takes a little extra attention, but once you're used to this new way of eating, it will be easier. Years ago, eating vegetarian might have been more difficult, but now it's mainstream. Supermarkets carry a wide variety of vegetarian foods plus convenience foods like precut vegetables and fruits. The number of whole-food and co-op stores has increased, offering even more options. Many grains, legumes, vegetables, soy-protein and nut products are less expensive per pound than meat, poultry, fish and seafood, so a vegetarian diet can be very easy on your budget!

Myth: I can eat only salads at restaurants.

FACT: More and more restaurants offer vegetarian entrées on their menus or are very willing to make something to order. You won't go hungry! Be creative as you check the menu. Read "Choosing Meatless While Dining Out," page 8.

Myth: I have to be young to become a vegetarian.

FACT: People of all ages are turning to a vegetarian diet, or reducing meat and animal products, because of health concerns. Many are combating weight gain, higher cholesterol and blood pressure, increased cancer risk and digestion problems. Start with just a meal or two a week that's meatless. It's an easy step toward committing your family to a healthier lifestyle!

Entertaining Without Meat

Delicious Holiday Menus and More

Don't know where to start in planning a vegetarian meal for Christmas or a Fourth of July bash? It's easy with the help of these vegetarian menu ideas. You can adapt them for any occasion—birthdays, anniversaries, girl's nights—or whenever you want a party! You can feel good about serving these healthy options to your family and friends—and they are easy enough to prepare, so you can enjoy the party, too!

Bountiful Thanksgiving

Balsamic & Rosemary Roasted Vegetable Platter, *page 25*

Five-Spice Mixed Nuts and Cranberries, *page 34*

Curried Carrot Soup, *page 218*

Butternut Squash Ravioli, *page 84*

Tossed Salad

Assorted Rolls

Apple, Pumpkin or Pecan Pie

Festive Christmas

Spicy Sweet Potato Rounds with Caribbean Dip, *page 41*

Assorted Olives

Spinach-Stuffed Manicotti with Vodka Blush Sauce, *page 124*

Tossed Salad with Pomegranate Seeds

Baguette Served with Olive Oil, Grated Parmesan and Freshly Ground Black Pepper for Dipping

Cheesecake and Toppings

Flavorful Easter Dinner

Olive and Herb Deviled Eggs, *page 35*

Artichoke-Rosemary Bruschetta, *page 17*

Sweet Potato–Cauliflower Curry, *page 46*

Asparagus

Fresh Berries

Lemon Meringue or Key Lime Pie

Carefree Sunday Brunch

Sweet Pea–Wasabi Hummus with Wonton Chips, *page 14*

Baked Buffalo Frittata, *page 137*

Muffins and Sweet Rolls

Fresh Fruit

Vegetable Tray with Dip

Hazelnut Dreamaccinos, *page 40*

Casual Get-Together with Friends

Chipotle–Black Bean Dip, *page 28*

Mexican Potato Tacos, *page 171*

Smoky Brown Rice–Stuffed Peppers, *page 113*

Tossed Salad

Brownies with Vanilla Ice Cream, Sprinkled with Ground Cinnamon

Cozy Winter Gathering

Greek Hummus Nachos, *page 36*

Italian Bean Soup with Greens, *page 245*

Broccoli-Cheese Calzones, *page 196*

Apple Crisp with Vanilla Ice Cream

Patriotic Summer Supper

Fresh Spring Rolls with Peanut Sauce, *page 23*

Salsa with Red, White and Blue Tortilla Chips

Portabella Mushroom Burgers, *page 161*

Quinoa and Corn Salad, *page 61*

Watermelon Slices

Ice Cream Sandwiches

Fun Kids Party

Veggie Joes, *page 232*

Sweet Potato Chips

Broccoli Florets with Ranch Dressing to Dip

Pineapple-Mango Smoothies, *page 42*

Chocolate Chip Cookies

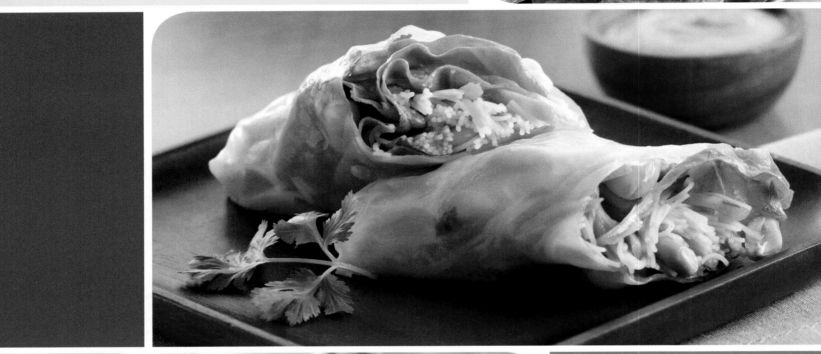

chapter 1

snacks, bites & nibbles

Sweet Pea–Wasabi Hummus with Wonton Chips

Prep Time: 20 minutes • Start to Finish: 40 minutes • **24 servings (2 tablespoons hummus and 3 chips each)**

HUMMUS

- 1 **bag (12 oz) frozen sweet peas (2 cups)**
- 1 **can (15 oz) garbanzo beans, drained, rinsed**
- 2 **tablespoons vegetable oil**
- 1 **tablespoon toasted sesame oil**
- 2 **teaspoons wasabi paste**
- 2 **teaspoons chopped gingerroot**
- ½ **teaspoon salt**
- 2 **cloves garlic, finely chopped**
- 2 **tablespoons water**

WONTON CHIPS

- 36 **wonton skins (3½-inch square)**
  Cooking spray
- ½ **teaspoon coarse sea salt**

1 Cook peas as directed on package for minimum cook time; drain.

2 In food processor, place cooked peas and remaining hummus ingredients except water. Process with on/off pulses 10 to 15 times or until partially smooth. With food processor running, add water, processing 10 to 15 seconds or until smooth. (Add additional water for a thinner dip.) Transfer to serving bowl. Cover; refrigerate up to 1 day.

3 Heat oven to 375°F. Cut wonton skins diagonally in half. Place half of the skins on ungreased large cookie sheet. Spray with cooking spray; sprinkle with sea salt.

4 Bake 8 to 10 minutes or until golden brown and crisp. Transfer to serving platter. Repeat with remaining wonton skins. Serve hummus with chips.

1 SERVING: Calories 90 (Calories from Fat 20); Total Fat 2.5g (Saturated Fat 0g; Trans Fat 0g); Cholesterol 0mg; Sodium 180mg; Total Carbohydrate 14g (Dietary Fiber 1g); Protein 3g **% Daily Value:** Vitamin A 6%; Vitamin C 0%; Calcium 0%; Iron 6% **Exchanges:** 1 Starch, ½ Fat **Carbohydrate Choices:** 1

This is a great make-ahead appetizer. Both the hummus and chips can be made a day in advance. To make the chips a day ahead, after they're baked and cooled, store them in a covered container at room temperature.

Guacamole-Cheese Crisps

Prep Time: 25 minutes • Start to Finish: 25 minutes • **16 servings**

1 **cup finely shredded Cheddar-Jack with jalapeño peppers cheese blend (from 8-oz package)**

½ cup guacamole

3 tablespoons sour cream

3 tablespoons chunky-style salsa

1 Heat oven to 400°F. Line cookie sheet with cooking parchment paper. For each cheese crisp, spoon 1 tablespoon cheese (loosely packed) onto paper-lined cookie sheet; pat into 1½-inch round.

2 Bake 6 to 8 minutes or until edges are light golden brown. Immediately remove from cookie sheet to cooling rack. Cool 5 minutes or until crisp.

3 Onto each cheese crisp, spoon 1½ teaspoons guacamole and about ½ teaspoon each sour cream and salsa.

1 SERVING: Calories 40 (Calories from Fat 30); Total Fat 3g (Saturated Fat 1.5g; Trans Fat 0g); Cholesterol 10mg; Sodium 95mg; Total Carbohydrate 0g (Dietary Fiber 0g); Protein 2g **%Daily Value:** Vitamin A 0%; Vitamin C 0%; Calcium 4%; Iron 0% **Exchanges:** ½ Very Lean Meat, ½ Fat **Carbohydrate Choices:** 0

You can make the cheese crisps up to 4 hours ahead without toppings. Store the crisps tightly covered at room temperature. Top just before serving.

Artichoke-Rosemary Bruschetta

Prep Time: 15 minutes • **Start to Finish:** 35 minutes • **12 slices**

1 **loaf (1 lb) French bread,
  cut horizontally in half**

1 **cup shredded mozzarella cheese
  (4 oz)**

½ **cup grated Parmesan cheese**

1 **tablespoon chopped fresh or
  1 teaspoon dried rosemary
  leaves, crumbled**

⅔ **cup mayonnaise or salad
  dressing**

1 **jar (6 oz) marinated artichoke
  hearts, drained, chopped**

1 Heat oven to 375°F. Place bread, cut sides up, on ungreased cookie sheet. Bake 10 minutes.

2 Meanwhile, mix ½ cup of the mozzarella cheese, the Parmesan cheese, rosemary, mayonnaise and artichokes.

3 Spread artichoke mixture on bread. Sprinkle with remaining ½ cup mozzarella cheese.

4 Bake 15 to 20 minutes or until cheese is melted.

1 SLICE: Calories 260 (Calories from Fat 130); Total Fat 15g (Saturated Fat 3.5g; Trans Fat 0g); Cholesterol 15mg; Sodium 460mg; Total Carbohydrate 23g (Dietary Fiber 1g); Protein 9g **%Daily Value:** Vitamin A 2%; Vitamin C 0%; Calcium 15%; Iron 8% **Exchanges:** 1½ Starch, ½ Very Lean Meat, 3 Fat **Carbohydrate Choices:** 1½

Turn this appetizer into a light meal by pairing it with a tossed salad and fruit.

Pinto Beans and Roasted Red Pepper Empanadas

Prep Time: **1 hour** • Start to Finish: **1 hour 50 minutes** • **12 servings (1 empanada and 1 tablespoon sauce each)**

DOUGH

- **2 cups all-purpose flour**
- **½ teaspoon salt**
- **⅔ cup shortening**
- **6 to 7 tablespoons ice water**
- **Milk**

FILLING

- **¾ cup canned pinto beans, drained, rinsed**
- **¼ cup roasted red peppers, drained, chopped**
- **3 tablespoons finely chopped fresh cilantro**
- **½ cup shredded Cheddar-Jack with jalapeño peppers cheese blend**

CILANTRO CREAM SAUCE

- **½ cup packed fresh cilantro leaves**
- **2 teaspoons fresh lime juice**
- **¼ cup mayonnaise**
- **½ cup sour cream**
- **1 clove garlic, cut in half**

1 In medium bowl, stir together flour and salt. Cut in shortening with pastry blender (or pulling 2 table knives through mixture in opposite directions) until mixture is crumbly. Sprinkle with ice water, 1 tablespoon at a time, tossing with fork until all flour is moistened and pastry leaves side of bowl. Form dough into 2 disks; wrap each in plastic wrap. Refrigerate 30 minutes.

2 Heat oven to 450°F. Spray cookie sheet with cooking spray. In small bowl, mix filling ingredients.

3 On well-floured surface, roll out dough disks until ⅛ inch thick. Cut into 4-inch rounds. Reroll scraps; cut out enough dough to make 12 rounds. For each empanada, spoon about 2 tablespoons filling onto center of dough round. Moisten edge with water; fold dough over to form crescent shape. Press edge with fork to seal. Brush top lightly with milk. Place on cookie sheet.

4 Bake 20 minutes or until golden brown and crisp.

5 Meanwhile, in blender or food processor, place sauce ingredients. Cover; blend or process until thoroughly mixed. Spoon into serving bowl. Cover; refrigerate until serving. Serve sauce with warm empanadas.

1 SERVING: Calories 260 (Calories from Fat 170); Total Fat 18g (Saturated Fat 5g; Trans Fat 2g); Cholesterol 10mg; Sodium 170mg; Total Carbohydrate 20g (Dietary Fiber 2g); Protein 4g **%Daily Value:** Vitamin A 4%; Vitamin C 0%; Calcium 6%; Iron 8% **Exchanges:** 1½ Starch, 3½ Fat **Carbohydrate Choices:** 1

If you wish, use a refrigerated, prepared pastry crust instead of making the crust. Use two 9-inch crusts, rolling them thin and then cutting them into the 4-inch rounds as directed in the recipe.

String Cheese Sticks with Dipping Sauce

Prep Time: 15 minutes • Start to Finish: 25 minutes • 4 servings (2 cheese sticks each)

2¼ cups Original Bisquick® mix

⅔ cup milk

1 package (8 oz) plain or smoked string cheese

1 can (8 oz) pizza sauce

1 tablespoon butter or margarine, melted

¼ teaspoon garlic powder

1 Heat oven to 450°F. In medium bowl, stir Bisquick mix and milk until soft dough forms; beat 30 seconds with spoon. Place dough on surface sprinkled with Bisquick mix; gently roll in Bisquick mix to coat. Shape into a ball; knead 10 times.

2 Roll dough into 12×8-inch rectangle, ¼ inch thick. Cut into 8 (6×2-inch) rectangles. Roll each rectangle around 1 piece of cheese. Pinch edge into roll to seal; seal ends. Roll on surface to completely enclose cheese sticks. On ungreased cookie sheet, place sticks seam sides down.

3 Bake 8 to 10 minutes or until golden brown. Meanwhile, in 1-quart saucepan, heat pizza sauce over low heat until warm. In small bowl, mix butter and garlic powder; brush over warm cheese sticks before removing from cookie sheet. Serve warm with pizza sauce for dipping.

1 SERVING: Calories 520 (Calories from Fat 210); Total Fat 24g (Saturated Fat 11g; Trans Fat 3g); Cholesterol 40mg; Sodium 1280mg; Total Carbohydrate 53g (Dietary Fiber 3g); Protein 22g **%Daily Value:** Vitamin A 20%; Vitamin C 6%; Calcium 60%; Iron 15% **Exchanges:** 3½ Starch, 1½ Lean Meat, 3½ Fat **Carbohydrate Choices:** 3½

If you don't have pizza sauce on hand, heat up your favorite pasta sauce instead.

If you've never made spring rolls before, you'll get a feel for how long to dip the rice paper wrappers as you make a few. Dipping the wrappers for too short a time means they won't bend and roll easily around the filling; dip them for too long and they become sticky, wrinkle up and won't lay flat for filling. As the water cools, they will require a few more seconds to soak to soften them.

Fresh Spring Rolls with Peanut Sauce

Prep Time: 40 minutes • Start to Finish: 40 minutes • **12 servings (1 spring roll and heaping tablespoon peanut sauce)**

SAUCE

½ **cup creamy peanut butter**

¼ **cup canned coconut milk (not cream of coconut)**

2 **tablespoons teriyaki sauce**

1 **tablespoon fresh lime juice**

2 **teaspoons finely chopped gingerroot**

2 **to 3 tablespoons water**

ROLLS

3 **oz uncooked thin rice stick noodles**

½ **cup shredded carrot (1 medium)**

⅓ **cup julienne-cut fresh basil leaves**

¼ **cup chopped fresh cilantro**

1 **small serrano chile, seeded, finely chopped**

¼ **cup teriyaki sauce**

12 **spring roll rice paper wrappers (about 8½ inch)**

12 **small butter lettuce leaves, tough centers removed**

¾ **cup salted dry-roasted peanuts**

1 **cup frozen shelled edamame (green) soybeans, cooked as directed on package**

1 In small bowl, beat sauce ingredients with whisk, adding enough water for desired consistency. Cover; refrigerate until ready to serve.

2 Fill 3-quart saucepan two-thirds with water; heat to boiling. Add rice stick noodles; boil gently 3 minutes or just until noodles are tender. Rinse with cold water; drain. Transfer to large bowl. With scissors, cut rice noodles into about 3-inch lengths. Stir in carrot, basil, cilantro, chile and ¼ cup teriyaki sauce.

3 Fill 9-inch round shallow pan with hot water (110°F); place clean, damp paper towel on work surface. Dip 1 rice paper wrapper in water about 5 seconds or just until pliable; place on towel. Place lettuce leaf on lower third of wrapper. Spoon scant ⅓ cup noodle mixture on lettuce. Sprinkle with about 1 tablespoon peanuts and heaping tablespoon edamame. Starting with edge covered with fillings, roll up wrapper over fillings, stopping after first turn to tuck in sides. Continue to roll up, tucking in sides. Place seam side down on serving platter. Repeat with remaining wrappers and fillings, placing on platter without sides touching.

4 Serve immediately, or cover with moist paper towels and refrigerate up to 2 hours. To serve, cut each roll in half diagonally. Stir sauce; serve with spring rolls.

1 SERVING: Calories 240 (Calories from Fat 110); Total Fat 12g (Saturated Fat 3g; Trans Fat 0g); Cholesterol 0mg; Sodium 520mg; Total Carbohydrate 24g (Dietary Fiber 3g); Protein 8g **%Daily Value:** Vitamin A 25%; Vitamin C 4%; Calcium 2%; Iron 6% **Exchanges:** 1½ Starch, 2½ Fat **Carbohydrate Choices:** 1½

Greek Marinated Roasted Peppers, Olives and Feta

Prep Time: 25 minutes • Start to Finish: 45 minutes • **32 servings (¼ cup each)**

5 large red bell peppers

¼ cup olive or vegetable oil

3 tablespoons lemon juice

½ cup chopped fresh parsley

¼ cup finely chopped red onion

2 tablespoons chopped fresh or 2 teaspoons dried oregano leaves

2 cloves garlic, finely chopped

2 cups pitted kalamata olives

2 cups feta cheese, cut into ½-inch cubes (1 cup)

Baguette slices, if desired

1 Set oven control to broil. Place bell peppers on ungreased cookie sheet. Broil with tops about 5 inches from heat, turning occasionally, until skin is blistered and evenly browned. Place peppers in plastic bag; close tightly. Let stand 20 minutes.

2 Meanwhile, in tightly covered container, shake oil, lemon juice, parsley, onion, oregano and garlic.

3 Remove skins, stems, seeds and membranes from peppers. Cut peppers into 1-inch pieces. In glass bowl or jar, place peppers, olives and cheese. Pour marinade over pepper mixture. To serve, use slotted spoon. Serve with baguette slices.

1 SERVING: Calories 45 (Calories from Fat 35); Total Fat 3.5g (Saturated Fat 1g; Trans Fat 0g); Cholesterol 0mg; Sodium 125mg; Total Carbohydrate 3g (Dietary Fiber 1g); Protein 1g **%Daily Value:** Vitamin A 15%; Vitamin C 60%; Calcium 4%; Iron 2% **Exchanges:** ½ Starch, ½ Fat **Carbohydrate Choices:** 0

For authentic flavor, use kalamata or Gaeta olives, but you can also use large pitted ripe olives if you prefer.

Balsamic & Rosemary Roasted Vegetable Platter

Prep Time: 10 minutes • **Start to Finish:** 50 minutes • **12 servings**

¼ **cup extra-virgin olive oil**

4 **teaspoons balsamic vinegar**

1 **tablespoon chopped fresh rosemary leaves**

1 **teaspoon Dijon mustard**

½ **teaspoon salt**

½ **teaspoon pepper**

12 **fingerling potatoes**

12 **small Brussels sprouts**

1 **medium red bell pepper, cut into 12 pieces**

24 **frozen pearl onions**

1 **package (12 oz) mozzarella-flavor soy cheese, cut into 24 cubes**

1 Heat oven to 450°F. Line 15×10-inch pan with sides with foil. In large bowl, stir together oil, vinegar, rosemary, mustard, salt and pepper. Stir in potatoes and Brussels sprouts until coated. Remove with slotted spoon to pan.

2 Bake 10 minutes. Meanwhile, coat bell pepper and onions in remaining oil mixture.

3 Stir partially baked vegetables in pan. With slotted spoon, add peppers and onions to pan. Bake 10 to 15 minutes longer, stirring occasionally, just until vegetables are tender. Cool 15 minutes.

4 Meanwhile, toss cheese cubes in bowl with remaining oil mixture; remove with slotted spoon to serving platter.

5 To serve, arrange roasted vegetables on platter with cheese. Serve warm or at room temperature. Refrigerate leftovers.

1 SERVING: Calories 170 (Calories from Fat 80); Total Fat 9g (Saturated Fat 0.5g; Trans Fat 0g); Cholesterol 0mg; Sodium 410mg; Total Carbohydrate 16g (Dietary Fiber 2g); Protein 8g **%Daily Value:** Vitamin A 35%; Vitamin C 25%; Calcium 20%; Iron 10% **Exchanges:** 1 Starch, ½ Vegetable, ½ Medium-Fat Meat, 1 Fat **Carbohydrate Choices:** 1

For a fancy presentation, arrange roasted veggies (when cool enough to handle) on bamboo skewers with marinated cheese cubes; for a more simple serving, use toothpicks.

California Sushi Canapés

Prep Time: **1 hour 5 minutes** • Start to Finish: **1 hour 40 minutes** • **16 servings (2 appetizers each)**

RICE

1 cup water

¾ cup uncooked sushi rice

2 tablespoons seasoned rice vinegar

SAUCE

3 tablespoons mayonnaise

2 teaspoons finely chopped gingerroot

1 teaspoon roasted red chili paste

CANAPÉS

1 small English (seedless) cucumber

1 sheet roasted seaweed nori sheets (8×7 inch; from 1-oz package), cut into 8 rows by 4 rows

2 tablespoons sesame seed, toasted*

½ red bell pepper, finely chopped (or thinly sliced carrot or very small pieces of avocado)

1 In 1-quart saucepan, heat 1 cup water and the rice to boiling. Reduce heat to low; cover and simmer 15 to 20 minutes or until tender. Transfer to large bowl, tossing rice with chopsticks or 2 forks to cool slightly. Gradually add vinegar, tossing constantly. Cover bowl with damp towel; cool rice about 45 minutes or until room temperature.

2 Meanwhile, in small bowl, stir together sauce ingredients; cover and refrigerate until ready to assemble canapés.

3 Cut cucumber into 32 slices, each about ¼ inch thick. Arrange on serving platter. For each canapé, place 1 piece of nori on each cucumber slice. Top each with about ¼ teaspoon sauce. Scoop rice using 1 measuring teaspoon, pressing rice against side of bowl to pack into spoon and hold shape of spoon. Carefully remove rice from spoon; dip flat side into sesame seed and place flat-side down on sauce. If necessary, carefully reshape rice with fingers. Top with bell pepper or other toppings (or a combination). Serve immediately, or cover and refrigerate up to 2 hours.

*To toast sesame seed, cook in skillet over medium-low heat 5 to 7 minutes, stirring frequently until browning begins, then stirring constantly until golden brown. Remove immediately from skillet to prevent seed from continuing to cook and getting overdone.

1 SERVING: Calories 70 (Calories from Fat 30); Total Fat 3g (Saturated Fat 0g; Trans Fat 0g); Cholesterol 0mg; Sodium 25mg; Total Carbohydrate 8g (Dietary Fiber 1g); Protein 1g **%Daily Value:** Vitamin A 4%; Vitamin C 4%; Calcium 0%; Iron 0% **Exchanges:** ½ Starch, ½ Fat **Carbohydrate Choices:** ½

Seasoned rice vinegar contains salt and sugar to flavor the sushi. In this recipe, you can make your own from rice vinegar by stirring in 2 teaspoons sugar and ¼ teaspoon salt.

Chipotle–Black Bean Dip

Prep Time: 20 minutes • Start to Finish: 45 minutes • **15 servings (2 tablespoons dip and 3 chips each)**

2 large dried chipotle chiles

1 cup chunky-style salsa

½ cup jalapeño–black bean dip

2 tablespoons chopped fresh cilantro

1 cup shredded Colby-Monterey Jack cheese blend (4 oz)

2 medium green onions, chopped (2 tablespoons)

Sweet red cherry chile half, if desired

Tortilla chips

1 Heat oven to 350°F. In small bowl, cover dried chiles with boiling water; let stand 10 minutes. Drain chiles; remove seeds. Chop chiles.

2 In small bowl, mix chiles, salsa and bean dip; stir in cilantro. Spoon into shallow 1-quart ovenproof serving dish. Sprinkle with cheese.

3 Bake about 15 minutes or until mixture is hot and cheese is melted. Sprinkle with onions. If desired, garnish with cherry chile half. Serve with tortilla chips.

1 SERVING: Calories 80 (Calories from Fat 35); Total Fat 3.5g (Saturated Fat 1.5g; Trans Fat 0g); Cholesterol 5mg; Sodium 220mg; Total Carbohydrate 9g (Dietary Fiber 1g); Protein 3g **%Daily Value:** Vitamin A 25%; Vitamin C 0%; Calcium 6%; Iron 4% **Exchanges:** ½ Starch, ½ Fat **Carbohydrate Choices:** ½

To make this tasty dip ahead of time, follow the directions through step 2, then cover and refrigerate up to 24 hours. Bake as directed.

Layered Black Bean and Roasted Salsa Dip

Prep Time: 10 minutes • Start to Finish: 30 minutes • **8 servings (about ¼ cup dip and about 20 chips each)**

- 1 **package (4 oz) goat cheese, softened**
- 1 **package (3 oz) cream cheese, softened**
- ½ **cup refried black beans with lime (from 15.5-oz can)**
- ½ **cup fire-roasted salsa (from 16-oz jar)**
- 2 **plum (Roma) tomatoes, seeded, chopped (⅔ cup)**
- 2 **medium green onions, sliced (2 tablespoons)**
- 1 **tablespoon chopped fresh cilantro**
- 8 **oz bite-size tortilla chips**

1 Heat oven to 350°F. In small bowl, stir together goat cheese and cream cheese. Spread into ungreased 9-inch pie plate. Spread refried beans and salsa over cheese.

2 Cover with foil; bake 14 to 16 minutes or until thoroughly heated. Sprinkle with tomatoes, onions and cilantro. Serve warm with tortilla chips.

1 SERVING: Calories 260 (Calories from Fat 130); Total Fat 14g (Saturated Fat 5g; Trans Fat 0g); Cholesterol 25mg; Sodium 330mg; Total Carbohydrate 25g (Dietary Fiber 2g); Protein 6g **%Daily Value:** Vitamin A 10%; Vitamin C 4%; Calcium 6%; Iron 10% **Exchanges:** 1½ Starch, 3 Fat **Carbohydrate Choices:** 1½

Look for a thick salsa to keep it from becoming too thin when baking. Or drain some of the liquid off the salsa before spreading it over the cheese.

Asparagus with Creamy Spanish Dip

Prep Time: 40 minutes • Start to Finish: 40 minutes • **15 servings (3 asparagus spears and 1 tablespoon dip each)**

½ **cup slivered almonds, toasted***

½ **cup roasted red bell peppers (from 7-oz jar), drained, chopped**

¼ **teaspoon crushed red pepper flakes**

½ **cup garlic-and-herbs spreadable cheese (from 4- or 6.5-oz container)**

¼ **cup chili sauce**

1 **to 2 tablespoons milk**

1 **lb fresh asparagus spears**

1 In food processor, place almonds. Cover; process 10 to 15 seconds or until finely ground. Add roasted peppers and crushed red pepper. Cover; process about 10 seconds or until finely ground. Add cheese, chili sauce and 1 tablespoon of the milk. Cover; process about 10 seconds or until well mixed. Add remaining 1 tablespoon milk if needed for dipping consistency.

2 In 12-inch skillet, heat ¾ inch water to boiling. Add asparagus; cover and cook 2 minutes. Drain. Plunge asparagus into ice water until cold; drain.

3 On serving platter, arrange asparagus spears. Serve with dip.

**To toast nuts, cook in an ungreased heavy skillet over medium-low heat 5 to 7 minutes, stirring frequently until browning begins, then stirring constantly until golden brown.*

1 SERVING: Calories 60 (Calories from Fat 40); Total Fat 4.5g (Saturated Fat 1.5g; Trans Fat 0g); Cholesterol 5mg; Sodium 95mg; Total Carbohydrate 3g (Dietary Fiber 1g); Protein 1g **%Daily Value:** Vitamin A 4%; Vitamin C 0%; Calcium 2%; Iron 4% **Exchanges:** 1 Fat **Carbohydrate Choices:** 0

> **This awesome dip is based on *romesco*, a classic Spanish sauce served with fish and poultry; almonds, red bell pepper, tomato, onion and garlic are what make it special.**

Chinese Dumplings with Sweet Soy Dipping Sauce

Prep Time: 45 minutes • Start to Finish: 1 hour 15 minutes • 24 servings

DUMPLINGS
- 1 **tablespoon vegetable oil**
- 2 **cups thinly sliced, chopped bok choy**
- 1 **cup finely chopped mushrooms**
- 1 **large carrot, shredded**
- ½ **cup sliced green onions (8 medium)**
- 1 **tablespoon finely chopped gingerroot**
- 1 **tablespoon white wine or water**
- 1 **tablespoon reduced-sodium soy sauce**
- 1 **teaspoon cornstarch**
- 1 **teaspoon toasted sesame oil**
- 24 **pot sticker (gyoza) wrappers**

SAUCE
- 2 **tablespoons sugar**
- 2 **tablespoons reduced-sodium soy sauce**
- 2 **tablespoons rice vinegar**
- 2 **tablespoons water**
- ½ **teaspoon toasted sesame oil**
- ⅛ **to ¼ teaspoon crushed red pepper flakes**

1 In 12-inch nonstick skillet, heat oil over medium-high heat. Add bok choy, mushrooms and carrot; cook and stir 3 to 4 minutes or until bok choy is tender and wilted. Stir in onions and gingerroot; cook and stir 1 minute longer.

2 In small bowl, stir together wine, 1 tablespoon soy sauce, the cornstarch and 1 teaspoon sesame oil. Stir into vegetable mixture just until combined; remove skillet from heat. Cool slightly.

3 Meanwhile, in another small bowl, mix sauce ingredients until sugar is dissolved; set aside.

4 For each dumpling, spoon about 1 tablespoon filling into center of pot sticker wrapper. Wet edge of wrapper with water; bring edge of wrapper together in thirds, pinching wrapper together in center to form a pyramid. Repeat with remaining wrappers. (Cover prepared dumplings with damp towel to keep them from drying out.)

5 In 5-quart Dutch oven, heat 1 inch water to boiling. Spray metal colander with cooking spray. Arrange about 8 dumplings in colander, about ½ inch apart. Place colander in Dutch oven; cover. Reduce heat; steam dumplings over simmering water 10 to 12 minutes or until dumplings are translucent. Transfer to serving plate; repeat with remaining dumplings. Serve dumplings with sauce.

1 SERVING: Calories 45 (Calories from Fat 10); Total Fat 1g (Saturated Fat 0g; Trans Fat 0g); Cholesterol 0mg; Sodium 80mg; Total Carbohydrate 7g (Dietary Fiber 0g); Protein 1g **%Daily Value:** Vitamin A 15%; Vitamin C 2%; Calcium 0%; Iron 2% **Exchanges:** ½ Starch **Carbohydrate Choices:** ½

Feel free to vary the shapes of the dumplings; wrappers can be shaped into round pouches or semicircles.

Roasted Carrot and Herb Spread

Prep Time: 20 minutes • Start to Finish: 1 hour 20 minutes • **16 servings (2 tablespoons spread and 2 crackers each)**

1 **lb ready-to-eat baby-cut carrots**

1 **dark-orange sweet potato, peeled, cut into 1-inch pieces (2½ cups)**

1 **small onion, cut into 8 wedges, separated**

2 **tablespoons olive oil**

1 **clove garlic, finely chopped**

1 **tablespoon chopped fresh or 1 teaspoon dried thyme leaves**

¼ **teaspoon salt**

⅛ **teaspoon freshly ground pepper**

Assorted whole-grain crackers or vegetable chips

1 Heat oven to 350°F. Spray 15×10×1-inch pan with cooking spray. Place carrots, sweet potato and onion in pan; drizzle with oil. Sprinkle with garlic, thyme, salt and pepper; stir to coat.

2 Bake uncovered about 1 hour, stirring occasionally, until vegetables are tender.

3 In food processor, place vegetable mixture. Cover; process until blended. Spoon into serving bowl. Serve warm, or cover and refrigerate until serving. Serve with crackers.

1 SERVING: Calories 90 (Calories from Fat 30); Total Fat 3.5g (Saturated Fat 0g; Trans Fat 0g); Cholesterol 0mg; Sodium 125mg; Total Carbohydrate 12g (Dietary Fiber 2g); Protein 1g **%Daily Value:** Vitamin A 160%; Vitamin C 4%; Calcium 2%; Iron 4% **Exchanges:** 1 Other Carbohydrate, ½ Fat **Carbohydrate Choices:** 1

Carrots and red garnet sweet potatoes—or any of the deep-orange variety—help give this dip its intense color, flavor and nutrition. You can use any kind of sweet potato that you like.

Five-Spice Mixed Nuts and Cranberries

Prep Time: **5 minutes** • Start to Finish: **1 hour** • **14 servings (¼ cup each)**

1 egg white, slightly beaten

2 tablespoons sugar

1 tablespoon five-spice powder

2½ cups assorted nuts (such as walnuts, cashews, macadamia nuts, pistachios and peanuts)

½ cup sweetened dried cranberries

1 Heat oven to 300°F. Spray 15×10×1-inch pan with cooking spray.

2 In medium bowl, beat egg white, sugar and five-spice powder with whisk. Stir in nuts until well coated. Spread nuts in single layer in pan.

3 Bake 25 minutes. Stir; bake 5 to 10 minutes longer or until toasted. Stir in cranberries. Cool completely, about 20 minutes. Store in tightly covered container up to 1 week.

1 SERVING: Calories 180 (Calories from Fat 110); Total Fat 13g (Saturated Fat 1.5g; Trans Fat 0g); Cholesterol 0mg; Sodium 170mg; Total Carbohydrate 12g (Dietary Fiber 2g); Protein 4g **%Daily Value:** Vitamin A 0%; Vitamin C 0%; Calcium 0%; Iron 6% **Exchanges:** 1 Starch, 2½ Fat **Carbohydrate Choices:** 1

These nuts would be a crunchy addition to a salad with vinaigrette dressing and feta cheese.

Olive and Herb Deviled Eggs

Prep Time: **15 minutes** • Start to Finish: **30 minutes** • **16 appetizers**

8 **hard-cooked eggs**

⅓ **cup mayonnaise or salad dressing**

2 **tablespoons finely chopped fresh parsley**

2 **tablespoons finely chopped fresh marjoram leaves**

2 **tablespoons finely chopped fresh chives**

½ **teaspoon garlic-pepper blend**

½ **cup chopped ripe olives**

8 **pitted ripe olives**

Fresh parsley or marjoram sprigs or leaves, if desired

1 With rippled vegetable cutter or sharp knife, cut peeled eggs lengthwise in half. Carefully remove yolks and place in small bowl; mash with fork. Reserve egg white halves.

2 Mix mashed yolks, mayonnaise, chopped herbs, garlic-pepper blend and chopped olives. Carefully spoon mixture into egg white halves, mounding lightly.

3 Cut whole pitted olives into slices; top each egg half with olive slices. Garnish with small herb sprig or leaves.

1 APPETIZER: Calories 80 (Calories from Fat 60); Total Fat 7g (Saturated Fat 1.5g; Trans Fat 0g); Cholesterol 110mg; Sodium 110mg; Total Carbohydrate 0g (Dietary Fiber 0g); Protein 3g **%Daily Value:** Vitamin A 4%; Vitamin C 0%; Calcium 2%; Iron 4% **Exchanges:** ½ Medium-Fat Meat, 1 Fat **Carbohydrate Choices:** 0

Don't be tempted to use kalamata or other specialty olives in this recipe because the flavor would be too strong. The ripe olives are mild enough to add just a pleasant olive flavor without overpowering the egg flavor. However, feel free to substitute basil for the marjoram or parsley, or top with a cherry tomato wedge instead of an olive slice.

Prepare the stuffed eggs up to 24 hours in advance. Refrigerate in a tightly covered container until serving time.

Greek Hummus Nachos

Prep Time: 15 minutes • **Start to Finish:** 20 minutes • **8 servings**

4 cups salted pita chips

1 container (8 oz) roasted red pepper hummus

½ cup chopped cucumber

1 plum (Roma) tomato, seeded, chopped

¼ cup chopped pitted kalamata olives

¼ cup crumbled feta cheese (1 oz)

1 tablespoon chopped fresh oregano

1 teaspoon finely shredded lemon peel, if desired

1 Heat oven to 400°F. Arrange pita chips on heatproof serving platter. Dollop hummus over chips. Top with cucumber, tomato, olives and cheese. Bake about 4 minutes or until hummus is warm.

2 In small bowl, stir together oregano and lemon peel. Sprinkle over hot nachos. Serve immediately.

1 SERVING: Calories 130 (Calories from Fat 60); Total Fat 7g (Saturated Fat 1g; Trans Fat 0g); Cholesterol 0mg; Sodium 390mg; Total Carbohydrate 13g (Dietary Fiber 2g); Protein 3g **%Daily Value:** Vitamin A 2%; Vitamin C 0%; Calcium 4%; Iron 4% **Exchanges:** 1 Starch, 1 Fat **Carbohydrate Choices:** 1

Going on a picnic? Bring all the ingredients and create the nachos on-site. It's not necessary to heat them.

Try white beans—cannellini beans or chickpeas (garbanzo beans)—as an alternative to the black beans.

Black Bean Sliders

Prep Time: 45 minutes • Start to Finish: 2 hours 45 minutes • 20 sandwiches

BUNS

5 frozen stone ground 100% whole wheat Texan rolls (from 3-lb bag)

2 tablespoons butter, melted

CORN SALSA

1 can (7 oz) whole kernel corn with red and green peppers, drained

⅔ cup chunky-style medium salsa

BEAN PATTIES

5 teaspoons olive oil

¼ cup finely chopped red or yellow onion

1 can (15 oz) black beans, drained, rinsed

1 egg, beaten

½ cup plain bread crumbs

2 cloves garlic, finely chopped

1 teaspoon ground cumin

½ teaspoon salt

¼ teaspoon freshly ground pepper

Bibb or leaf lettuce, torn into 20 small pieces

5 slices (¾ oz each) Cheddar cheese, cut into quarters

1 Thaw rolls at room temperature until soft but still cold, about 10 minutes. Spray cookie sheet with cooking spray. Cut each roll into quarters; shape dough pieces into balls. Place on cookie sheet. Brush tops of dough balls with butter. Cover with plastic wrap sprayed with cooking spray. Let rise in warm place 2 hours to 2 hours 30 minutes until doubled in size.

2 Heat oven to 350°F. Remove plastic wrap. Bake buns 12 to 15 minutes or until golden brown. Remove from pan to cooling rack.

3 Meanwhile, in medium bowl, mix salsa ingredients. Cover; refrigerate until serving time.

4 In 10-inch nonstick skillet, heat 1 teaspoon of the oil over medium heat. Add onion; cook 3 to 4 minutes, stirring often, until softened. Remove from heat; cool slightly.

5 In medium bowl, mash beans with potato masher or fork, leaving a few beans whole. Stir in egg, bread crumbs, garlic, cumin, salt and pepper. Add cooled onion; mix until thoroughly combined. Shape mixture into 20 (1-inch) balls, using about 1 scant tablespoon per ball.

6 In same skillet, heat 2 teaspoons oil over medium heat. Place half of the bean balls in skillet; with back of spatula, flatten balls into patties, about 1½ inches in diameter. Cook 4 to 6 minutes, turning once, until browned. Remove from skillet; cover to keep warm. Repeat with remaining 2 teaspoons oil and bean balls.

7 Split buns in half. On bottom half of each bun, place lettuce piece, bean patty, cheese quarter and 1 heaping tablespoon corn salsa. Cover with top halves of buns.

1 SANDWICH: Calories 130 (Calories from Fat 45); Total Fat 5g (Saturated Fat 2g; Trans Fat 0g); Cholesterol 20mg; Sodium 270mg; Total Carbohydrate 17g (Dietary Fiber 3g); Protein 5g **%Daily Value:** Vitamin A 10%; Vitamin C 0%; Calcium 6%; Iron 4% **Exchanges:** 1 Starch, ½ Vegetable, 1 Fat **Carbohydrate Choices:** 1

Hazelnut Dreamaccinos

Prep Time: 5 minutes • **Start to Finish:** 5 minutes • **2 servings**

1¼ **cups dark chocolate all natural almond milk**

⅓ **cup water**

2 **tablespoons hazelnut-flavored coffee syrup**

1 **tablespoon instant espresso powder**

Ice cubes

3 **tablespoons whipped soy or whipped cream topping in aerosol can**

2 **teaspoons miniature semisweet chocolate chips or 6 chocolate-covered coffee beans**

1 In blender, place milk, water, coffee syrup and espresso powder. Cover; blend until frothy.

2 Pour into glasses over ice. Garnish with whipped topping and chocolate chips.

1 SERVING: Calories 150 (Calories from Fat 40); Total Fat 4.5g (Saturated Fat 2g; Trans Fat 0g); Cholesterol 0mg; Sodium 125mg; Total Carbohydrate 27g (Dietary Fiber 0g); Protein 1g **%Daily Value:** Vitamin A 6%; Vitamin C 10%; Calcium 30%; Iron 6% **Exchanges:** 2 Other Carbohydrate, 1 Fat **Carbohydrate Choices:** 2

Flavored coffee syrups are what coffeehouses use to make their yummy drinks. You can find them for sale in the coffee aisle at many grocery stores, specialty food stores and some coffeehouses. For a more intense hazelnut flavor, feel free to add another tablespoon of the flavored syrup.

Spicy Sweet Potato Rounds with Caribbean Dip

Prep Time: 15 minutes • **Start to Finish:** 50 minutes • **10 servings (about 3 potato rounds and about 1 tablespoon dip each)**

SWEET POTATOES

2 tablespoons olive or vegetable oil

1 teaspoon ground cumin

1 teaspoon ground cinnamon

½ teaspoon salt

¼ to ½ teaspoon ground red pepper (cayenne)

1½ lb sweet potatoes (3 medium), peeled, cut into ½-inch slices

CARIBBEAN DIP

⅓ cup sour cream

⅓ cup mayonnaise

3 tablespoons chopped green onions (3 medium)

3 tablespoons chopped fresh cilantro

1 Heat oven to 425°F. Spray cookie sheet with cooking spray. In gallon-size resealable plastic bag, mix oil, cumin, cinnamon, salt and ground red pepper. Add potato slices to bag. Seal bag; shake well to coat. Spread potatoes in single layer on cookie sheet.

2 Bake 20 minutes. Turn potatoes; bake 10 to 15 minutes longer or until golden brown and tender.

3 Meanwhile, stir together dip ingredients. Serve dip with potato rounds.

1 SERVING: Calories 140 (Calories from Fat 90); Total Fat 10g (Saturated Fat 2g; Trans Fat 0g); Cholesterol 5mg; Sodium 180mg; Total Carbohydrate 12g (Dietary Fiber 2g); Protein 1g **%Daily Value:** Vitamin A 210%; Vitamin C 10%; Calcium 4%; Iron 4% **Exchanges:** ½ Starch, 2 Fat **Carbohydrate Choices:** 1

Sweet potatoes come in all sorts of shapes; for easiest slicing, avoid those that are irregularly shaped.

Pineapple-Mango Smoothies

Prep Time: **5 minutes** • Start to Finish: **5 minutes** • **2 servings (1 cup each)**

1 **container (6 oz) Greek plain fat-free yogurt**

⅓ **cup fresh or canned drained pineapple chunks**

⅓ **cup chopped mango slices (from 1 lb 4-oz jar)**

¼ **cup mango syrup (from jar of mango slices)**

3 **or 4 ice cubes**

In blender, place all ingredients. Cover; blend about 30 seconds or until thoroughly combined. Pour into glasses.

1 SERVING: Calories 80 (Calories from Fat 0); Total Fat 0g (Saturated Fat 0g; Trans Fat 0g); Cholesterol 5mg; Sodium 45mg; Total Carbohydrate 13g (Dietary Fiber 0g); Protein 7g **%Daily Value:** Vitamin A 8%; Vitamin C 4%; Calcium 20%; Iron 0% **Exchanges:** 1 Other Carbohydrate, 1 Very Lean Meat **Carbohydrate Choices:** 1

Go for the Greek—yogurt that is. This thick yogurt contains more protein than regular yogurt, but either can be used.

Great Vegetarian Snacks

When the hungries strike, it's hard to stick to a food plan if healthy snacks aren't quickly within reach. Keeping some of these on hand will allow you and your family to resist the temptation to grab something less healthful.

Savory

- Cheese (or soy cheese) and whole-grain crackers
- Whole grain tortilla chips and bean dip, guacamole or salsa
- Edamame (fresh or frozen green soybeans), plain or seasoned with salt or other seasonings
- Hummus or baba ghanoush (eggplant-based dip/spread) and whole grain pita wedges
- Nachos made with whole-grain tortilla chips, black or refried vegetarian beans, cheese and salsa
- Nuts or toasted soy nuts
- Olive tapenade and whole grain crackers or baguette slices
- Popcorn
- Pretzels
- Raw veggies
- Rice cakes
- String cheese
- Yogurt

Sweet

- Fresh fruit
- Dried fruit, and dried fruit leathers and trail mixes
- Fruit-filled breakfast bars
- Granola and granola bars
- Nut butter and whole-grain bread
- Smoothies (look for ready-to-drink smoothies in the dairy case or smoothie mixes in the freezer case)
- Yogurt with fruit or granola

Fresh Fruit with Ginger Dip

Prep Time: 25 minutes • **Start to Finish:** 25 minutes • **24 servings (3 fruit pieces and 1½ tablespoons dip each)**

1 cup sour cream

¼ cup apricot preserves

2 tablespoons finely chopped crystallized ginger

1 tablespoon chopped fresh cilantro

24 fresh strawberries

24 cantaloupe balls (1 inch in diameter)

24 honeydew melon balls (1 inch in diameter)

1 In small bowl, mix sour cream, preserves and ginger until well blended. Stir in cilantro.

2 Arrange strawberries and melon balls on platter. Serve with dip.

1 SERVING: Calories 45 (Calories from Fat 20); Total Fat 2g (Saturated Fat 1g; Trans Fat 0g); Cholesterol 0mg; Sodium 15mg; Total Carbohydrate 7g (Dietary Fiber 0g); Protein 0g **%Daily Value:** Vitamin A 10%; Vitamin C 25%; Calcium 0%; Iron 0% **Exchanges:** ½ Fruit, ½ Fat **Carbohydrate Choices:** ½

Dress up the fruit plate with sprigs of fresh cilantro; if you like, add some kiwifruit slices, watermelon or fresh pineapple to the platter. Serve the fruit with frilly toothpicks or cocktail forks.

chapter 2

grains, risotto & pasta

Sweet Potato–Cauliflower Curry

Prep Time: 35 minutes • Start to Finish: 1 hour 15 minutes • 6 servings

CURRY

2 tablespoons vegetable oil

1 large onion, chopped (1 cup)

2 cloves garlic, finely chopped

2 medium dark-orange sweet potatoes, peeled, cut into 1-inch cubes (4 cups)

4 cups fresh cauliflower florets

1 tablespoon finely chopped gingerroot

4 teaspoons curry powder

½ teaspoon salt

¼ teaspoon pepper

1 can (13.5 oz) coconut milk (not cream of coconut)

1 cup vegetable broth

2 teaspoons cornstarch

2 tablespoons cold water

RICE

½ cup uncooked brown or white rice

1⅓ cups water

1 teaspoon butter

TOPPINGS

⅓ cup sliced almonds, toasted*

⅓ cup sliced green onions (about 5 medium)

⅓ cup chopped fresh cilantro

1 In 5-quart Dutch oven, heat oil over medium-high heat. Add onion; cook 5 minutes, stirring frequently, until onion is tender. Add garlic; cook 1 minute. Stir in all remaining curry ingredients except cornstarch and cold water. Reduce heat to low; cover and cook 30 minutes or until vegetables are tender.

2 Uncover; increase heat to medium-high. In small bowl, blend cornstarch and cold water until smooth paste forms. Stir cornstarch mixture into curry. Cook uncovered 5 to 10 minutes, stirring frequently, until thickened and bubbly.

3 Meanwhile, in 1-quart saucepan, heat rice, water and butter to boiling. Reduce heat; cover and simmer about 30 minutes or until rice is tender and water is absorbed.

4 Serve curry in individual deep bowls. Top each serving with about ¼ cup hot cooked rice, almonds, green onions and cilantro.

*To toast almonds, sprinkle in ungreased heavy skillet. Cook over medium heat 5 to 7 minutes, stirring frequently until almonds begin to brown, then stirring constantly until almonds are light brown.

1 SERVING: Calories 400 (Calories from Fat 210); Total Fat 23g (Saturated Fat 13g; Trans Fat 0g); Cholesterol 0mg; Sodium 440mg; Total Carbohydrate 40g (Dietary Fiber 7g); Protein 7g **%Daily Value:** Vitamin A 270%; Vitamin C 45%; Calcium 10%; Iron 15% **Exchanges:** 2 Starch, 1½ Vegetable, 4½ Fat **Carbohydrate Choices:** 2½

Curry powders are blends of many spices, and their flavors vary with the spices used. Those labeled "Madras" are hotter than the others. Experiment with different brands and blends to find the one you enjoy the most. If you are not familiar with the flavor in the particular blend of curry powder you have, use the minimal amount at first, then taste it near the end of the cooking period and add more if you like.

Substitute couscous for the cooked rice, if desired. You might also top the curry with other typical Indian toppings, such as raisins, coconut or chutney.

Wild About Mushrooms

Prep Time: 25 minutes • Start to Finish: 55 minutes • **8 servings**

1 box (1 lb) fettuccine
3 tablespoons olive oil
1 lb assorted wild mushrooms (crimini, oyster, portabella, shiitake), sliced
1 large onion, cut into wedges (about 1½ cups)
1 teaspoon dried thyme leaves
1 teaspoon salt
¼ teaspoon pepper
2 tablespoons all-purpose flour
1½ cups vegetable broth (from 32-oz carton)
1½ cups whipping cream
¼ cup chopped fresh parsley
4 oz chèvre (goat) cheese, crumbled (1 cup)
1 cup shredded Parmesan cheese (4 oz)

1 Heat oven to 400°F. Spray 13×9-inch (3-quart) glass baking dish with cooking spray. Cook and drain fettuccine as directed on package.

2 Meanwhile, in 12-inch nonstick skillet, heat oil over medium-high heat. Add mushrooms, onion, thyme, salt and pepper; cook 10 minutes, stirring occasionally, until tender. Remove from heat. Stir in flour; gradually stir in broth. Heat to boiling; boil 1 minute. Remove from heat; stir in whipping cream.

3 Add cooked fettuccine and parsley to skillet; toss. Add goat cheese; toss gently. Spoon into baking dish.

4 Cover; bake 15 minutes. Uncover; sprinkle with Parmesan cheese. Bake 10 to 15 minutes longer or until thoroughly heated and bubbly.

1 SERVING: Calories 540 (Calories from Fat 280); Total Fat 31g (Saturated Fat 16g; Trans Fat 1g); Cholesterol 115mg; Sodium 800mg; Total Carbohydrate 45g (Dietary Fiber 3g); Protein 18g **%Daily Value:** Vitamin A 20%; Vitamin C 2%; Calcium 30%; Iron 20% **Exchanges:** 3 Starch, ½ Vegetable, 1 Medium-Fat Meat, 5 Fat **Carbohydrate Choices:** 3

The goat cheese in this recipe is not meant to be melted smoothly throughout the sauce. Some of the crumbles melt and others will surprise you when you take a bite of this casserole.

This casserole is hearty enough for a main dish but can also be served as a side dish to your favorite main course.

Easy Italian Skillet Supper

Prep Time: 20 minutes • Start to Finish: 30 minutes • 4 servings

1 can (14 oz) vegetable broth

1¼ cups uncooked rosamarina (orzo) pasta (8 oz)

1 can (14.5 oz) diced tomatoes with basil, garlic and oregano, undrained

1 can (15 oz) black beans, drained, rinsed

2 cups frozen broccoli, cauliflower and carrots (from 1-lb bag)

2 tablespoons chopped fresh parsley, if desired

2 tablespoons shredded Parmesan cheese

1 In 10-inch skillet, heat broth to boiling. Stir in pasta. Return to boiling. Reduce heat to low; cover and simmer 10 to 12 minutes or until liquid is absorbed.

2 Stir in tomatoes, beans and vegetables. Cover; cook over medium heat 5 to 10 minutes, stirring occasionally, until vegetables are tender.

3 Stir in parsley; sprinkle with cheese.

1 SERVING: Calories 370 (Calories from Fat 25); Total Fat 3g (Saturated Fat 1g; Trans Fat 0g); Cholesterol 0mg; Sodium 940mg; Total Carbohydrate 67g (Dietary Fiber 16g); Protein 18g **%Daily Value:** Vitamin A 80%; Vitamin C 25%; Calcium 20%; Iron 25% **Exchanges:** 4 Starch, 1 Vegetable, ½ Lean Meat **Carbohydrate Choices:** 4½

This is the perfect dish for kids to make for the family supper. It's easy and requires no chopping or cutting if they select to omit the parsley; try a different cheese for a topping, such as Romano, mozzarella, fontina or even Asiago.

Vegetable Paella

Prep Time: 20 minutes • Start to Finish: 1 hour 20 minutes • 6 servings

1 cup uncooked regular long-grain brown or white rice

2¾ cups water

1 lb fresh asparagus spears, cut into 2-inch pieces

3 cups fresh broccoli florets

2 teaspoons olive or vegetable oil

1 medium red bell pepper, chopped (1 cup)

2 small zucchini, chopped (1¼ cups)

1 box (9 oz) frozen baby sweet peas

1 medium onion, chopped (½ cup)

¾ teaspoon salt

½ teaspoon saffron threads or ¼ teaspoon ground turmeric

2 large tomatoes, seeded, chopped (2 cups)

2 cans (15 oz each) garbanzo beans, drained, rinsed

Lettuce leaves, if desired

1 Cook rice in water as directed on package; set aside and keep warm.

2 In 2-quart saucepan, heat 1 inch water to boiling. Add asparagus and broccoli; return to boiling. Boil about 4 minutes or until crisp-tender; drain.

3 In 10-inch skillet, heat oil over medium-high heat. Add asparagus, broccoli, bell pepper, zucchini, peas, onion, salt and saffron; cook 5 minutes, stirring occasionally, until onion is crisp-tender.

4 Stir in remaining ingredients except lettuce leaves. Serve on platter or individual serving plates lined with lettuce if desired.

1 SERVING: Calories 460 (Calories from Fat 60); Total Fat 7g (Saturated Fat 1g; Trans Fat 0g); Cholesterol 0mg; Sodium 360mg; Total Carbohydrate 79g (Dietary Fiber 17g); Protein 21g **%Daily Value:** Vitamin A 60%; Vitamin C 70%; Calcium 15%; Iron 40% **Exchanges:** 4 Starch, 3½ Vegetable, 1 Fat **Carbohydrate Choices:** 5

No kidding? It's true, sweet peas are a good source of fiber, and they also rank as one of the top three favorite vegetables in the United States!

Fruited Tabbouleh with Walnuts and Feta

Prep Time: 20 minutes • Start to Finish: 3 hours 20 minutes • **10 servings (½ cup each)**

1 **cup uncooked bulgur**

1 **cup boiling water**

¼ **cup orange juice**

¼ **cup olive oil**

½ **medium cucumber, unpeeled, seeded and chopped (about 1 cup chopped)**

½ **cup chopped red onion**

½ **cup sweetened dried cranberries**

⅓ **cup loosely packed Italian (flat-leaf) parsley, minced**

⅓ **cup loosely packed mint leaves, minced**

1 **tablespoon grated orange peel**

½ **teaspoon salt**

1 **orange, peeled, divided into sections and chopped**

½ **cup chopped walnuts, toasted**

½ **cup feta cheese crumbles**

1 Place bulgur in large heatproof bowl. Pour boiling water over bulgur; stir. Let stand about 1 hour or until water is absorbed.

2 Stir in orange juice, oil, cucumber, onion, cranberries, parsley, mint, orange peel and salt; toss well. Cover; refrigerate 2 to 3 hours or until well chilled.

3 Just before serving, stir in chopped orange; sprinkle with walnuts and feta cheese.

1 SERVING: Calories 200 (Calories from Fat 100); Total Fat 11g (Saturated Fat 2.5g; Trans Fat 0g); Cholesterol 5mg; Sodium 210mg; Total Carbohydrate 21g (Dietary Fiber 4g); Protein 4g **%Daily Value:** Vitamin A 6%; Vitamin C 10%; Calcium 6%; Iron 4% **Exchanges:** 1 Starch, ½ Other Carbohydrate, 2 Fat **Carbohydrate Choices:** 1½

> Toasting intensifies the flavor of the nuts. To toast them, spread in a single layer in an ungreased shallow pan and bake uncovered in 350°F oven 6 to 10 minutes, stirring occasionally, until golden and toasted.

Moroccan Garbanzo Beans with Raisins

Prep Time: 20 minutes • Start to Finish: 20 minutes • **4 servings**

1⅓ cups uncooked regular long-grain white rice

2⅔ cups water

1 tablespoon peanut or vegetable oil

1 large onion, sliced

1 medium onion, chopped (½ cup)

1 clove garlic, finely chopped

1 cup diced seeded peeled acorn or butternut squash

¼ cup raisins

1 cup vegetable broth

1 teaspoon ground turmeric

1 teaspoon ground cinnamon

½ teaspoon ground ginger

1 can (15 oz) garbanzo beans, drained, rinsed

1 Cook rice in water as directed on package.

2 Meanwhile, in 3-quart saucepan, heat oil over medium heat. Add sliced onion, chopped onion and garlic; cook about 7 minutes, stirring occasionally, until onions are tender. Stir in remaining ingredients except garbanzo beans.

3 Heat to boiling. Reduce heat; cover and simmer about 8 minutes, stirring occasionally, until squash is tender. Stir in beans; heat thoroughly. Serve over rice.

1 SERVING: Calories 530 (Calories from Fat 60); Total Fat 7g (Saturated Fat 1g; Trans Fat 0g); Cholesterol 0mg; Sodium 260mg; Total Carbohydrate 101g (Dietary Fiber 10g); Protein 16g **%Daily Value:** Vitamin A 6%; Vitamin C 8%; Calcium 10%; Iron 35% **Exchanges:** 4½ Starch, 1½ Other Carbohydrate, 1½ Vegetable, 1 Fat **Carbohydrate Choices:** 7

Garbanzo, chickpea, *ceci*. This bean with many names has a culinary history that is shared by the cultures of the Mediterranean, the Middle East, India and Mexico. Unlike most cooked legumes, this nutty-flavored bean has a firm texture.

Mexican Tofu-Rice Skillet

Prep Time: 30 minutes • Start to Finish: 35 minutes • **4 servings**

1 package (12 oz) extra-firm tofu packed in water, drained

1 cup frozen whole kernel corn

1 can (14.5 oz) diced tomatoes with green chiles, undrained

1 package (5.6 oz) Spanish rice–flavor rice and pasta blend mix in tomato sauce

1¼ cups water

1 cup shredded Mexican cheese blend (4 oz)

1½ cups shredded lettuce

1 large tomato, seeded, chopped (1 cup)

4 medium green onions, sliced (¼ cup)

1 Place drained tofu between 2 layers of paper towels; press gently to remove as much water as possible. Cut into ½-inch cubes; set aside.

2 In 12-inch nonstick skillet, mix corn, diced tomatoes with chiles, contents of rice mix package and water. Gently stir in tofu. Heat to boiling. Reduce heat to low; cover and simmer 12 to 14 minutes, stirring occasionally, until rice is tender.

3 Remove skillet from heat. Sprinkle cheese over rice mixture. Cover; let stand 4 to 5 minutes or until liquid is absorbed and cheese is melted. Top with lettuce, chopped tomato and onions.

1 SERVING: Calories 420 (Calories from Fat 130); Total Fat 14g (Saturated Fat 6g; Trans Fat 0g); Cholesterol 30mg; Sodium 1010mg; Total Carbohydrate 50g (Dietary Fiber 5g); Protein 22g **%Daily Value:** Vitamin A 25%; Vitamin C 15%; Calcium 40%; Iron 25% **Exchanges:** 3 Starch, 1 Vegetable, 1½ Medium-Fat Meat, 1 Fat **Carbohydrate Choices:** 3

Looking for an icebreaker for introducing tofu into your eating plan? This recipe is it! Why? The dish starts with familiar Mexican ingredients and lets tofu do its chameleon act of absorbing all the wonderful flavors in the dish.

Indian Lentils and Rice

Prep Time: **25 minutes** · Start to Finish: **55 minutes** · **6 servings**

8 **medium green onions, chopped (½ cup)**

1 **tablespoon finely chopped gingerroot**

⅛ **teaspoon crushed red pepper flakes**

2 **cloves garlic, finely chopped**

3 **cans (14 oz each) vegetable broth (5¼ cups)**

1½ **cups dried lentils (12 oz), sorted, rinsed**

1 **teaspoon ground turmeric**

½ **teaspoon salt**

1 **large tomato, chopped (1 cup)**

¼ **cup shredded coconut**

2 **tablespoons chopped fresh mint leaves or 2 teaspoons dried mint leaves**

3 **cups hot cooked rice**

1½ **cups plain fat-free yogurt (from 2-lb container)**

1 Spray 3-quart saucepan with cooking spray. Add onions, gingerroot, pepper flakes and garlic; cook over medium heat 3 to 5 minutes, stirring occasionally, until onions are tender.

2 Stir in 5 cups of the broth, the lentils, turmeric and salt. Heat to boiling. Reduce heat; cover and simmer 25 to 30 minutes, adding remaining broth if needed, until lentils are tender.

3 Stir in tomato, coconut and mint. Serve over rice and with yogurt.

1 SERVING: Calories 330 (Calories from Fat 20); Total Fat 2g (Saturated Fat 1.5g; Trans Fat 0g); Cholesterol 0mg; Sodium 1050mg; Total Carbohydrate 61g (Dietary Fiber 9g); Protein 17g **%Daily Value:** Vitamin A 15%; Vitamin C 6%; Calcium 15%; Iron 35% **Exchanges:** 4 Starch, ½ Very Lean Meat **Carbohydrate Choices:** 4

This lentil dish is easy to love because it's a rich source of iron, as well as a good source of vitamin A and calcium.

Tofu and Sweet Potato Jambalaya

Prep Time: 45 minutes • Start to Finish: 55 minutes • **4 servings**

1 **package (14 oz) firm tofu packed in water, drained**

1 **tablespoon olive or vegetable oil**

1 **large dark-orange sweet potato, peeled, cut into ½-inch cubes (2 cups)**

2 **cloves garlic, finely chopped**

1 **can (14 oz) vegetable broth**

¾ **cup uncooked regular long-grain rice**

2 **tablespoons Worcestershire sauce**

¼ **teaspoon ground red pepper (cayenne)**

1 **can (15 oz) black beans, drained, rinsed**

12 **medium green onions, sliced (¾ cup)**

1 Place tofu between 2 layers of paper towels; press gently to remove as much water as possible. Cut into ¾-inch cubes.

2 In 12-inch skillet, heat oil over medium heat. Add tofu; cook 6 to 8 minutes, turning frequently, until light golden brown. Remove tofu from skillet; set aside.

3 In same skillet, cook sweet potato and garlic 2 to 3 minutes, stirring occasionally, just until sweet potato begins to brown. Stir in broth, uncooked rice, Worcestershire sauce and red pepper. Heat to boiling. Reduce heat; cover and simmer 10 minutes.

4 Stir in beans. Cover; cook 8 to 10 minutes, stirring occasionally, until rice is tender and liquid is absorbed. Stir in tofu and onions. Cook 1 to 2 minutes or until thoroughly heated.

1 SERVING: Calories 460 (Calories from Fat 80); Total Fat 9g (Saturated Fat 1.5g; Trans Fat 0g); Cholesterol 0mg; Sodium 520mg; Total Carbohydrate 75g (Dietary Fiber 14g); Protein 21g **%Daily Value:** Vitamin A 210%; Vitamin C 15%; Calcium 35%; Iron 35% **Exchanges:** 4½ Starch, 1 Vegetable, ½ Very Lean Meat, 1½ Fat **Carbohydrate Choices:** 5

Canned beans and tofu stand in for meat, poultry and shellfish, which are widely used in jambalaya recipes. The result—a truly tasty dish that will transport you to the bayou. Take a tip from New Orleans's nickname, and kick back with a "Big Easy" night when you cook this low-key skillet meal.

Quinoa and Corn Salad

Prep Time: 35 minutes • **Start to Finish:** 35 minutes • **12 servings (½ cup each)**

SALAD

- ½ **cup uncooked quinoa**
- 1 **cup water**
- ¾ **cup frozen whole kernel corn**
- 1 **cucumber, peeled, if desired**
- 2 **stalks celery, sliced (¾ cup)**
- ½ **medium red bell pepper, chopped**
- ½ **cup red onion, cut into thin bite-size pieces**

DRESSING

- 2 **tablespoons white wine vinegar**
- 2 **tablespoons fresh lime juice**
- 1 **clove garlic, finely chopped**
- 1 **teaspoon ground cumin**
- ¼ **teaspoon salt**
- ¼ **teaspoon pepper**
- ¼ **cup olive oil**
- 2 **tablespoons finely chopped fresh cilantro**

1 Rinse quinoa in cold water; drain in fine-mesh strainer. In 1-quart saucepan, heat quinoa and 1 cup water to boiling. Reduce heat; cover and simmer 15 to 20 minutes or until water is absorbed and quinoa is tender. Cool slightly. Meanwhile, cook corn as directed on package; cool.

2 Halve cucumber lengthwise; remove seeds and cut into 1½×¼-inch strips. In large salad bowl, place cucumber, celery, bell pepper, red onion, cooked quinoa and corn.

3 In small bowl, beat vinegar, lime juice, garlic, cumin, salt and pepper with whisk until blended. Beat in oil. Pour dressing over quinoa mixture; toss to coat. Sprinkle with cilantro.

1 SERVING: Calories 80 (Calories from Fat 45); Total Fat 5g (Saturated Fat 0.5g; Trans Fat 0g); Cholesterol 0mg; Sodium 55mg; Total Carbohydrate 8g (Dietary Fiber 1g); Protein 1g **%Daily Value:** Vitamin A 4%; Vitamin C 6%; Calcium 0%; Iron 4% **Exchanges:** ½ Starch, 1 Fat **Carbohydrate Choices:** ½

Quinoa is a very old grain, first used by the Incas. It is popular today because it is a whole grain.

Barley, Corn and Pepper Salad

Prep Time: 15 minutes • **Start to Finish:** 40 minutes • **10 servings (½ cup each)**

SALAD

1 cup uncooked barley

2 cups frozen whole kernel corn

½ cup diced red bell pepper

½ cup diced green bell pepper

½ cup sliced green onions (8 medium)

CILANTRO DRESSING

⅓ cup olive or vegetable oil

⅓ cup lemon juice

¼ cup chopped fresh cilantro

½ teaspoon salt

Coarsely ground black pepper

1 Cook barley as directed on package. Drain; rinse with cold water.

2 Cook corn as directed on bag. Drain; rinse with cold water. Meanwhile, in large bowl, mix barley, corn and remaining salad ingredients.

3 In jar with tight-fitting lid, combine dressing ingredients; shake well. Pour dressing over salad; toss to combine. Serve at room temperature or chilled. Store in refrigerator.

1 SERVING: Calories 170 (Calories from Fat 70); Total Fat 8g (Saturated Fat 1g; Trans Fat 0g); Cholesterol 0mg; Sodium 120mg; Total Carbohydrate 23g (Dietary Fiber 4g); Protein 3g **%Daily Value:** Vitamin A 8%; Vitamin C 35%; Calcium 0%; Iron 4% **Exchanges:** 1 Starch, ½ Vegetable, 1½ Fat **Carbohydrate Choices:** 1½

Regular or quick-cooking barley can be used to make this colorful vegetable salad.

Exploring the Variety of Grains

In a meatless diet, whole grains are an important source of fiber, protein and other nutrients. For variety of texture and flavor, try some of these less-known grains in your vegetarian cooking. They may be found in bulk or in packages near the natural foods in your grocery store, in whole food stores and in food co-ops:

Barley: Hulled barley (regular barley) is a whole grain. Pearled barley* (quick-cooking) has some of the hull removed, so it isn't a whole grain but is considered an incomplete protein (see "The 'Meat' of Vegetarian Nutrition," page 7).

Bulgur: Whole wheat kernels that have been boiled, dried and cracked.

Kasha*: A generic term given to any crushed grain—but typically buckwheat kernels.

Millet*: The mild flavor mixes well with other flavors. Toasting it first adds another layer of flavor.

Quinoa*: Rinse, if desired, before cooking to remove the bitter coating. A quick-cooking whole grain that has a light and fluffy texture. Use in side dishes, soups or salads.

Wheat Berries: Whole wheat kernels with a chewy texture and nutty flavor. Good in main or side dishes and salads.

*Grains with *=20 minutes or less cooking time*

Storing and Cooking Grains

- Grains can be kept at room temperature for up to 1 year. Store them in their original packaging or in airtight glass or plastic containers in a cool (60°F or less) dry place. All grains can be refrigerated or frozen—a good idea if you live in a hot, humid climate. Whole grains naturally contain oil, so they can become rancid more quickly if stored at room temperature. Store these in the refrigerator or freezer for up to 6 months.

- Use a medium bowl if soaking the grains; a 2-quart saucepan for cooking.

- Heat the water (or add additional flavor by cooking in vegetable broth or half vegetable broth or fruit juice instead of water) and grains to boiling, then reduce the heat. Cover and simmer as directed in the chart at right. Don't remove the lid or stir during cooking (stirring releases more starch, making grains—particularly rice—sticky). After cooking, fluff with a fork, lifting the grains to release steam.

- Grains lose moisture with age, so a little more or less liquid than the chart calls for may be needed. If all the liquid is absorbed but the grain is not yet tender, add a little more liquid and continue cooking. If the grain is tender but all the liquid hasn't been absorbed, just drain it away.

- Check the packaging for additional information about cooking specific grains.

Grain Cooking Chart

TYPE OF GRAIN (1 CUP)	AMOUNT OF WATER IN CUPS	COOKING DIRECTIONS	YIELD IN CUPS
RICE			
White Rice			
Long-Grain	2	Simmer 15 minutes.	3
Parboiled (Converted)	2½	Simmer 20 to 25 minutes. Let stand 5 minutes.	3 to 4
Precooked (Instant)	1	After stirring in rice, cover and remove from heat. Let stand 5 minutes.	2
Basmati (White)	1½ cups	Simmer 15 to 20 minutes.	3
Brown Rice			
Long-Grain Brown (Regular and Basmati)	2¾	Simmer 45 to 50 minutes.	4
Precooked (Instant) Brown	1¼	Simmer 10 minutes.	2
Jasmine	1¾	Simmer 15 to 20 minutes.	3
Wild Rice	2½	Simmer 40 to 50 minutes.	3
OTHER GRAINS			
Barley			
Quick-Cooking	2	Simmer 10 to 12 minutes. Let stand 5 minutes.	3
Regular	4	Simmer 45 to 50 minutes.	4
Bulgur	3	Bring water to boil, then add bulgur; cover and remove from heat. Let stand 30 to 60 minutes. Drain if needed. Or cook as directed on package.	3
Kasha	2	Bring water to boil, then add kasha; cover and let stand 10 to 15 minutes. Drain if needed. Or cook as directed on package.	4
Millet	2½	Simmer 15 to 20 minutes.	4
Quinoa	2	Simmer 15 minutes.	3 to 4
Wheat Berries	2½	Simmer 50 to 60 minutes.	2¾ to 3

Wheat Berry Salad

Prep Time: **15 minutes** • Start to Finish: **2 hours 45 minutes** • **5 servings**

WHEAT BERRIES

¾ **cup uncooked wheat berries**

3 **cups water**

CREAMY VINAIGRETTE DRESSING

⅓ **cup vegetable oil**

2 **tablespoons mayonnaise or salad dressing**

2 **tablespoons red wine vinegar**

½ **teaspoon salt**

¼ **teaspoon garlic powder**

⅛ **teaspoon pepper**

SALAD

1 **cup chopped broccoli**

1 **cup chopped cauliflower**

1 **cup grape or cherry tomatoes, cut in half**

1 **small green bell pepper, chopped (½ cup)**

4 **medium green onions, sliced (¼ cup)**

½ **cup crumbled feta cheese (2 oz)**

1 In 3-quart saucepan, soak wheat berries in water 30 minutes.

2 Heat berries and water to boiling over high heat. Reduce heat to low; partially cover and simmer 55 to 60 minutes or until wheat berries are tender. Drain; rinse with cold water.

3 In small bowl, mix dressing ingredients until well blended.

4 In large serving bowl, toss wheat berries, salad ingredients and dressing. Cover; refrigerate at least 1 hour before serving.

1 SERVING: Calories 330 (Calories from Fat 200); Total Fat 22g (Saturated Fat 5g; Trans Fat 0g); Cholesterol 15mg; Sodium 460mg; Total Carbohydrate 25g (Dietary Fiber 5g); Protein 7g **%Daily Value:** Vitamin A 10%; Vitamin C 35%; Calcium 10%; Iron 8% **Exchanges:** 1½ Starch, 1 Vegetable, 4 Fat **Carbohydrate Choices:** 1½

Wheat berries are simply whole grains of wheat and can be found in the natural food section of the supermarket.

Classic Risotto

Prep Time: 55 minutes • Start to Finish: 55 minutes • **4 servings**

6 cups vegetable broth

2 tablespoons butter or margarine

¼ cup olive or vegetable oil

1 medium onion, thinly sliced

2 tablespoons chopped fresh parsley

2 cups uncooked Arborio or medium-grain white rice

1 cup dry white wine or vegetable broth

1 cup freshly grated or shredded Parmesan cheese

½ teaspoon coarsely ground pepper

1 In 3-quart saucepan, heat broth over medium heat.

2 Meanwhile, in 12-inch nonstick skillet or 4-quart saucepan, heat butter and oil over medium-high heat until butter is melted. Add onion and parsley; cook about 5 minutes, stirring frequently, until onion is tender.

3 Stir in rice. Cook, stirring occasionally, until edges of rice kernels are translucent. Stir in wine. Cook about 3 minutes, stirring constantly, until wine is absorbed.

4 Reduce heat to medium. Pour ½ cup of the hot broth over rice mixture. Cook uncovered, stirring frequently, until broth is absorbed. Continue cooking 30 to 35 minutes, adding broth ½ cup at a time and stirring frequently, until rice is almost tender and mixture is creamy. Remove from heat.

5 Stir in cheese and pepper.

1 SERVING: Calories 720 (Calories from Fat 250); Total Fat 27g (Saturated Fat 10g; Trans Fat 0g); Cholesterol 35mg; Sodium 1910mg; Total Carbohydrate 90g (Dietary Fiber 1g); Protein 18g **%Daily Value:** Vitamin A 25%; Vitamin C 4%; Calcium 40%; Iron 25% **Exchanges:** 6 Starch, ½ Vegetable, 5 Fat **Carbohydrate Choices:** 6

Classic Risotto with Peas: Just before serving, stir in a 1-pound bag of frozen sweet peas, cooked and drained.

Risottos are very easy to make and will stick to your ribs. To create authentic taste and texture, use Arborio rice, a short-grain rice with a high starch content that lends risotto its creaminess. Add the hot broth a half cup at a time and don't add more until the liquid has been absorbed. This will ensure a wonderful creamy rice dish.

Risotto Primavera

Prep Time: 45 minutes • Start to Finish: 45 minutes • **4 servings**

¼ **cup water**

1 **medium onion, chopped (½ cup)**

1 **lb fresh asparagus spears, cut into 1-inch pieces**

1 **cup uncooked Arborio or other short-grain white rice**

2 **cans (14 oz each) vegetable broth**

2 **cups fresh broccoli florets**

1 **cup frozen sweet peas**

3 **tablespoons grated Parmesan cheese**

1 In 3-quart saucepan, heat water to boiling. Add onion and asparagus; cook about 5 minutes, stirring frequently, until crisp-tender. Remove mixture from saucepan.

2 Spray saucepan with cooking spray; add rice to saucepan. Cook about 3 minutes, stirring frequently, until rice begins to brown.

3 Pour ½ cup of the broth over rice. Cook uncovered, stirring occasionally, until liquid is absorbed. Continue cooking 15 to 20 minutes, adding broth ½ cup at a time and stirring occasionally, until rice is tender and creamy; add asparagus mixture, broccoli and peas with the last addition of broth. Sprinkle with cheese.

1 SERVING: Calories 290 (Calories from Fat 20); Total Fat 2g (Saturated Fat 1g; Trans Fat 0g); Cholesterol 0mg; Sodium 910mg; Total Carbohydrate 56g (Dietary Fiber 5g); Protein 11g **%Daily Value:** Vitamin A 45%; Vitamin C 35%; Calcium 15%; Iron 30% **Exchanges:** 3 Starch, 2 Vegetable **Carbohydrate Choices:** 4

> Risotto is done when enough broth has been absorbed to make the rice just tender and the mixture creamy.

Sweet Potato Risotto

Prep Time: **1 hour** • Start to Finish: **1 hour** • **4 servings**

7½ cups vegetable broth

¼ cup dry white wine or water

⅔ cup chopped onion

2 cloves garlic, finely chopped

2 cups uncooked short-grain Arborio or medium-grain white rice

1 cup mashed cooked sweet potato

¼ cup grated Parmesan cheese

1 teaspoon chopped fresh or **½** teaspoon dried rosemary leaves, crumbled

¼ teaspoon ground nutmeg

Additional fresh rosemary, if desired

Shredded Parmesan cheese, if desired

1 In 3-quart saucepan, heat broth over medium heat.

2 Meanwhile, in 12-inch nonstick skillet or 4-quart saucepan, heat wine to boiling over medium-high heat. Add onion and garlic; cook 3 to 4 minutes, stirring frequently, until onion is tender.

3 Stir in rice. Cook 1 minute, stirring frequently, until rice begins to brown.

4 Reduce heat to medium. Stir in sweet potato and ½ cup of the hot broth. Cook uncovered, stirring frequently, until broth is absorbed. Continue cooking 30 to 35 minutes, adding broth ½ cup at a time and stirring frequently, until rice is almost tender and mixture is creamy. Remove from heat.

5 Stir in remaining ingredients. Garnish with additional fresh rosemary and shredded Parmesan cheese.

1 SERVING: Calories 490 (Calories from Fat 25); Total Fat 3g (Saturated Fat 1.5g; Trans Fat 0g); Cholesterol 5mg; Sodium 1890mg; Total Carbohydrate 103g (Dietary Fiber 3g); Protein 11g **%Daily Value:** Vitamin A 260%; Vitamin C 15%; Calcium 15%; Iron 25% **Exchanges:** 3 Starch, 3½ Other Carbohydrate, 1 Vegetable **Carbohydrate Choices:** 7

Sweet potatoes are full of vitamin A. You can use either mashed fresh cooked or canned sweet potatoes in this dish. For another orange-hued version, use mashed cooked carrots instead of sweet potatoes.

Vegetable-Cashew-Noodle Bowl

Prep Time: 20 minutes • **Start to Finish:** 30 minutes • **4 servings (1¼ cups each)**

7 to 8 oz uncooked Japanese udon noodles (from 10-oz package)

1 red bell pepper, seeded, cut into 2×¼-inch strips

1 yellow bell pepper, seeded, cut into 2×¼-inch strips

2 small carrots, thinly sliced

2 cups fresh cilantro leaves

1 tablespoon grated lemon peel

3 cloves garlic

1 teaspoon lemon juice

Salt and pepper to taste

¼ cup olive oil

1 green onion, sliced

¼ cup lightly salted roasted cashews

1 In 6- to 8-quart Dutch oven or sauce pot, heat 4 quarts water to boiling. Add noodles; return to boiling. Reduce heat; boil 13 to 14 minutes or until noodles are tender. During last 4 minutes of cooking time, add bell peppers and carrots. Drain; place in large bowl.

2 Meanwhile, in food processor, process cilantro, lemon peel and garlic until very finely chopped. Add lemon juice, salt, pepper and oil; process until mixture forms a smooth puree.

3 Pour cilantro sauce over noodle mixture; toss to coat evenly. Divide mixture into 4 individual serving bowls. Garnish each with green onion and cashews.

1 SERVING: Calories 410 (Calories from Fat 160); Total Fat 18g (Saturated Fat 2.5g; Trans Fat 0g); Cholesterol 0mg; Sodium 140mg; Total Carbohydrate 53g (Dietary Fiber 6g); Protein 8g **%Daily Value:** Vitamin A 50%; Vitamin C 80%; Calcium 4%; Iron 10% **Exchanges:** 3 Starch, 1 Vegetable, 3 Fat **Carbohydrate Choices:** 3½

Udon noodles are wheat noodles popular in Asia. They are readily available now at many larger grocery stores and at stores that specialize in Asian cuisines. If desired, substitute linguine or fettuccine for the udon noodles.

Chipotle-Peanut-Noodle Bowls

easy quick

Prep Time: **15 minutes** • Start to Finish: **30 minutes** • **4 servings**

½ **cup creamy peanut butter**

½ **cup apple juice**

2 **tablespoons soy sauce**

2 **chipotle chiles in adobo sauce (from 7-oz can), seeded, chopped**

1 **teaspoon adobo sauce from can of chiles**

¼ **cup chopped fresh cilantro**

2 **medium carrots, cut into julienne (matchstick) strips**

1 **medium red bell pepper, cut into julienne (matchstick) strips**

1 **package (8 to 10 oz) Chinese curly noodles**

2 **tablespoons chopped peanuts**

1 In large bowl, mix peanut butter, apple juice, soy sauce, chiles and adobo sauce until smooth. Stir in cilantro; set aside.

2 In 2-quart saucepan, heat 4 cups water to boiling. Add carrots and bell pepper; cook 1 minute. Remove from water with slotted spoon. Add noodles to water; cook and drain as directed on package.

3 Add noodles to peanut butter mixture; toss. Divide noodles among 4 bowls; top with carrots and bell pepper. Sprinkle with peanuts.

1 SERVING: Calories 480 (Calories from Fat 170); Total Fat 19g (Saturated Fat 4g; Trans Fat 0g); Cholesterol 0mg; Sodium 710mg; Total Carbohydrate 59g (Dietary Fiber 8g); Protein 17g **%Daily Value:** Vitamin A 40%; Vitamin C 30%; Calcium 4%; Iron 10% **Exchanges:** 4 Starch, ½ Vegetable, ½ Lean Meat, 3 Fat **Carbohydrate Choices:** 4

To save the rest of the chiles in adobo sauce for other uses, spoon the chiles and sauce into a resealable plastic freezer bag, flatten to a thin layer and freeze. To use, just break off the amount you need; freezing makes them a bit milder, so you may need more.

Pad Thai

Prep Time: 40 minutes • Start to Finish: 40 minutes • **4 servings**

4 **cups water**

1 **package (6 to 8 oz) linguine-style stir-fry rice noodles (rice stick noodles)***

⅓ **cup fresh lime juice**

⅓ **cup water**

3 **tablespoons packed brown sugar**

3 **tablespoons fish sauce or soy sauce**

3 **tablespoons soy sauce**

1 **tablespoon rice vinegar or white vinegar**

¾ **teaspoon ground red pepper (cayenne)**

3 **tablespoons vegetable oil**

3 **cloves garlic, finely chopped**

1 **medium shallot, finely chopped, or ¼ cup finely chopped onion**

2 **eggs, beaten**

¼ **cup finely chopped dry-roasted peanuts**

3 **cups fresh bean sprouts**

4 **medium green onions, thinly sliced (¼ cup), if desired**

¼ **cup firmly packed fresh cilantro leaves, if desired**

1 In 3-quart saucepan, heat 4 cups water to boiling. Remove from heat; add noodles (push noodles into water with back of spoon to cover completely with water if necessary). Soak noodles 3 to 5 minutes or until noodles are soft but firm. Drain noodles; rinse with cold water.

2 Meanwhile, in small bowl, mix lime juice, ⅓ cup water, the brown sugar, fish sauce, soy sauce, vinegar, red pepper and 1 tablespoon of the oil; set aside.

3 In nonstick wok or 12-inch nonstick skillet, heat remaining 2 tablespoons oil over medium heat. Add garlic and shallot; cook about 30 seconds, stirring constantly, until they begin to brown. Stir in beaten eggs, cooking and stirring gently about 2 minutes or until scrambled but still moist.

4 Stir in noodles and lime juice mixture. Increase heat to high; cook about 1 minute, tossing constantly with 2 wooden spoons, until sauce begins to thicken. Add remaining ingredients except cilantro; cook 2 to 3 minutes, tossing with wooden spoons, until noodles are tender. Place on serving platter. Sprinkle with cilantro. If desired, garnish with additional chopped dry-roasted peanuts and green onions.

**Thin or thick rice stick noodles can be substituted for the linguine-style stir-fry rice noodles.*

1 SERVING: Calories 510 (Calories from Fat 190); Total Fat 21g (Saturated Fat 3.5g; Trans Fat 0g); Cholesterol 105mg; Sodium 1880mg; Total Carbohydrate 65g (Dietary Fiber 3g); Protein 15g **%Daily Value:** Vitamin A 8%; Vitamin C 15%; Calcium 10%; Iron 15% **Exchanges:** 4 Starch, 1 Vegetable, 3½ Fat **Carbohydrate Choices:** 4

Fish sauce gives this noodle dish its distinctive Thai flavor. If you like, vegetarian fish sauce can be used instead. Look for it in an Asian food store or order it online.

Fettuccine Primavera

Prep Time: 25 minutes • Start to Finish: 25 minutes • **4 servings (1½ cups each)**

8 oz uncooked fettuccine

1 tablespoon olive or vegetable oil

1 cup fresh broccoli florets

1 cup fresh cauliflower florets

1 cup frozen sweet peas

2 medium carrots, thinly sliced (1 cup)

1 small onion, chopped (¼ cup)

1 container (10 oz) refrigerated Alfredo pasta sauce

¼ cup milk

1 tablespoon Dijon mustard

1 oz shaved Parmesan cheese

1 Cook and drain fettuccine as directed on package.

2 Meanwhile, in 12-inch skillet, heat oil over medium-high heat. Add broccoli, cauliflower, peas, carrots and onion; cook 6 to 8 minutes, stirring frequently, until vegetables are crisp-tender.

3 Stir Alfredo sauce, milk and mustard into vegetable mixture; cook until hot. Stir in fettuccine; cook until thoroughly heated. Top with cheese.

1 SERVING: Calories 570 (Calories from Fat 280); Total Fat 31g (Saturated Fat 16g; Trans Fat 1g); Cholesterol 120mg; Sodium 580mg; Total Carbohydrate 55g (Dietary Fiber 5g); Protein 18g **%Daily Value:** Vitamin A 140%; Vitamin C 35%; Calcium 30%; Iron 20% **Exchanges:** 3 Starch, 2 Vegetable, ½ High-Fat Meat, 5 Fat **Carbohydrate Choices:** 3½

Look for refrigerated Alfredo sauce next to the fresh pasta in your grocery store refrigerator case. If you're counting calories and fat, purchase "light" Alfredo sauce.

Gorgonzola Linguine with Toasted Walnuts

Prep Time: 30 minutes • **Start to Finish:** 30 minutes • **4 servings (1½ cups each)**

12 oz uncooked linguine
2 tablespoons butter or margarine
2 cloves garlic, finely chopped
2 tablespoons all-purpose flour
½ teaspoon salt
1 pint (2 cups) fat-free half-and-half
½ cup dry white wine or vegetable broth
1 cup crumbled Gorgonzola cheese (4 oz)
¼ cup chopped walnuts, toasted*

1 Cook and drain linguine as directed on package.

2 Meanwhile, in 3-quart saucepan, melt butter over medium heat. Add garlic; cook, stirring occasionally, until golden brown. Stir in flour and salt. Cook, stirring constantly, until smooth and bubbly. Remove from heat. Stir in half-and-half and wine. Cook, stirring constantly, until mixture thickens slightly. Reduce heat to medium-low. Stir in cheese. Cook, stirring occasionally, until cheese is melted.

3 Add linguine to sauce; toss. Garnish with walnuts.

*To toast walnuts, sprinkle in ungreased heavy skillet. Cook over medium heat 5 to 7 minutes, stirring frequently until nuts begin to brown, then stirring constantly until nuts are light brown.

1 SERVING: Calories 690 (Calories from Fat 200); Total Fat 23g (Saturated Fat 11g; Trans Fat 0g); Cholesterol 45mg; Sodium 910mg; Total Carbohydrate 91g (Dietary Fiber 5g); Protein 24g **%Daily Value:** Vitamin A 8%; Vitamin C 0%; Calcium 30%; Iron 20% **Exchanges:** 6 Starch, 1 Medium-Fat Meat, 3 Fat **Carbohydrate Choices:** 6

You'll love the flavor combination of Gorgonzola and walnuts! If desired, sprinkle additional cheese and fresh parsley over the pasta.

Angel Hair Pasta with Autumn Vegetable Ragout

Prep Time: 30 minutes • **Start to Finish:** 30 minutes • **4 servings**

3 cups water

1 medium dark-orange sweet potato, peeled, diced

8 oz uncooked angel hair (capellini) pasta

2 tablespoons olive or vegetable oil

3 cloves garlic, finely chopped

4 medium tomatoes, chopped (4 cups)

1 small zucchini, cut lengthwise in half, then cut crosswise into slices (1 cup)

1 small yellow summer squash, cut lengthwise in half, then cut crosswise into slices (1 cup)

½ teaspoon salt

¼ teaspoon freshly ground pepper

⅓ cup freshly shredded Parmesan cheese

1 In 4-quart Dutch oven, heat water to boiling over medium-high heat. Add sweet potato; cook 3 to 5 minutes or until crisp-tender. Drain.

2 Cook and drain pasta as directed on package.

3 Meanwhile, in 10-inch skillet, heat oil over medium-high heat. Add garlic; cook 30 seconds, stirring frequently. Stir in tomatoes. Cook about 3 minutes, stirring frequently, until slightly soft. Stir in zucchini, yellow squash, sweet potato, salt and pepper. Cook 2 to 3 minutes, stirring frequently, until vegetables are crisp-tender.

4 Serve vegetables over pasta. Sprinkle with cheese.

1 SERVING: Calories 420 (Calories from Fat 100); Total Fat 11g (Saturated Fat 3g; Trans Fat 0g); Cholesterol 5mg; Sodium 480mg; Total Carbohydrate 65g (Dietary Fiber 6g); Protein 15g **%Daily Value:** Vitamin A 140%; Vitamin C 35%; Calcium 15%; Iron 15% **Exchanges:** 4 Starch, 1 Vegetable, 2 Fat **Carbohydrate Choices:** 4

Store tomatoes at room temperature, not in the refrigerator—cold temperatures destroy the flavor and make the flesh mealy.

Spaghetti and Spicy Rice Balls

Prep Time: 30 minutes • Start to Finish: 30 minutes • **5 servings**

2 cups cooked regular long-grain white or brown rice*

½ cup quick-cooking oats

1 medium onion, chopped (½ cup)

¼ cup plain bread crumbs

¼ cup milk

1 tablespoon chopped fresh or 1 teaspoon dried basil leaves

2 teaspoons chopped fresh or ½ teaspoon dried oregano leaves

¼ teaspoon ground red pepper (cayenne)

1 egg, beaten

½ cup wheat germ

1 tablespoon vegetable oil

1 package (16 oz) spaghetti

2 cups tomato pasta sauce (any variety), heated

Finely shredded Parmesan cheese, if desired

1 In medium bowl, mix cooked rice, oats, onion, bread crumbs, milk, basil, oregano, red pepper and egg. Shape mixture into 10 balls; roll in wheat germ to coat.

2 In 10-inch skillet, heat oil over medium heat. Add rice balls; cook about 10 minutes, turning occasionally, until light golden brown.

3 Meanwhile, cook and drain spaghetti as directed on package.

4 Serve rice balls and pasta sauce over spaghetti. Sprinkle with cheese.

*Do not use instant rice.

1 **SERVING:** Calories 670 (Calories from Fat 80); Total Fat 9g (Saturated Fat 2g; Trans Fat 0g); Cholesterol 45mg; Sodium 560mg; Total Carbohydrate 123g (Dietary Fiber 9g); Protein 24g **%Daily Value:** Vitamin A 15%; Vitamin C 10%; Calcium 6%; Iron 35% **Exchanges:** 8 Starch, 1 Fat **Carbohydrate Choices:** 8

The rice and oat "meatballs" get a light wheat germ coating, giving them a golden brown color and a bit of nutty-flavored crunch. Wheat germ is oily, so it can turn rancid quickly; store it in the fridge or freezer.

Lemon-Pepper Pasta and Asparagus

Prep Time: 25 minutes • Start to Finish: 25 minutes • **4 servings**

2 **cups uncooked bow-tie (farfalle) pasta (4 oz)**

¼ **cup olive or vegetable oil**

1 **medium red bell pepper, chopped (1 cup)**

1 **lb fresh asparagus spears, cut into 1-inch pieces**

1 **teaspoon grated lemon peel**

½ **teaspoon salt**

½ **teaspoon freshly ground pepper**

3 **tablespoons lemon juice**

1 **can (15 oz) cannellini (white kidney) beans or 1 can (15.5 oz) navy beans, drained, rinsed**

Freshly ground pepper, if desired

1 Cook and drain pasta as directed on package.

2 Meanwhile, in 12-inch skillet, heat oil over medium-high heat. Add bell pepper, asparagus, lemon peel, salt and ½ teaspoon pepper; cook, stirring occasionally, until vegetables are crisp-tender.

3 Stir lemon juice and beans into vegetable mixture. Cook until beans are hot. Add pasta; toss. Sprinkle with pepper.

1 SERVING: Calories 400 (Calories from Fat 130); Total Fat 15g (Saturated Fat 2g; Trans Fat 0g); Cholesterol 0mg; Sodium 420mg; Total Carbohydrate 52g (Dietary Fiber 9g); Protein 15g **%Daily Value:** Vitamin A 30%; Vitamin C 50%; Calcium 10%; Iron 30% **Exchanges:** 3 Starch, 1 Vegetable, ½ Very Lean Meat, 2½ Fat **Carbohydrate Choices:** 3½

For a delicious change of flavor, use fresh lime juice and peel instead of the lemon.

Tofu-Teriyaki-Mushroom Noodles

Prep Time: 30 minutes • Start to Finish: 30 minutes • **4 servings**

6 dried Chinese black or shiitake mushrooms (½ oz)

8 oz uncooked soba (buckwheat) noodles or whole wheat spaghetti

1 package (14 oz) firm tofu packed in water, drained

1 tablespoon vegetable oil

1 large onion, sliced

1 package (8 oz) sliced fresh mushrooms (3 cups)

8 oz fresh shiitake, crimini or baby portabella mushrooms, sliced

⅓ cup teriyaki sauce

¼ cup chopped fresh cilantro

1 tablespoon sesame seed, toasted, if desired

1 In small bowl, pour 1 cup hot water over dried mushrooms; let stand about 20 minutes or until soft.

2 Meanwhile, cook and drain noodles as directed on package. Place drained tofu between 2 layers of paper towels; press gently to remove as much water as possible. Cut into ¼-inch cubes; set aside.

3 Drain water from dried mushrooms; rinse with warm water and drain again. Squeeze out excess moisture from mushrooms. Remove and discard stems; cut caps into ½-inch strips.

4 In 12-inch skillet or wok, heat oil over medium-high heat. Add onion; cook and stir 3 minutes. Add all mushrooms and tofu; cook and stir 3 minutes. Stir in teriyaki sauce. Reduce heat; partially cover and simmer about 2 minutes or until vegetables are tender. Stir in noodles, cilantro and sesame seed.

1 SERVING: Calories 420 (Calories from Fat 90); Total Fat 10g (Saturated Fat 1.5g; Trans Fat 0g); Cholesterol 0mg; Sodium 1150mg; Total Carbohydrate 58g (Dietary Fiber 7g); Protein 24g **%Daily Value:** Vitamin A 2%; Vitamin C 4%; Calcium 20%; Iron 30% **Exchanges:** 3 Starch, 2 Vegetable, 1½ Medium-Fat Meat, ½ Fat **Carbohydrate Choices:** 4

> Soba noodles are made with buckwheat and wheat flour. These quick-cooking noodles have a similar taste to wheat noodles. Look for them near the Asian ingredients in the grocery store.

Butternut Squash Ravioli

Prep Time: 1 hour • Start to Finish: 1 hour 30 minutes • 6 servings (6 ravioli and 1 tablespoon sauce each)

RAVIOLI

- 1 medium butternut squash (about 1½ lb), halved, seeds removed
- 1 tablespoon olive oil
- ½ cup low-fat ricotta cheese
- ¼ cup shredded Parmesan cheese
- ½ teaspoon salt
- ¼ teaspoon pepper
- ¼ teaspoon ground nutmeg
- 36 wonton skins (about 3½-inch square)
- 1 egg
- 2 tablespoons water

BROWNED BUTTER–SAGE SAUCE

- ½ cup butter
- 12 to 15 fresh sage leaves
- 1 clove garlic, finely chopped
- ¼ teaspoon salt
- ¼ teaspoon pepper

TOPPINGS

- 6 tablespoons shredded Parmesan cheese
- 6 fresh sage leaves

1 Heat oven to 400°F. Place squash halves, cut side up, on ungreased cookie sheet. Brush with oil. Roast 30 minutes or until squash is very tender. Cool slightly.

2 When squash is cool enough to handle, use spoon to remove pulp; place in small bowl. Stir in ricotta cheese, ¼ cup Parmesan cheese, ½ teaspoon salt, ¼ teaspoon pepper and the nutmeg.

3 Spoon 1 tablespoon squash mixture onto center of each wonton skin. In another small bowl, beat together egg and water. Brush edges of wonton skins with egg-water mixture. Fold skins tightly over filling, pressing gently to remove any air trapped inside, forming triangles, and sealing filling tightly inside skins. (If filled wonton skins have large air pockets, they can float to surface when boiled, causing them to cook unevenly.)

4 In 1-quart saucepan, heat butter over medium heat about 3 minutes until melted. Add 12 to 15 sage leaves; cook 3 to 4 minutes, watching carefully and stirring frequently, until butter is golden and sage wilts and then crisps. Add garlic; cook 1 minute or until butter is amber in color and garlic is tender. Stir in ¼ teaspoon salt and ¼ teaspoon pepper. Set aside; keep warm.

5 In Dutch oven or sauce pot, heat 4 quarts water to boiling. Slip filled wonton skins into boiling water in batches so as not to crowd them. Boil 3 minutes or until tender. (Do not overcook.) Use slotted spoon to lift ravioli from boiling water; place on serving plates.

6 Drizzle butter mixture evenly over ravioli. Immediately sprinkle each serving with 1 tablespoon Parmesan cheese; garnish each with sage leaf.

1 SERVING: Calories 430 (Calories from Fat 220); Total Fat 24g (Saturated Fat 13g; Trans Fat 0.5g); Cholesterol 95mg; Sodium 910mg; Total Carbohydrate 40g (Dietary Fiber 2g); Protein 13g **%Daily Value:** Vitamin A 230%; Vitamin C 15%; Calcium 25%; Iron 15% **Exchanges:** 2½ Starch, 1 Medium-Fat Meat, 3½ Fat **Carbohydrate Choices:** 2½

Filled ravioli made from wonton skins can be frozen. Cook the number you would like to serve, then freeze the rest. Arrange filled ravioli in a single layer on a tray and freeze 1 to 2 hours or until they are firm. Transfer to a freezer storage bag, label and freeze. No need to thaw when cooking, just increase the cooking time about 1 minute.

Alfredo Pasta Pie with Toasted French Bread Crust

Prep Time: 15 minutes • Start to Finish: 40 minutes • 6 servings

4 oz uncooked angel hair (capellini) pasta

18 slices French bread, about ¼ inch thick

2 tablespoons butter or margarine, softened

¾ cup shredded Swiss cheese (3 oz)

2 tablespoons chopped fresh or 2 teaspoons dried basil leaves

1 container (10 oz) refrigerated Alfredo sauce

3 medium plum (Roma) tomatoes, chopped (1 cup)

4 medium green onions, sliced (¼ cup)

1 tablespoon grated Romano or Parmesan cheese

1 Heat oven to 400°F. Cook and drain pasta as directed on package.

2 Meanwhile, brush bread with butter. Line bottom and side of 10-inch pie plate with bread, buttered sides up and slightly overlapping slices. Bake about 10 minutes or until light brown.

3 Reduce oven temperature to 350°F. In medium bowl, mix Swiss cheese, 1 tablespoon of the basil and the Alfredo sauce. Gently stir in pasta. Spoon into baked crust.

4 In small bowl, mix tomatoes, onions and remaining 1 tablespoon basil. Sprinkle over pasta mixture; lightly press onto surface. Sprinkle with Romano cheese.

5 Bake at 350°F 15 to 20 minutes or until hot. Let stand 5 minutes before cutting.

1 SERVING: Calories 480 (Calories from Fat 220); Total Fat 24g (Saturated Fat 15g; Trans Fat 1g); Cholesterol 70mg; Sodium 580mg; Total Carbohydrate 49g (Dietary Fiber 2g); Protein 16g **%Daily Value:** Vitamin A 20%; Vitamin C 4%; Calcium 25%; Iron 15% **Exchanges:** 3 Starch, ½ Vegetable, 1 Medium-Fat Meat, 3½ Fat **Carbohydrate Choices:** 3

This is vegetarian comfort food and a delicious way to use up leftover French bread! The bread becomes a toasted crust for this creamy pasta pie. Just add veggies or a salad for a family-pleasing dinner.

Curried Ravioli with Spinach

Prep Time: 20 minutes • Start to Finish: 20 minutes • **4 servings**

- **1 package (9 oz) refrigerated cheese-filled ravioli**
- **1 box (9 oz) frozen chopped spinach**
- **2 oz cream cheese, softened**
- **⅔ cup canned coconut milk (not cream of coconut)**
- **⅓ cup vegetable broth**
- **¾ teaspoon curry powder**
- **¼ teaspoon salt**
- **¼ cup chopped peanuts**
- **¼ cup sliced green onions (4 medium)**

1 Cook and drain ravioli as directed on package. Cook and drain spinach as directed on box.

2 In 1-quart saucepan, mix cream cheese, coconut milk, broth, curry powder and salt. Cook over medium heat, stirring occasionally, until hot.

3 Spoon spinach onto serving plate. Top with ravioli and sauce. Sprinkle with peanuts and onions.

1 SERVING: Calories 420 (Calories from Fat 220); Total Fat 25g (Saturated Fat 14g; Trans Fat 0g); Cholesterol 50mg; Sodium 560mg; Total Carbohydrate 35g (Dietary Fiber 4g); Protein 14g **%Daily Value:** Vitamin A 110%; Vitamin C 2%; Calcium 20%; Iron 20% **Exchanges:** 2 Starch, ½ Vegetable, 1 Medium-Fat Meat, 4 Fat **Carbohydrate Choices:** 2

Coconut milk, which is richly flavored and slightly sweet, is made from simmering fresh coconut meat and water. It is used extensively in Thai and Indonesian cooking. Don't buy cream of coconut by mistake; that is for making tropical-flavored drinks and desserts.

Vegetable Curry with Couscous

Prep Time: 15 minutes • Start to Finish: 15 minutes • 4 servings

1 tablespoon vegetable oil

1 medium red bell pepper, cut into thin strips

¼ cup vegetable broth

1 tablespoon curry powder

1 teaspoon salt

1 bag (1 lb) frozen broccoli, cauliflower and carrots (or other combination)

½ cup raisins

⅓ cup mango chutney

2 cups hot cooked couscous or rice

¼ cup chopped peanuts

1 In 12-inch skillet, heat oil over medium-high heat. Add bell pepper; cook 4 to 5 minutes, stirring frequently, until tender.

2 Stir in broth, curry powder, salt and vegetables. Heat to boiling. Boil about 4 minutes, stirring frequently, until vegetables are crisp-tender.

3 Stir in raisins and chutney. Serve over couscous. Sprinkle with peanuts.

1 SERVING: Calories 330 (Calories from Fat 80); Total Fat 9g (Saturated Fat 1.5g; Trans Fat 0g); Cholesterol 0mg; Sodium 750mg; Total Carbohydrate 54g (Dietary Fiber 7g); Protein 9g **%Daily Value:** Vitamin A 150%; Vitamin C 60%; Calcium 8%; Iron 15% **Exchanges:** 3 Starch, 1½ Vegetable, 1½ Fat **Carbohydrate Choices:** 3½

Mango chutney is a delicious sweet-spicy blend of mango, raisins, vinegar and spices.

Vegetable Tetrazzini

Prep Time: 15 minutes • **Start to Finish:** 45 minutes • **6 servings**

7 oz uncooked spaghetti

2 cups vegetable broth

2 cups half-and-half

½ cup all-purpose flour

¼ cup butter or margarine

½ teaspoon salt

¼ teaspoon pepper

2 cups frozen mixed vegetables

1 can (2¼ oz) sliced ripe olives, drained

½ cup slivered almonds

½ cup shredded Cheddar cheese (2 oz)

1 Heat oven to 350°F. Cook and drain spaghetti as directed on package. Rinse with cold water; drain.

2 In 3-quart saucepan, mix broth, half-and-half, flour, butter, salt and pepper. Heat to boiling over medium heat, stirring constantly. Boil 1 minute, stirring constantly. Stir in spaghetti, frozen vegetables and olives. In ungreased 2-quart casserole, spread mixture. Sprinkle with almonds and cheese.

3 Bake uncovered 25 to 30 minutes or until hot and bubbly.

1 SERVING: Calories 490 (Calories from Fat 230); Total Fat 26g (Saturated Fat 13g; Trans Fat 0.5g); Cholesterol 60mg; Sodium 750mg; Total Carbohydrate 50g (Dietary Fiber 4g); Protein 14g **%Daily Value:** Vitamin A 30%; Vitamin C 2%; Calcium 15%; Iron 15% **Exchanges:** 3½ Starch, 5 Fat **Carbohydrate Choices:** 3

Less fat doesn't mean less taste! Lower the fat by substituting fat-free half-and-half for the regular half-and-half, cutting the butter from ¼ cup to 2 tablespoons and using ½ cup reduced-fat Cheddar cheese.

Spaghetti-Basil Torte

Prep Time: **15 minutes** • Start to Finish: **1 hour** • **8 servings**

1 package (16 oz) spaghetti

½ cup grated Parmesan cheese

½ cup ricotta cheese

1 tablespoon Italian seasoning

2 eggs, beaten

¼ cup chopped fresh or
1½ teaspoons dried basil
leaves

2 medium tomatoes, each cut into
5 slices

4 slices (1 oz each) provolone
cheese, each cut in half

1 Heat oven to 350°F. Spray 9-inch springform pan with cooking spray. Cook and drain spaghetti as directed on package. Rinse with cold water; drain.

2 In large bowl, toss spaghetti, Parmesan cheese, ricotta cheese, Italian seasoning and eggs until spaghetti is well coated.

3 Press half of spaghetti mixture in bottom of pan. Sprinkle with half of the basil. Layer with half of the tomato and cheese slices. Press remaining spaghetti mixture on top. Sprinkle with remaining basil. Layer with remaining tomato and cheese slices.

4 Bake uncovered 30 minutes or until hot and light brown. Let stand 15 minutes. Remove side of pan. Cut torte into wedges.

1 SERVING: Calories 370 (Calories from Fat 90); Total Fat 10g (Saturated Fat 5g; Trans Fat 0g); Cholesterol 70mg; Sodium 280mg; Total Carbohydrate 52g (Dietary Fiber 3g); Protein 19g **%Daily Value:** Vitamin A 15%; Vitamin C 4%; Calcium 25%; Iron 15% **Exchanges:** 3½ Starch, 1 Medium-Fat Meat, ½ Fat **Carbohydrate Choices:** 3½

Skillet "Chicken" Parmigiana

Prep Time: **15 minutes** • Start to Finish: **25 minutes** • **4 servings**

1 tablespoon olive or vegetable oil

1 package (10 oz) frozen chicken-style breaded soy-protein patties

2 cups tomato pasta sauce (any variety)

½ cup shredded mozzarella cheese (2 oz)

1 In 10-inch skillet, heat oil over medium heat. Add patties; cook 5 to 7 minutes, turning once, until thoroughly heated.

2 Pour pasta sauce over patties in skillet; sprinkle with cheese. Reduce heat to low; cover and cook 5 to 7 minutes or until sauce is hot and cheese is melted.

1 SERVING: Calories 270 (Calories from Fat 110); Total Fat 12g (Saturated Fat 3g; Trans Fat 0g); Cholesterol 10mg; Sodium 1230mg; Total Carbohydrate 27g (Dietary Fiber 4g); Protein 14g **%Daily Value:** Vitamin A 20%; Vitamin C 10%; Calcium 10%; Iron 15% **Exchanges:** 2 Starch, 1 Lean Meat, 1½ Fat **Carbohydrate Choices:** 2

Is company coming? Serve the patties over steaming-hot spaghetti and top with the pasta sauce and cheese. Add a bagged salad with Italian dressing and some sorbet for dessert and you're all set.

Sweet-and-Sour "Chicken"

Prep Time: 20 minutes • Start to Finish: 20 minutes • **4 servings**

1 **package (10 to 10.5 oz) frozen chicken-style breaded soy-protein nuggets**

1 **bag (1 lb) frozen broccoli, carrots and water chestnuts**

1 **can (20 oz) pineapple chunks, drained**

1 **jar (10 oz) sweet-and-sour sauce (1⅓ cups)**

1 Bake nuggets as directed on package.

2 Meanwhile, in 3-quart saucepan, heat ¼ cup water to boiling. Add frozen vegetables; reduce heat to medium. Cover; cook 7 to 8 minutes, stirring occasionally and breaking apart large pieces, until hot. Drain; return vegetables to saucepan.

3 Stir in nuggets, pineapple and sweet-and-sour sauce. Cook over medium heat 3 to 4 minutes, stirring occasionally, until hot.

1 SERVING: Calories 410 (Calories from Fat 60); Total Fat 6g (Saturated Fat 0.5g; Trans Fat 0g); Cholesterol 0mg; Sodium 790mg; Total Carbohydrate 76g (Dietary Fiber 9g); Protein 13g **%Daily Value:** Vitamin A 130%; Vitamin C 25%; Calcium 8%; Iron 20% **Exchanges:** 4½ Starch, 1 Vegetable, ½ Fat **Carbohydrate Choices:** 5

This dish is great served over hot cooked rice or Japanese curly noodles; try sprinkling toasted regular sesame seed or untoasted black sesame seed over the top for extra Asian taste.

Tempeh Stir-Fry with Yogurt-Peanut Sauce

Prep Time: 40 minutes • Start to Finish: 40 minutes • **4 servings**

¼ cup creamy peanut butter

¼ cup vanilla fat-free yogurt

3 tablespoons teriyaki marinade (from 12-oz bottle)

1 tablespoon honey

2 tablespoons vegetable oil

1 package (8 oz) tempeh, cut into 2×¼×¼-inch strips

1 medium onion, cut into thin wedges

4 medium carrots, cut into 2×¼×¼-inch strips (2 cups)

12 oz fresh green beans, cut in half crosswise (2 cups)

¼ cup water

1 medium red bell pepper, cut into thin bite-size strips

2 cups hot cooked white or brown rice

¼ cup chopped fresh cilantro

1 In small bowl, beat peanut butter, yogurt, teriyaki marinade and honey with whisk until smooth; set aside.

2 In wok or 12-inch skillet, heat 1 tablespoon of the oil over medium heat. Add tempeh; cook 5 to 6 minutes, turning frequently, until light golden brown. Remove tempeh from skillet.

3 In same skillet, heat remaining 1 tablespoon oil over medium heat. Add onion; cook 1 minute, stirring occasionally. Stir in carrots, green beans and water. Cover; cook 5 minutes. Stir in bell pepper. Cook 2 to 3 minutes, stirring occasionally, until vegetables are crisp-tender.

4 Stir in tempeh and reserved peanut butter mixture until well mixed. Cook 1 to 2 minutes, stirring occasionally, until hot. Serve over rice. Sprinkle with cilantro.

1 SERVING: Calories 490 (Calories from Fat 200); Total Fat 22g (Saturated Fat 4g; Trans Fat 0g); Cholesterol 0mg; Sodium 590mg; Total Carbohydrate 53g (Dietary Fiber 7g); Protein 20g **%Daily Value:** Vitamin A 230%; Vitamin C 40%; Calcium 15%; Iron 20% **Exchanges:** 3 Starch, 2 Vegetable, 1 Medium-Fat Meat, 3 Fat **Carbohydrate Choices:** 3½

Tempeh, pronounced TEHM-pay and also spelled tempe, is a fermented, high-protein soybean cake with a chewy texture and slightly nutty flavor. If you can't find it in your supermarket (sometimes it's sold in the freezer case with other vegetarian foods), check a co-op or natural foods grocer.

Tailgate Pasta Salad

Prep Time: 25 minutes • Start to Finish: 2 hours 25 minutes • **6 servings (1⅓ cups each)**

SALAD

8 **oz uncooked gemelli or rotini pasta**

1 **medium zucchini, cut in half lengthwise, thinly sliced (2 cups)**

1 **can (14 oz) artichoke hearts, drained, chopped**

1 **cup cherry tomatoes, each cut in half**

4 **oz fresh baby spinach leaves**

½ **cup chopped fresh basil leaves**

DRESSING

¼ **cup olive or vegetable oil**

3 **tablespoons red wine vinegar**

1 **teaspoon coarse-grained mustard**

1 **teaspoon salt**

½ **teaspoon pepper**

1 **clove garlic, crushed**

1 Cook and drain pasta as directed on package. Rinse with cold water to cool; drain well.

2 Meanwhile, in small bowl, mix dressing ingredients until well blended.

3 In large bowl, mix cooked pasta with remaining salad ingredients except use only ¼ cup of the basil. Pour dressing over salad; toss until coated. Cover; refrigerate 2 to 3 hours to blend flavors.

4 Just before serving, sprinkle remaining ¼ cup basil over top of salad.

1 SERVING: Calories 310 (Calories from Fat 100); Total Fat 11g (Saturated Fat 1.5g; Trans Fat 0g); Cholesterol 0mg; Sodium 590mg; Total Carbohydrate 43g (Dietary Fiber 9g); Protein 9g **%Daily Value:** Vitamin A 45%; Vitamin C 20%; Calcium 6%; Iron 15% **Exchanges:** 2½ Starch, 1 Vegetable, 2 Fat **Carbohydrate Choices:** 3

Hearty Soybean and Cheddar Pasta Salad

Prep Time: 30 minutes • Start to Finish: 1 hour 30 minutes • **4 servings**

1 cup uncooked penne pasta (3 oz)

2 cups frozen shelled edamame (green) soybeans (from 12-oz bag)

6 oz Cheddar cheese, cut into ½-inch cubes (1½ cups)

1 large tomato, coarsely chopped (1 cup)

½ medium cucumber, coarsely chopped (½ cup)

1 small yellow bell pepper, coarsely chopped (½ cup)

⅔ cup Italian dressing

1 Cook and drain pasta as directed on package. Rinse with cold water; drain.

2 Meanwhile, cook soybeans as directed on package. Rinse with cold water; drain.

3 In large bowl, toss pasta, soybeans and remaining ingredients. Cover; refrigerate at least 1 hour before serving.

1 SERVING: Calories 520 (Calories from Fat 290); Total Fat 32g (Saturated Fat 12g; Trans Fat 0g); Cholesterol 50mg; Sodium 1020mg; Total Carbohydrate 33g (Dietary Fiber 5g); Protein 24g **%Daily Value:** Vitamin A 20%; Vitamin C 40%; Calcium 30%; Iron 15% **Exchanges:** 1½ Starch, 2 Vegetable, 1 Very Lean Meat, 1 Medium-Fat Meat, 5 Fat **Carbohydrate Choices:** 2

Edamame is the Japanese name for fresh green soybeans, tasty little bright green gems that are high in protein and easily digested. Try eating them as a snack or appetizer—you will love them!

Edamame Stir-Fry Salad

Prep Time: 20 minutes • **Start to Finish:** 20 minutes • **6 servings**

1 **bag (1 lb 5 oz) frozen stir-fry sesame meal starter**

1 **bag (12 oz) frozen shelled edamame (green) soybeans**

2 **tablespoons rice vinegar**

4 **cups thinly sliced Chinese (napa) cabbage**

2 **tablespoons chopped fresh cilantro**

¼ **cup salted roasted soy nuts**

1 Cut large slit in frozen sesame sauce packet from meal starter. Microwave on High 30 to 60 seconds. In large bowl, reserve ¼ cup sesame sauce.

2 Spray 12-inch skillet with cooking spray; heat over medium-high heat. Add soybeans, remaining sesame sauce and frozen vegetables from meal starter. Cover; cook 5 to 7 minutes, stirring frequently, just until vegetables are crisp-tender. Remove from heat.

3 To sesame sauce in bowl, stir in vinegar. Add cabbage, cilantro and cooked vegetable mixture; toss to mix. Top with soy nuts. Serve immediately.

1 SERVING: Calories 180 (Calories from Fat 40); Total Fat 4.5g (Saturated Fat 0g; Trans Fat 0g); Cholesterol 0mg; Sodium 470mg; Total Carbohydrate 24g (Dietary Fiber 5g); Protein 10g **%Daily Value:** Vitamin A 50%; Vitamin C 30%; Calcium 10%; Iron 10% **Exchanges:** 1½ Starch, 1 Vegetable, ½ Fat **Carbohydrate Choices:** 1½

Lightly salted soy nuts add lots of crunch to this "soy-ful" warm salad. Look for them alongside packages of dried fruit near produce or in the natural food section of the store.

Pasta with Sweet Beans and Basil "Cream"

Prep Time: 20 minutes • **Start to Finish:** 20 minutes • **6 servings**

6 cups uncooked bow-tie (farfalle) pasta (12 oz)

1½ cups frozen shelled edamame (green) soybeans (from 12-oz bag)

1 cup original-flavored soymilk

¼ cup chopped fresh or 1 tablespoon dried basil leaves

1 tablespoon olive or vegetable oil

1 teaspoon salt

1 package (12 oz) soft silken tofu

¼ cup grated Parmesan cheese

1 In 5-quart Dutch oven, heat 4 quarts (16 cups) salted water to boiling. Add pasta; boil uncovered 6 minutes, stirring occasionally. Add soybeans; return to boiling. Cook uncovered about 6 minutes longer, stirring occasionally, until pasta is tender. Drain; return to saucepan.

2 Meanwhile, in blender or food processor, place remaining ingredients except cheese. Cover; blend on high speed until smooth, stopping to scrape down sides as needed.

3 Stir tofu mixture into pasta in saucepan. Reduce heat to low; cook about 3 minutes, stirring constantly, until warm. Just before serving, sprinkle with cheese and toss.

1 SERVING: Calories 350 (Calories from Fat 80); Total Fat 9g (Saturated Fat 1.5g; Trans Fat 0g); Cholesterol 0mg; Sodium 510mg; Total Carbohydrate 50g (Dietary Fiber 4g); Protein 18g **%Daily Value:** Vitamin A 6%; Vitamin C 2%; Calcium 15%; Iron 20% **Exchanges:** 3 Starch, ½ Vegetable, 1 Lean Meat, 1 Fat **Carbohydrate Choices:** 3

Pureed soft silken tofu gives dips and sauces like the one in this recipe the creamy, smooth texture of sour cream, without the fat—and it adds protein!

Stir-Fried Tofu with Almonds

Prep Time: 30 minutes • Start to Finish: 30 minutes • **4 servings**

4 oz uncooked spinach fettuccine or fettuccine, broken into 3-inch pieces

½ cup vegetable broth

⅓ cup dry white wine or vegetable broth

1 tablespoon cornstarch

3 tablespoons hoisin sauce

⅛ teaspoon pepper

1 package (14 oz) firm or extra-firm tofu, drained if needed

2 tablespoons vegetable oil

1½ cups small fresh cauliflower florets

1 large red or green bell pepper, cut into ¼-inch strips

2 cloves garlic, finely chopped

⅓ cup sliced almonds, toasted∗

1 Cook and drain fettuccine as directed on package. Meanwhile, in small bowl, mix broth, wine, cornstarch, hoisin sauce and pepper; set aside.

2 Place drained tofu between 2 layers of paper towels; press gently to remove as much water as possible. Cut into ¾-inch cubes; set aside.

3 Heat wok or 12-inch skillet over high heat. Add 1 tablespoon of the oil; rotate wok to coat side. Cook and stir cauliflower and bell pepper in oil about 4 minutes or until crisp-tender. Remove vegetables from wok.

4 Add remaining 1 tablespoon oil to wok; rotate wok to coat side. Cook tofu and garlic in oil over high heat 5 minutes, stirring gently. Stir in reserved broth mixture; cook and stir about 1 minute or until thickened. Stir in vegetables and fettuccine; cook until thoroughly heated. Sprinkle with almonds.

∗*To toast almonds, sprinkle in ungreased heavy skillet. Cook over medium heat 5 to 7 minutes, stirring frequently until nuts begin to brown, then stirring constantly until nuts are light brown.*

1 SERVING: Calories 390 (Calories from Fat 170); Total Fat 19g (Saturated Fat 3g; Trans Fat 0g); Cholesterol 20mg; Sodium 380mg; Total Carbohydrate 35g (Dietary Fiber 5g); Protein 15g **%Daily Value:** Vitamin A 25%; Vitamin C 60%; Calcium 25%; Iron 20% **Exchanges:** 2 Starch, 1 Vegetable, 1 Medium-Fat Meat, 2½ Fat **Carbohydrate Choices:** 2

Uniquely flavored hoisin sauce can best be described as an Asian barbecue sauce, yet it's nothing like its American counterpart! It can be found near the other Asian sauces.

Pepper and Soybean Stir-Fry

Prep Time: 20 minutes • Start to Finish: 20 minutes • **4 servings**

⅔ **cup uncooked jasmine rice**

1 **cup water**

1 **tablespoon vegetable oil**

1 **tablespoon curry powder**

1 **bag (1 lb) frozen bell pepper and onion stir-fry**

1 **bag (12 oz) frozen shelled edamame (green) soybeans**

4 **cloves garlic, finely chopped**

1 **cup unsweetened coconut milk (not cream of coconut)**

½ **cup salted roasted cashews**

Chopped fresh cilantro or parsley, if desired

1 Cook rice in water as directed on package.

2 Meanwhile, in 12-inch nonstick skillet, heat oil over medium-high heat. Add curry powder; cook 1 minute, stirring frequently. Stir in bell pepper and onion stir-fry, soybeans and garlic. Cook 2 minutes, stirring frequently. Cover; cook about 3 minutes longer or until vegetables are tender.

3 Stir in coconut milk. Reduce heat to medium-low; simmer uncovered 2 minutes, stirring occasionally.

4 Serve mixture over rice. Sprinkle with cashews and if desired, cilantro.

1 SERVING: Calories 520 (Calories from Fat 250); Total Fat 28g (Saturated Fat 13g; Trans Fat 0g); Cholesterol 0mg; Sodium 140mg; Total Carbohydrate 50g (Dietary Fiber 8g); Protein 16g **%Daily Value:** Vitamin A 8%; Vitamin C 20%; Calcium 8%; Iron 25% **Exchanges:** 3 Starch, 1 Vegetable, ½ Medium-Fat Meat, 5 Fat **Carbohydrate Choices:** 3

Be sure you're on the right page—coconut milk is made from the flesh of coconut, not the thin liquid found inside the ripe fruit. It gives the sauce subtle coconut flavor and a creamy texture. Look for regular and reduced-fat ("lite") coconut milk in the Asian foods aisle.

Crunchy Oriental "Chicken" Salad

Prep Time: 25 minutes • Start to Finish: 25 minutes • **4 servings**

DRESSING

⅓ **cup mayonnaise or salad dressing**

¼ **cup Asian sesame dressing and marinade**

SALAD

1 **package (10 or 10.5 oz) frozen chicken-style breaded soy-protein nuggets**

8 **cups torn mixed salad greens**

1 **cup shredded red cabbage**

1 **cup shredded carrots (1½ medium)**

2 **medium green onions, sliced (2 tablespoons)**

1 **cup wide chow mein noodles**

1 In small bowl, mix dressing ingredients with whisk until creamy.

2 Heat nuggets as directed on package.

3 Divide salad greens, cabbage, carrots and onions among 4 plates or 4 shallow bowls. Top with nuggets; sprinkle with noodles. Drizzle with dressing.

1 SERVING: Calories 440 (Calories from Fat 250); Total Fat 28g (Saturated Fat 4g; Trans Fat 0g); Cholesterol 5mg; Sodium 860mg; Total Carbohydrate 33g (Dietary Fiber 8g); Protein 14g **%Daily Value:** Vitamin A 220%; Vitamin C 25%; Calcium 10%; Iron 30% **Exchanges:** 1½ Starch, 2 Vegetable, 1 Medium-Fat Meat, 4½ Fat **Carbohydrate Choices:** 2

When time is tight, the produce department of the supermarket can come to the rescue! To save you time in the kitchen, look for all the convenience items you can find—such as preshredded carrots.

Couscous-Vegetable Salad

Prep Time: 25 minutes • Start to Finish: 25 minutes • **6 servings**

1 **cup uncooked couscous**

2 **teaspoons olive or vegetable oil**

1 **medium zucchini, cut into ¼-inch slices (2 cups)**

1 **medium yellow summer squash, cut into ¼-inch slices (1½ cups)**

1 **large red bell pepper, cut into 1-inch pieces**

½ **medium red onion, cut into 8 wedges**

1 **container (7 oz) refrigerated pesto with sun-dried tomatoes or regular basil pesto**

2 **tablespoons balsamic or cider vinegar**

1 Cook couscous as directed on package.

2 In 10-inch nonstick skillet, heat oil over medium-high heat. Add zucchini, yellow squash, bell pepper and onion; cook about 5 minutes, stirring frequently, until crisp-tender.

3 In large bowl, toss couscous, vegetable mixture, pesto and vinegar. Serve warm or cool.

1 SERVING: Calories 300 (Calories from Fat 140); Total Fat 16g (Saturated Fat 3g; Trans Fat 0g); Cholesterol 10mg; Sodium 280mg; Total Carbohydrate 31g (Dietary Fiber 4g); Protein 8g **%Daily Value:** Vitamin A 35%; Vitamin C 40%; Calcium 10%; Iron 10% **Exchanges:** 1½ Starch, 1½ Vegetable, 3 Fat **Carbohydrate Choices:** 2

Couscous is on the most-wanted list because it's versatile, tastes great and is fast to fix— it only takes 5 minutes! This tiniest form of pasta is granular semolina, a staple of North African cuisine.

gratins, casseroles & pot pies

Curried Lentils with Rice

Prep Time: 20 minutes • Start to Finish: 45 minutes • **4 servings (1¼ cups each)**

1 tablespoon vegetable oil
1 cup coarsely chopped cauliflower
1 cup shredded carrots
1 large onion, chopped (1 cup)
2 teaspoons curry powder
2½ cups water
¾ cup dried red lentils
½ cup uncooked long-grain rice
½ teaspoon salt
1 cup frozen shelled edamame (green) soybeans
1 tablespoon butter
¼ cup chopped dry-roasted peanuts

1 In 12-inch nonstick skillet, heat oil over medium-high heat. Add cauliflower, carrots and onion. Cook about 3 minutes, stirring occasionally, until softened. Stir in curry powder; cook and stir 1 minute.

2 Add water; heat to boiling. Stir in lentils, rice and salt; return to boiling. Reduce heat; cover and simmer 12 to 15 minutes or until lentils and rice are almost tender.

3 Stir in edamame; cook uncovered 5 to 10 minutes or until liquid is absorbed and lentils and rice are tender. Gently stir in butter until melted. Just before serving, sprinkle with peanuts.

1 SERVING: Calories 410 (Calories from Fat 120); Total Fat 14g (Saturated Fat 3.5g; Trans Fat 0g); Cholesterol 10mg; Sodium 430mg; Total Carbohydrate 54g (Dietary Fiber 11g); Protein 18g **%Daily Value:** Vitamin A 100%; Vitamin C 20%; Calcium 8%; Iron 30% **Exchanges:** 3 Starch, 1½ Vegetable, 1 Medium-Fat Meat, 1½ Fat **Carbohydrate Choices:** 3½

Red lentils are reddish-orange in color. While they are also known as European lentils, they are especially popular in Middle Eastern and Indian cooking. Look for these lentils in larger supermarkets or in those that specialize in Middle Eastern or Asian cuisines.

Italian "Veggie Burger" Bake

Prep Time: 25 minutes • Start to Finish: 1 hour 15 minutes • **4 servings**

1 **cup uncooked orzo or rosamarina pasta (6 oz)**

4 **frozen soy-protein burgers**

3 **cups frozen bell pepper and onion stir-fry (from 1-lb bag)**

1 **can (14.5 oz) diced tomatoes with basil, garlic and oregano, undrained**

1 **container (7 or 8 oz) plain hummus (¾ cup)**

1 **cup crumbled tomato-basil feta cheese (4 oz)**

⅓ **cup pitted kalamata olives, coarsely chopped**

1 Heat oven to 350°F. Spray 8-inch square (2-quart) glass baking dish with cooking spray. Cook and drain pasta as directed on package.

2 Meanwhile, on large microwavable plate, microwave burgers uncovered on High 2 to 3 minutes, turning once, until thawed.

3 Spray 12-inch skillet with cooking spray; heat over medium-high heat until hot. Add pepper and onion stir-fry; cook 2 to 3 minutes, stirring frequently, until crisp-tender. Stir in diced tomatoes. Cook 4 to 6 minutes, stirring frequently, until slightly thickened. Remove from heat.

4 In medium bowl, stir cooked pasta and hummus until coated. In baking dish, layer half each of the pasta mixture, vegetable mixture and cheese; top with burgers. Repeat with remaining pasta mixture, vegetable mixture and cheese. Sprinkle olives evenly over top.

5 Cover tightly with foil; bake 35 minutes. Uncover; bake 5 to 10 minutes longer or until thoroughly heated. Let stand 5 minutes before serving.

1 SERVING: Calories 470 (Calories from Fat 150); Total Fat 17g (Saturated Fat 6g; Trans Fat 0g); Cholesterol 25mg; Sodium 1510mg; Total Carbohydrate 59g (Dietary Fiber 10g); Protein 21g **%Daily Value:** Vitamin A 15%; Vitamin C 15%; Calcium 15%; Iron 20% **Exchanges:** 4 Starch, ½ Vegetable, 1 Lean Meat, 2 Fat **Carbohydrate Choices:** 4

The burgers in this recipe are microwaved for a brief flash to thaw them before the dish is assembled and baked. This step ensures they will heat through during baking.

Sweet Potato, Apple and Leek Gratin

Prep Time: 30 minutes • Start to Finish: 1 hour 25 minutes • **5 servings**

1¼ cups whipping cream

2 large leeks, sliced (2 cups)

2 tablespoons chopped fresh or 2 teaspoons dried thyme leaves

1 teaspoon salt

¼ teaspoon pepper

¼ teaspoon ground nutmeg

2 medium dark-orange sweet potatoes (about ¾ lb), peeled, thinly sliced (2 cups)

4 medium parsnips, peeled, thinly sliced (2 cups)

2 cups shredded white Cheddar cheese (8 oz)

1 large cooking apple, thinly sliced (1½ cups)

1 Heat oven to 375°F. Grease 3-quart casserole with shortening. In 2-quart heavy saucepan, cook whipping cream, leeks, thyme, salt, pepper and nutmeg over low heat, stirring occasionally, until mixture begins to simmer. Stir in sweet potatoes and parsnips. Cover; simmer about 10 minutes or until vegetables are slightly tender.

2 Layer half of vegetable mixture and half of cheese in casserole. Top with apple. Repeat layers of vegetables and cheese.

3 Bake uncovered about 45 minutes or until golden brown and bubbly. Let stand 10 minutes before serving.

1 SERVING: Calories 490 (Calories from Fat 310); Total Fat 34g (Saturated Fat 21g; Trans Fat 1g); Cholesterol 115mg; Sodium 800mg; Total Carbohydrate 30g (Dietary Fiber 5g); Protein 14g **%Daily Value:** Vitamin A 190%; Vitamin C 20%; Calcium 35%; Iron 10% **Exchanges:** 1½ Starch, 1½ Vegetable, 1 Medium-Fat Meat, 5½ Fat **Carbohydrate Choices:** 2

Splurging now and again is what this rich gratin is all about. For a less rich entrée, use equal parts whipping cream and half-and-half instead of all whipping cream. Along with the gratin, serve a lightly dressed salad.

Cauliflower au Gratin

Prep Time: 10 minutes • Start to Finish: 40 minutes • 4 servings

1   medium head cauliflower (2 lb)

1   medium red onion, cut into
    8 wedges

1   tablespoon fresh lemon juice

1   tablespoon olive or vegetable oil

2   large cloves garlic, finely
    chopped

1   tablespoon chopped fresh parsley

½   teaspoon coarsely ground pepper

2   tablespoons freshly grated or
    shredded Parmesan cheese

2   tablespoons freshly grated or
    shredded Asiago cheese

¼   cup shredded provolone cheese
    (1 oz)

1 Separate cauliflower into florets. In 3-quart saucepan, heat 1 inch salted water (½ teaspoon salt to 1 cup water) to boiling. Add cauliflower, onion and lemon juice; cover and return to boiling. Reduce heat; simmer about 6 minutes or until cauliflower is just tender. Drain.

2 Heat oven to 425°F. In ungreased 9-inch square pan, mix oil, garlic and parsley. Heat uncovered in oven 5 minutes. Spread cauliflower and onion in pan; sprinkle with pepper and cheeses.

3 Bake uncovered about 20 minutes or until cheese is melted and forms a golden brown crust.

1 SERVING: Calories 170 (Calories from Fat 70); Total Fat 8g (Saturated Fat 3.5g; Trans Fat 0g); Cholesterol 10mg; Sodium 230mg; Total Carbohydrate 15g (Dietary Fiber 5g); Protein 8g **%Daily Value:** Vitamin A 4%; Vitamin C 100%; Calcium 20%; Iron 8% **Exchanges:** 3 Vegetable, ½ Medium-Fat Meat, 1 Fat **Carbohydrate Choices:** 1

Serve this authentic Italian gratin with extra shredded cheeses. Cooked green beans drizzled with a little olive oil and sprinkled with toasted walnuts would go nicely with this dish.

Mediterranean Gratin

easy

Prep Time: 15 minutes • Start to Finish: 40 minutes • 4 servings

1 box (5.8 oz) roasted garlic and olive oil flavor couscous mix

6 cups fresh baby spinach leaves (5 oz)

2 tablespoons water

½ cup roasted red bell peppers (from 7.25-oz jar), drained, chopped

1½ teaspoons grated lemon peel

¼ teaspoon salt

1 can (15 oz) garbanzo beans, drained, rinsed

1 cup crumbled feta cheese (4 oz)

½ cup coarsely chopped walnuts

1 tablespoon olive or vegetable oil

1 Heat oven to 350°F. Make couscous as directed on box for version without olive oil.

2 Meanwhile, spray 11×7-inch (2-quart) glass baking dish or gratin dish with cooking spray. In 12-inch skillet, place spinach and 2 tablespoons water. Cover; cook over medium heat 2 to 4 minutes, stirring occasionally, until spinach is wilted.

3 Stir in cooked couscous, roasted red peppers, lemon peel, salt, beans and ½ cup of the cheese. Spread mixture in baking dish.

4 In small bowl, mix remaining cheese, walnuts and oil. Sprinkle over couscous mixture.

5 Bake uncovered 20 to 25 minutes or until thoroughly heated.

1 SERVING: Calories 590 (Calories from Fat 220); Total Fat 25g (Saturated Fat 7g; Trans Fat 0g); Cholesterol 35mg; Sodium 1010mg; Total Carbohydrate 66g (Dietary Fiber 10g); Protein 24g **%Daily Value:** Vitamin A 90%; Vitamin C 15%; Calcium 30%; Iron 30% **Exchanges:** 4 Starch, 1½ Vegetable, 1 Very Lean Meat, 4½ Fat **Carbohydrate Choices:** 4½

Look for boxes of plain and flavored couscous near the rice and legumes in your supermarket. Some stores may carry couscous in the ethnic-foods aisle.

Smoky Brown Rice–Stuffed Peppers

Prep Time: 25 minutes • Start to Finish: 1 hour 10 minutes • **6 servings**

½ cup uncooked whole-grain
   brown rice
1⅓ cups water
1 teaspoon butter, if desired
6 large red or green bell peppers
2 tablespoons olive oil
1 onion, chopped
1 clove garlic, chopped
1 package (12 oz) frozen sausage-
   style soy-protein crumbles
2 cups cooked brown rice
1 can (14.5 oz) organic diced
   tomatoes, undrained
1 teaspoon dried basil leaves
½ teaspoon dried oregano leaves
½ teaspoon pepper
4 oz smoked Gouda cheese,
   shredded (1 cup)

1 Heat oven to 375°F. Spray 11×7-inch (2-quart) glass baking dish with cooking spray.

2 In 2-quart saucepan, combine rice, water and butter. Heat to boiling over medium-high heat. Reduce heat to medium-low; cover and simmer 30 minutes or until water is absorbed.

3 Meanwhile, cut off top of each bell pepper, slicing evenly across top of pepper; remove seeds. If peppers will not sit upright, slice very thin strip off bottom but not cutting through. Arrange peppers cut side up in baking dish. Cut pepper flesh off pepper tops; chop. Discard stems.

4 In 10-inch skillet, heat oil over medium-high heat. Add onion, garlic and chopped pepper; cook 5 minutes, stirring frequently, until onion is tender. Stir in soy-protein crumbles, cooked rice, tomatoes, basil, oregano and pepper. Cook 5 to 7 minutes, stirring frequently, until hot. Remove from heat; stir in ½ cup of the cheese.

5 Spoon about 1 cup filling into each pepper shell, pressing very lightly with back of spoon.

6 Bake uncovered 35 to 40 minutes or until filling is hot and peppers are crisp-tender. Sprinkle remaining ½ cup cheese on top of peppers. Bake uncovered 5 minutes longer or until cheese is melted.

1 SERVING: Calories 390 (Calories from Fat 110); Total Fat 12g (Saturated Fat 4g; Trans Fat 0g); Cholesterol 20mg; Sodium 590mg; Total Carbohydrate 48g (Dietary Fiber 10g); Protein 23g **%Daily Value:** Vitamin A 110%; Vitamin C 190%; Calcium 25%; Iron 20% **Exchanges:** 3 Starch, 1 Vegetable, 1½ Medium-Fat Meat, ½ Fat **Carbohydrate Choices:** 3

If you have any remaining filling that won't fit into the peppers, spoon the filling into a ramekin that has been sprayed with cooking spray and bake next to the peppers.

Three-Bean Casserole

Prep Time: 20 minutes • Start to Finish: 1 hour 5 minutes • 8 servings

Cooking spray

2 medium stalks celery, sliced (1 cup)

1 medium onion, chopped (½ cup)

1 large clove garlic, finely chopped

2 cups frozen sausage-style soy-protein crumbles (from 12-oz package)

2 cans (21 oz each) baked beans (any variety)

1 can (15.5 oz) lima or butter beans, drained

1 can (15 oz) dark red kidney beans, drained

1 can (8 oz) tomato sauce

1 tablespoon ground mustard

2 tablespoons honey or packed brown sugar

1 tablespoon white or cider vinegar

¼ teaspoon red pepper sauce

1 Heat oven to 400°F. Generously spray 10-inch skillet with cooking spray. Add celery, onion and garlic; spray vegetables with cooking spray. Cook vegetables over medium heat 8 to 10 minutes, stirring occasionally, until crisp-tender.

2 In ungreased 3-quart casserole, mix vegetable mixture and remaining ingredients.

3 Bake uncovered about 45 minutes, stirring once, until hot and bubbly.

Slow Cooker Directions: Substitute ½ cup ketchup for the tomato sauce; decrease honey to 1 tablespoon. Generously spray 10-inch skillet with cooking spray. Add celery, onion and garlic; spray vegetables with cooking spray. Cook vegetables over medium heat 8 to 10 minutes, stirring occasionally, until crisp-tender. In 3½- to 4-quart slow cooker, mix vegetable mixture and remaining ingredients. Cover; cook on High heat setting 2 hours to 2 hours 30 minutes to blend flavors.

1 SERVING: Calories 370 (Calories from Fat 15); Total Fat 1.5g (Saturated Fat 0g; Trans Fat 0g); Cholesterol 0mg; Sodium 1050mg; Total Carbohydrate 65g (Dietary Fiber 15g); Protein 23g %Daily Value: Vitamin A 6%; Vitamin C 4%; Calcium 10%; Iron 30% Exchanges: 3½ Starch, 2 Vegetable, 1½ Very Lean Meat Carbohydrate Choices: 4

Sausage-style soy-protein crumbles flavor this hearty casserole instead of traditional bulk pork sausage. If you can't find the crumbles, look for soy-protein breakfast sausage links and cut into thin slices or crumble before using.

Green Chile Casserole

Prep Time: **15 minutes** • Start to Finish: **1 hour 5 minutes** • **6 servings**

12 corn tortillas (5 or 6 inch)

2 cans (4.5 oz each) chopped green chiles, undrained

2½ cups shredded reduced-fat Monterey Jack cheese (10 oz)

1 jalapeño chile, seeded, finely chopped, if desired

½ cup shredded sharp Cheddar cheese (2 oz)

2 eggs

3 egg whites

2 cups fat-free (skim) milk

½ teaspoon salt

Dash pepper

Chunky-style salsa

1 Heat oven to 375°F. Spray 13×9-inch (3-quart) glass baking dish with cooking spray. Tear 6 of the tortillas into bite-size pieces; spread in bottom of baking dish.

2 Layer 1 can of the green chiles and half of the Monterey Jack cheese over tortillas. Sprinkle with jalapeño chile. Repeat with remaining tortillas, green chiles and Monterey Jack cheese. Sprinkle with Cheddar cheese.

3 In small bowl, beat eggs, egg whites, milk, salt and pepper until blended; pour slowly over casserole.

4 Bake uncovered 45 to 50 minutes or until set and golden brown. Serve with salsa.

1 SERVING: Calories 360 (Calories from Fat 150); Total Fat 16g (Saturated Fat 9g; Trans Fat 0g); Cholesterol 115mg; Sodium 930mg; Total Carbohydrate 29g (Dietary Fiber 2g); Protein 23g **%Daily Value:** Vitamin A 20%; Vitamin C 8%; Calcium 50%; Iron 6% **Exchanges:** 2 Starch, 2½ Lean Meat, 1½ Fat **Carbohydrate Choices:** 2

Not only would this casserole make a delicious dinner—it could star as the main dish of a tasty brunch buffet!

Veggies and Orecchiette with Arugula-Walnut Pesto

Prep Time: 35 minutes • Start to Finish: 35 minutes • **6 servings (about 1⅓ cups each)**

PESTO

- 1½ **cups firmly packed fresh arugula leaves**
- ½ **cup grated Romano or Parmesan cheese**
- ¼ **cup chopped walnuts**
- 1 **clove garlic**
- ⅓ **cup extra-virgin olive oil**

PASTA AND SAUCE

- 3 **cups uncooked orecchiette (tiny disk) pasta (12 oz)**
- 1 **tablespoon olive or vegetable oil**
- ½ **cup chopped onion (1 medium)**
- 1 **package (8 oz) sliced fresh mushrooms (3 cups)**
- 1 **pint (2 cups) grape tomatoes, halved**
- ½ **teaspoon salt**
- ¼ **teaspoon pepper**

1 In food processor, place pesto ingredients. Cover; process on medium speed about 1 minute, stopping occasionally to scrape down sides, until smooth. Set aside.

2 Cook and drain pasta as directed on box. Return to saucepan or stockpot.

3 Meanwhile, in 10-inch skillet, heat oil over medium heat. Add onion; cook and stir 2 minutes. Stir in mushrooms, tomatoes, salt and pepper. Cook and stir 5 minutes or until mushrooms are tender and tomatoes are soft.

4 Stir vegetables and pesto into pasta until evenly coated in pesto. Transfer to serving dish.

1 SERVING: Calories 390 (Calories from Fat 170); Total Fat 19g (Saturated Fat 2.5g; Trans Fat 0g); Cholesterol 0mg; Sodium 200mg; Total Carbohydrate 47g (Dietary Fiber 3g); Protein 9g **%Daily Value:** Vitamin A 10%; Vitamin C 8%; Calcium 2%; Iron 15% **Exchanges:** 2½ Starch, 1½ Vegetable, 3½ Fat **Carbohydrate Choices:** 3

This colorful pasta dish is a perfect choice when entertaining friends or family. Only you need to know how easy it is to prepare! You can substitute campanelle pasta (small bells or flowers) if orecchiette isn't available.

Shortcut Vegetable Lasagna

Prep Time: 40 minutes • Start to Finish: 2 hours • **8 servings**

1 tablespoon olive oil

4 medium green onions, sliced (¼ cup)

2 medium zucchini, shredded (about 3 cups)

2 medium carrots, shredded (about 1 cup)

1 medium dark-orange sweet potato, peeled, shredded (about 1 cup)

1 package (8 oz) sliced fresh mushrooms (about 3 cups)

2 cloves garlic, finely chopped

1 egg

1 container (15 oz) light ricotta cheese

1 cup shredded Swiss cheese (4 oz)

¼ cup grated Parmesan cheese

1 teaspoon dried basil leaves

1 jar (16 oz) Alfredo pasta sauce

1½ cups water

9 uncooked lasagna noodles

1 cup shredded mozzarella cheese (4 oz)

2 tablespoons chopped fresh parsley

1 Heat oven to 350°F. Spray 13×9-inch (3-quart) glass baking dish with cooking spray.

2 In 12-inch nonstick skillet, heat oil over medium-high heat. Add onions, zucchini, carrots, sweet potato, mushrooms and garlic; cook 6 to 8 minutes, stirring occasionally, until mushrooms are tender. Drain off any excess liquid.

3 In medium bowl, beat egg. Stir in ricotta cheese, Swiss cheese, Parmesan cheese and basil. In separate medium bowl, mix Alfredo sauce and water.

4 Arrange 3 uncooked noodles in bottom of baking dish. Top with ⅓ of sauce mixture (about 1 cup), ½ of ricotta mixture and ½ of vegetable mixture. Repeat layers once. Top with remaining 3 noodles and remaining sauce mixture. Sprinkle with mozzarella cheese.

5 Spray sheet of foil with cooking spray; cover baking dish tightly with foil, sprayed side down. Bake 1 hour to 1 hour 10 minutes or until bubbly around edges. Sprinkle with parsley. Let stand 10 minutes before serving.

1 SERVING: Calories 530 (Calories from Fat 290); Total Fat 33g (Saturated Fat 19g; Trans Fat 1g); Cholesterol 120mg; Sodium 500mg; Total Carbohydrate 34g (Dietary Fiber 3g); Protein 25g **%Daily Value:** Vitamin A 120%; Vitamin C 10%; Calcium 60%; Iron 10% **Exchanges:** 2 Starch, 1 Vegetable, ½ Lean Meat, 2 Medium-Fat Meat, 4 Fat **Carbohydrate Choices:** 2

You don't need to cook the lasagna noodles before layering them in this recipe. Lasagna or casseroles prepared with uncooked noodles or pasta have a slightly drier texture than those made with cooked pasta. You can assemble the lasagna up to 24 hours in advance, cover it with foil and refrigerate it. When you're ready, bake the lasagna as directed.

Lasagna Primavera

Prep Time: 20 minutes • Start to Finish: 1 hour 35 minutes • 8 servings

12 uncooked lasagna noodles

3 cups frozen broccoli cuts, thawed, well drained

3 large carrots, coarsely shredded (2 cups)

2 cups organic diced tomatoes (from 28-oz can), well drained

2 medium bell peppers, cut into ½-inch pieces

1 container (15 oz) ricotta cheese

½ cup grated Parmesan cheese

1 egg

2 containers (10 oz each) refrigerated Alfredo pasta sauce

1 package (16 oz) shredded mozzarella cheese (4 cups)

1 Heat oven to 350°F. Cook and drain noodles as directed on package.

2 Meanwhile, if necessary, cut broccoli florets into bite-size pieces. In large bowl, mix broccoli, carrots, tomatoes and bell peppers. In small bowl, mix ricotta cheese, Parmesan cheese and egg.

3 In ungreased 13×9-inch (3-quart) glass baking dish, spread ⅔ cup Alfredo sauce. Top with 4 noodles. Spread half of the cheese mixture and 2½ cups of the vegetables over noodles. Spoon ⅔ cup sauce in dollops over vegetables. Sprinkle with 1 cup of the mozzarella cheese.

4 Top with 4 noodles; spread with remaining cheese mixture and 2½ cups of vegetables. Spoon ⅔ cup sauce in dollops over vegetables. Sprinkle with 1 cup mozzarella cheese. Top with remaining 4 noodles and the vegetables. Spoon remaining sauce in dollops over vegetables. Sprinkle with remaining 2 cups mozzarella cheese.

5 Bake uncovered 45 to 60 minutes or until bubbly and hot in center. Let stand 15 minutes before cutting.

1 SERVING: Calories 700 (Calories from Fat 370); Total Fat 41g (Saturated Fat 24g; Trans Fat 1g); Cholesterol 150mg; Sodium 960mg; Total Carbohydrate 45g (Dietary Fiber 5g); Protein 36g **%Daily Value:** Vitamin A 140%; Vitamin C 45%; Calcium 80%; Iron 15% **Exchanges:** 2½ Starch, 1 Vegetable, 3½ Medium-Fat Meat, 4½ Fat **Carbohydrate Choices:** 3

Make sure you thoroughly drain the broccoli and tomatoes so the lasagna won't be watery. Use a paper towel to remove any excess moisture from the broccoli.

Slightly undercook the pasta when making lasagna because it cooks again in the oven.

Family-Loving Meatless Monday Options

Working meatless choices into your week is easy if you pick one or two days to be meatless, as a start! Pick any day(s) of the week that work best for your family. Not only are you making healthier choices for your family, but it's a great way to stretch your food budget as well. Here are some fast and easy meatless "go-to" ideas your whole family will love:

- Baked potatoes or sweet potatoes topped with cheese sauce, cheese, meatless chili, canned dried beans, salsa, pesto or vegetables

- Cheese or vegetable pizza

- Cottage cheese, plain or with fruit, beans or vegetables

- Eggs, any style, served plain or with soy-protein sausage, vegetables or cheese

- Grilled cheese sandwiches with soup

- Macaroni and cheese

- Meatless chili

- Pancakes, waffles and French toast (whole grain), with peanut butter, cream cheese or yogurt

- Pasta, cheese-filled ravioli or cheese-filled tortellini topped with pasta sauce, or pasta tossed with pesto or olive oil or melted butter and grated or shredded cheese; serve plain or add vegetables or beans

- Quesadillas filled with foods like cheese, beans, vegetables or bits of leftovers

- Brown rice tossed with olive oil or melted butter and grated or shredded cheese; serve plain or add vegetables or beans

- Smoothies made with yogurt, fruit (fresh or frozen) and a little fruit juice

- Soy-protein burgers, soy hot dogs and "chicken" nuggets

- Tacos filled with foods like shredded lettuce, tomatoes, beans, cheese, guacamole and salsa

- Vegetable stir-fry with brown rice or whole wheat pasta

- Vegetarian baked beans

- Whole grain cereal with fresh fruit and vanilla-flavored soy milk or yogurt

- Wraps or burritos—fill flour tortillas with foods like shredded lettuce, cabbage, or carrots; chopped vegetables; rice; beans; cheese; peanut sauce; peanut butter and jelly; salsa or bits of leftovers

- Yogurt parfaits—layer yogurt, granola or slightly crushed cereal and fresh fruit

Lasagna Cupcakes

Prep Time: 15 minutes • Start to Finish: 1 hour • **12 servings**

1 cup ricotta cheese

½ cup grated Parmesan cheese

1 egg

1 jar (25.5 oz) pasta sauce (any variety)

½ lb frozen Italian sausage-style soy-protein crumbles (2 cups)

36 round pot sticker (gyoza) wrappers

1 cup shredded mozzarella cheese (4 oz)

1 Heat oven to 375°F. Spray 12 regular-size muffin cups with cooking spray. In small bowl, mix ricotta cheese, Parmesan cheese and egg. In another small bowl, mix pasta sauce and soy-protein crumbles.

2 Place 1 round wrapper in bottom of each muffin cup; top each with 1 heaping tablespoon pasta sauce mixture and 1 tablespoon cheese mixture. Repeat layers, ending with pasta sauce mixture. Sprinkle each with mozzarella cheese.

3 Spray sheet of foil large enough to cover pan with cooking spray; place sprayed side down over pan. Bake 15 minutes. Uncover; bake 15 minutes longer. Let stand about 15 minutes before serving.

1 SERVING: Calories 170 (Calories from Fat 60); Total Fat 7g (Saturated Fat 3g; Trans Fat 0g); Cholesterol 30mg; Sodium 500mg; Total Carbohydrate 13g (Dietary Fiber 2g); Protein 12g **%Daily Value:** Vitamin A 8%; Vitamin C 4%; Calcium 20%; Iron 8% **Exchanges:** 1 Starch, 1 Medium-Fat Meat **Carbohydrate Choices:** 1

These are fantastic little casseroles to freeze and eat for a quick dinner—or to take to work for lunch. Microwave 1 frozen cupcake uncovered on Medium (50%) for 5 to 6 minutes or until hot.

Spinach-Stuffed Manicotti with Vodka Blush Sauce

Prep Time: 25 minutes • Start to Finish: 1 hour • **7 servings (2 manicotti each)**

1 **box (8 oz) uncooked manicotti pasta shells (14 shells)**

2 **jars (25.5 oz each) garden vegetable pasta sauce**

¼ **cup vodka**

½ **cup whipping cream**

2 **cups shredded Italian cheese blend (8 oz)**

½ **cup sun-dried tomatoes in oil, drained, chopped**

1 **container (15 oz) ricotta cheese**

1 **box (9 oz) frozen chopped spinach, thawed, drained and squeezed dry**

2 **tablespoons julienne-cut fresh basil leaves**

1 Cook manicotti as directed on box. Rinse with cool water; drain. Heat oven to 375°F.

2 Meanwhile, in 2-quart nonreactive saucepan, heat 1 jar of pasta sauce and the vodka to boiling. Reduce heat; simmer 3 minutes, stirring occasionally. Remove from heat; stir in whipping cream. Set aside.

3 In medium bowl, stir together 1 cup of the Italian cheese blend, the sun-dried tomatoes, ricotta and spinach.

4 In bottom of ungreased 13×9-inch (3-quart) glass baking dish, spread 1 cup of sauce from second jar (save remaining sauce for another use). Fill each manicotti with about 3 tablespoons ricotta mixture; place over sauce in dish. Pour vodka pasta sauce over manicotti.

5 Cover tightly with foil; bake 30 minutes or until sauce is bubbling. Uncover dish; sprinkle with remaining 1 cup cheese blend. Bake uncovered 5 minutes longer or until cheese is melted. Sprinkle with basil.

1 SERVING: Calories 420 (Calories from Fat 130); Total Fat 15g (Saturated Fat 7g; Trans Fat 0g); Cholesterol 35mg; Sodium 880mg; Total Carbohydrate 48g (Dietary Fiber 6g); Protein 19g **%Daily Value:** Vitamin A 90%; Vitamin C 20%; Calcium 60%; Iron 20% **Exchanges:** 3 Starch, ½ Vegetable, 1 Medium-Fat Meat, 2 Fat **Carbohydrate Choices:** 3

For ease when filling the manicotti shells, shape the ricotta mixture into a log with your fingers and simply place it inside the cooked shells.

Moussaka

Prep Time: 30 minutes • Start to Finish: 1 hour 40 minutes • **4 servings**

4 **frozen soy-protein burgers or soy-protein vegetable burgers**

1 **medium unpeeled eggplant (about 1½ lb), cut into ¼-inch slices**

¼ **cup all-purpose flour**

½ **teaspoon salt**

½ **teaspoon pepper**

¼ **teaspoon ground nutmeg**

¼ **teaspoon ground cinnamon**

3 **cups milk**

4 **oz (half of 8-oz package) cream cheese, cut into cubes**

1 **can (15 oz) tomato sauce**

2 **eggs, beaten**

1 Heat oven to 375°F. Grease 3-quart casserole with shortening. On large microwavable plate, microwave burgers uncovered on High 2 to 3 minutes, turning once, until thawed. Cut into 1-inch pieces; set aside.

2 In 2-quart saucepan, place eggplant and enough water to cover. Heat to boiling; cook 5 to 8 minutes or until tender. Drain in colander; set aside.

3 In same saucepan, mix flour, salt, pepper, nutmeg, cinnamon and milk. Heat to boiling, stirring constantly. Boil 1 minute, stirring constantly. Remove from heat. Stir in cream cheese until melted and smooth.

4 Place half of the eggplant in casserole. Layer with burger pieces, tomato sauce, 1½ cups of the white sauce and remaining eggplant. Stir eggs into remaining white sauce; pour over eggplant.

5 Bake uncovered about 1 hour or until firm. Let stand 10 minutes before serving.

1 SERVING: Calories 420 (Calories from Fat 150); Total Fat 16g (Saturated Fat 8g; Trans Fat 0g); Cholesterol 140mg; Sodium 1470mg; Total Carbohydrate 48g (Dietary Fiber 11g); Protein 20g **%Daily Value:** Vitamin A 25%; Vitamin C 10%; Calcium 30%; Iron 10% **Exchanges:** 2½ Starch, 2 Vegetable, 1 Medium-Fat Meat, 2 Fat **Carbohydrate Choices:** 3

Eggplant has been called "the vegetarian's beef" because of its meaty texture. Choose firm, even-colored eggplants that are heavy for their size and free of blemishes. Caps and stems should be intact with no mold. Refrigerate eggplant unwashed in a plastic bag up to 5 days.

Caramelized Onion, Barley and Bella Casserole

Prep Time: 35 minutes • Start to Finish: 1 hour 35 minutes • 8 servings

3 tablespoons butter

3 medium onions, thinly sliced

1 teaspoon sugar

2 cloves garlic, finely chopped

6 cups sliced baby portabella mushrooms (three 8-oz packages)

1½ cups uncooked pearl barley

1 medium red bell pepper, chopped (1 cup)

2 tablespoons chopped fresh parsley

2 tablespoons soy sauce

1 tablespoon sesame oil

½ teaspoon coarsely ground pepper

½ teaspoon dried thyme leaves

4 cups vegetable broth

¾ cup shredded Swiss cheese (3 oz)

1 Heat oven to 350°F. Spray 13×9-inch (3-quart) glass baking dish with cooking spray.

2 In 5-quart Dutch oven, melt butter over low heat. Add onions and sugar; cook about 20 minutes, stirring occasionally, until onions are golden brown. Add garlic and mushrooms; cook 5 to 10 minutes longer, stirring occasionally. Add barley; cook 2 minutes. Remove from heat; stir in bell pepper, parsley, soy sauce, sesame oil, pepper and thyme. Pour into baking dish.

3 In microwavable bowl, microwave broth uncovered on High 4 minutes. Pour broth over onion-mushroom mixture. Cover with foil.

4 Bake 1 hour. Let stand 10 minutes before serving. Sprinkle with cheese.

1 SERVING: Calories 280 (Calories from Fat 90); Total Fat 10g (Saturated Fat 5g; Trans Fat 0g); Cholesterol 20mg; Sodium 760mg; Total Carbohydrate 40g (Dietary Fiber 8g); Protein 9g **%Daily Value:** Vitamin A 25%; Vitamin C 25%; Calcium 10%; Iron 8% **Exchanges:** 2½ Starch, 1½ Fat **Carbohydrate Choices:** 2½

Mushrooms add an earthy flavor to this dish. Feel free to use any variety of mushrooms, substituting them for the baby portabella mushrooms suggested in this recipe. Button mushrooms are readily available and offer a mild flavor, while wild mushrooms, such as enoki or shiitake, offer a richer flavor.

In a taste panel, we thought this was reminiscent of the flavors of French Onion Soup, with the added meatiness of the mushrooms, in a delicious casserole.

Indian-Style Vegetable Casserole

Prep Time: 25 minutes • Start to Finish: 1 hour 20 minutes • **8 servings (1⅓ cups each)**

1 **can (13.5 oz) unsweetened coconut milk (not cream of coconut)**

¾ **cup water**

1½ **teaspoons salt**

1 **cup uncooked basmati rice**

1 **bag (1 lb) frozen sliced carrots, thawed, drained (about 4 cups)**

1 **bag (1 lb) frozen cauliflower florets, thawed, drained (about 5 cups)**

1 **can (15.8 oz) black-eyed peas, drained, rinsed**

1 **serrano chile, seeded, finely chopped**

2 **tablespoons olive oil**

1½ **teaspoons garam masala**

Chopped fresh cilantro, if desired

Lime wedges, if desired

1 Heat oven to 375°F. Spray 13×9-inch (3-quart) glass baking dish with cooking spray.

2 In 2-quart saucepan, stir 1 cup of the coconut milk, the water, ½ teaspoon of the salt and the rice. Heat to boiling over high heat. Stir; reduce heat to low. Cover; simmer 15 minutes or until liquid is absorbed. Remove from heat; fluff rice with fork.

3 In large bowl, stir carrots, cauliflower, peas, chile, oil, remaining 1 teaspoon salt and the garam masala. Stir in cooked rice and remaining coconut milk until well blended. Spoon into baking dish.

4 Cover with foil; bake 40 minutes or until thoroughly heated. Garnish with cilantro; squeeze lime juice over top.

1 SERVING: Calories 320 (Calories from Fat 130); Total Fat 14g (Saturated Fat 9g; Trans Fat 0g); Cholesterol 0mg; Sodium 630mg; Total Carbohydrate 39g (Dietary Fiber 6g); Protein 7g **%Daily Value:** Vitamin A 190%; Vitamin C 15%; Calcium 4%; Iron 15% **Exchanges:** 2 Starch, 1½ Vegetable, 2½ Fat **Carbohydrate Choices:** 2½

Be sure to use plastic gloves when seeding and chopping the chile. Its essential oils can burn if you use your hands and then touch your face. If you'd like extra heat, don't remove all of the seeds . . . or try using 2 serranos!

Mushroom-Spinach Stroganoff

Prep Time: 45 minutes • Start to Finish: 45 minutes • **4 servings (1[2/3] cups each)**

4 cups wide or dumpling egg noodles (8 oz)

3 tablespoons chopped fresh Italian (flat-leaf) parsley

1 tablespoon olive oil

½ cup chopped onion (1 medium)

1 lb mixed fresh mushrooms (such as crimini, portabella and regular white), cut into ¼-inch slices

2 cloves garlic, finely chopped

2 tablespoons tomato paste

2 cups fresh spinach leaves

1 container (8 oz) sour cream

¾ cup milk

½ teaspoon salt

¼ teaspoon pepper

1 Cook noodles as directed on package; drain. Toss with 2 tablespoons of the parsley; place in serving dish. Cover to keep warm.

2 Meanwhile, in 10-inch skillet, heat oil over medium-high heat. Add onion and mushrooms; cook 10 minutes, stirring occasionally. Add garlic; cook 1 minute, stirring occasionally. Reduce heat to medium. Stir in tomato paste. Stir in spinach; cook 1 to 2 minutes or until spinach is wilted. Gently fold in sour cream, milk, salt and pepper. Cook just until hot, stirring constantly. Cover; remove from heat.

3 Pour onion-mushroom mixture over noodles. Sprinkle with remaining tablespoon parsley.

1 SERVING: Calories 370 (Calories from Fat 160); Total Fat 18g (Saturated Fat 8g; Trans Fat 0g); Cholesterol 65mg; Sodium 450mg; Total Carbohydrate 40g (Dietary Fiber 3g); Protein 11g **%Daily Value:** Vitamin A 45%; Vitamin C 10%; Calcium 15%; Iron 15% **Exchanges:** 2 Starch, 2 Vegetable, 3½ Fat **Carbohydrate Choices:** 2½

Tomato paste, available in a tube, is a convenient way to use a small amount. Store the rest of the tube, tightly covered, in the refrigerator for up to a year. If you use a can of tomato paste, freeze the rest in 1-tablespoon portions; add a frozen amount to a soup, stew or chili without thawing it first. Be sure to seal the tomato paste in an air-tight container, label and date it.

Black Bean–Corn Enchiladas

Prep Time: 20 minutes • Start to Finish: 40 minutes • 5 servings (2 enchiladas each)

ENCHILADAS

- 1 tablespoon vegetable oil
- 1½ cups frozen whole kernel corn
- 2 cloves garlic, finely chopped
- 2 cups packed fresh spinach leaves
- 1 can (15 oz) black beans, drained, rinsed
- 1 teaspoon ground cumin
- 2 cups shredded taco-seasoned cheese blend (8 oz)
- 2 cans (10 oz each) enchilada sauce
- 1 package (8.2 oz) flour tortillas for soft tacos & fajitas (10 tortillas; 6 inch) or 10 corn tortillas (6 inch)

GARNISHES, IF DESIRED

Sliced green onions

Finely chopped fresh cilantro

Sour cream

1 Heat oven to 375°F. Spray 13×9-inch (3-quart) glass baking dish with cooking spray.

2 In 12-inch skillet, heat oil over medium-high heat. Add corn and garlic; cook 3 minutes. Stir in spinach and beans; sprinkle with cumin. Cook 3 minutes longer, stirring constantly, until spinach wilts. Remove from heat; cool slightly.

3 Stir in 1½ cups cheese. Pour 1 can of the enchilada sauce into baking dish. Spoon scant ½ cup filling onto each tortilla. Roll up each tightly; place seam side down in baking dish. Pour remaining can of enchilada sauce over top. Sprinkle with remaining ½ cup cheese.

4 Bake uncovered 20 minutes or until thoroughly heated and cheese is melted. Garnish with onions, cilantro and sour cream.

1 SERVING: Calories 460 (Calories from Fat 160); Total Fat 18g (Saturated Fat 8g; Trans Fat 1.5g); Cholesterol 40mg; Sodium 1110mg; Total Carbohydrate 54g (Dietary Fiber 9g); Protein 19g **%Daily Value:** Vitamin A 30%; Vitamin C 4%; Calcium 35%; Iron 20% **Exchanges:** 3½ Starch, ½ Vegetable, 1 Very Lean Meat, 3 Fat **Carbohydrate Choices:** 3½

Leftover enchiladas? Bring a few to work to reheat for a quick, homemade lunch. Store cooled enchiladas in a resealable plastic bag in the refrigerator. To reheat, simply move to a plate and microwave until hot.

Bell Pepper–Mac and Cheese with Fondue Cheese Sauce

Prep Time: 30 minutes • Start to Finish: 1 hour • **7 servings (about 1½ cups each)**

3 medium red, yellow, orange or green bell peppers

3 cups uncooked penne pasta (9 oz)

10 oz Gruyère cheese, shredded (2½ cups)

3 tablespoons all-purpose flour

1 cup dry white wine

¾ cup whipping cream

2 cloves garlic, finely chopped

½ teaspoon salt

¼ teaspoon ground red pepper (cayenne)

⅛ teaspoon ground nutmeg

2 tablespoons chopped fresh parsley

½ cup Italian style bread crumbs

2 tablespoons butter or margarine, melted

1 Set oven control to broil. Broil bell peppers with tops about 5 inches from heat about 20 minutes, turning occasionally, until skins are blistered and evenly browned. Place peppers in plastic bag; close tightly. Let stand 20 minutes. Remove skin, stems, seeds and membranes from peppers. Cut peppers into 1-inch pieces; set aside.

2 Meanwhile, cook and drain pasta as directed on package, using minimum cook time. Heat oven to 350°F. Spray 3-quart casserole with cooking spray.

3 While pasta is cooking, in medium bowl, toss cheese with flour until cheese is coated. In 3-quart nonreactive saucepan, heat wine, whipping cream and garlic to a simmer. Reduce heat; gradually stir in cheese, salt, pepper and nutmeg until cheese is melted. Cook and stir 2 minutes longer.

4 Stir pasta, roasted peppers and parsley into sauce. Spoon into casserole. In small bowl, stir together bread crumbs and butter. Sprinkle over pasta mixture.

5 Bake uncovered 20 to 30 minutes or until edges are bubbly.

1 SERVING: Calories 490 (Calories from Fat 240); Total Fat 26g (Saturated Fat 14g; Trans Fat 0.5g); Cholesterol 80mg; Sodium 450mg; Total Carbohydrate 39g (Dietary Fiber 2g); Protein 18g **%Daily Value:** Vitamin A 50%; Vitamin C 60%; Calcium 40%; Iron 10% **Exchanges:** 2½ Starch, ½ Vegetable, 1½ Medium-Fat Meat, 3½ Fat **Carbohydrate Choices:** 2½

For a flavor twist, try half Gruyère and half Emmentaler cheese.

Caribbean Soybean and Rice Bake

Prep Time: 15 minutes • Start to Finish: 50 minutes • **4 servings**

1½ **cups uncooked instant brown rice**

1 **cup frozen shelled edamame (green) soybeans (from 12-oz bag)**

½ **medium green bell pepper, coarsely chopped (½ cup)**

4 **medium green onions, sliced (¼ cup)**

1 **tablespoon Caribbean jerk seasoning**

1 **cup water**

1 **can (15 oz) soybeans, drained, rinsed**

1 **can (14½ oz) Italian-style stewed tomatoes, undrained, cut up**

1 **cup shredded Cheddar cheese (4 oz)**

1 Heat oven to 375°F. Spray 11×7-inch (2-quart) glass baking dish with cooking spray. In dish, mix all ingredients except cheese.

2 Cover tightly with foil; bake 25 to 30 minutes or until liquid is absorbed and rice is tender. Uncover; stir in ½ cup cheese. Sprinkle remaining cheese over top. Bake uncovered 5 minutes longer or until cheese is melted.

1 SERVING: Calories 660 (Calories from Fat 210); Total Fat 23g (Saturated Fat 8g; Trans Fat 0g); Cholesterol 30mg; Sodium 630mg; Total Carbohydrate 77g (Dietary Fiber 16g); Protein 36g **%Daily Value:** Vitamin A 25%; Vitamin C 25%; Calcium 35%; Iron 45% **Exchanges:** 5 Starch, 1 Vegetable, 1½ Lean Meat, 1 Medium-Fat Meat, 2 Fat **Carbohydrate Choices:** 5

If you can't find Caribbean jerk seasoning, you can substitute any type of seasoning labeled "jerk," or try Cajun or Creole seasoning.

Italian "Sausage" Egg Bake

Prep Time: **10 minutes** · Start to Finish: **1 hour 10 minutes** · **12 servings**

1 **package (6 oz) seasoned stuffing mix**

1 **package (12 oz) frozen sausage-style soy-protein crumbles**

1 **medium red bell pepper, cut into ½-inch pieces**

2 **medium green onions, sliced (2 tablespoons)**

1 **cup shredded Swiss cheese (4 oz)**

2 **cups original-flavored soymilk**

½ **teaspoon Italian seasoning**

½ **teaspoon salt**

1 **can (10¾ oz) condensed cream of mushroom soup**

6 **eggs**

1 Heat oven to 350°F. Spray 13×9-inch (3-quart) glass baking dish with cooking spray. In dish, layer stuffing mix, crumbles, bell pepper, onions and cheese.

2 In small bowl, mix remaining ingredients with whisk until blended; pour over ingredients in dish.

3 Bake uncovered 45 to 55 minutes or until knife inserted in center comes out clean and top is set and lightly browned. Let stand 5 minutes before serving.

1 SERVING: Calories 220 (Calories from Fat 70); Total Fat 8g (Saturated Fat 3g; Trans Fat 0g); Cholesterol 115mg; Sodium 690mg; Total Carbohydrate 21g (Dietary Fiber 3g); Protein 15g **%Daily Value:** Vitamin A 10%; Vitamin C 10%; Calcium 20%; Iron 15% **Exchanges:** 1½ Starch, ½ Lean Meat, 1 Medium-Fat Meat **Carbohydrate Choices:** 1½

Here's a light, golden, flavor-rich egg dish for your next weekend brunch! Vary the flavor by using broccoli or mushrooms instead of bell pepper and different varieties of cheese or seasoned stuffing mix.

Baked Buffalo Frittata

Prep Time: **10 minutes** • Start to Finish: **35 minutes** • **4 servings**

1 tablespoon butter or margarine

6 eggs

2 tablespoons Buffalo wing sauce

1 cup shredded Mexican cheese blend (4 oz)

2 tablespoons crumbled blue cheese

2 stalks celery, cut into 3-inch pieces

1 Heat oven to 375°F. Place butter in 8-inch square (2-quart) glass baking dish; place in oven until butter is melted.

2 In medium bowl, beat eggs and wing sauce until well blended. Stir in cheese blend. Pour egg mixture into melted butter in baking dish.

3 Bake 18 to 22 minutes or until set. Drizzle frittata with remaining wing sauce. Sprinkle with blue cheese. Serve with celery pieces.

1 SERVING: Calories 270 (Calories from Fat 190); Total Fat 21g (Saturated Fat 11g; Trans Fat 0g); Cholesterol 355mg; Sodium 460mg; Total Carbohydrate 2g (Dietary Fiber 0g); Protein 17g **%Daily Value:** Vitamin A 15%; Vitamin C 0%; Calcium 25%; Iron 6% **Exchanges:** 2½ Medium-Fat Meat, 1½ Fat **Carbohydrate Choices:** 0

Like it spicy? Choose a hot variety of Buffalo wing sauce, and then drizzle with 2 or 3 additional tablespoons of sauce after baking.

If desired, use an ovenproof skillet instead of the baking dish.

Denver Eggs Frittata

Prep Time: 15 minutes • Start to Finish: 25 minutes • 4 servings

8 eggs

½ teaspoon salt

2 tablespoons vegetable oil

½ medium green bell pepper, cut into 1-inch strips

½ medium red bell pepper, cut into 1-inch strips

1 medium onion, sliced

1 can (1¾ oz) shoestring potatoes (1¼ cups)

½ cup shredded Cheddar cheese (2 oz)

1 In medium bowl, beat eggs and salt with fork or whisk; set aside. In 12-inch nonstick skillet, heat oil over medium-high heat. Add bell peppers and onion; cook about 5 minutes, stirring occasionally, until tender. Spread vegetables evenly in skillet.

2 Pour eggs over vegetables. Reduce heat to low; cover and cook 7 to 9 minutes or until eggs are set. Remove from heat.

3 Sprinkle with potatoes and cheese. Cover; let stand about 2 minutes or until cheese is melted. Cut into wedges to serve.

1 SERVING: Calories 360 (Calories from Fat 240); Total Fat 27g (Saturated Fat 9g; Trans Fat 2g); Cholesterol 440mg; Sodium 560mg; Total Carbohydrate 13g (Dietary Fiber 1g); Protein 17g **%Daily Value:** Vitamin A 25%; Vitamin C 30%; Calcium 15%; Iron 8% **Exchanges:** ½ Starch, ½ Vegetable, 2 Medium-Fat Meat, 3½ Fat **Carbohydrate Choices:** 1

You can use any color of bell peppers that you have on hand to equal 1 cup.

Portabella and Vegetable Pot Pie

Prep Time: 40 minutes • Start to Finish: 1 hour 20 minutes • 6 servings

1⅓ cups all-purpose flour

½ teaspoon salt

¼ teaspoon dried thyme leaves

⅓ cup vegetable oil

2 tablespoons cold water

1 tablespoon butter or margarine

8 oz baby portabella mushrooms, each cut into quarters (3½ cups)

1½ cups half-and-half

1 package (1.6 oz) garlic herb sauce mix

1 bag (12 oz) frozen mixed vegetables, thawed

1 teaspoon half-and-half

1 In medium bowl, mix flour, salt, thyme and oil until all flour is moistened. Sprinkle with cold water, 1 tablespoon at a time, tossing with fork until all water is absorbed. Gather pastry into a ball. Place pastry between 2 sheets of waxed paper. With rolling pin, roll into 8½-inch round; set aside, covered with towel.

2 Heat oven to 425°F. In 12-inch skillet, melt butter over medium-high heat. Add mushrooms; cook 5 to 7 minutes, stirring frequently, until mushrooms are tender. Stir in 1½ cups half-and-half and the sauce mix. Heat to boiling over medium-high heat, stirring constantly. Stir in vegetables. Cook 2 to 3 minutes, stirring frequently, until thoroughly heated.

3 Spoon vegetable mixture into ungreased 9½-inch deep-dish pie plate. Remove top waxed paper from crust; cut about 1-inch hole in center of crust. Carefully invert crust over filling; remove remaining waxed paper. Cut small slits in several places in crust. Brush crust with 1 teaspoon half-and-half.

4 Bake 25 to 30 minutes or until crust is golden brown. Let stand 10 minutes before cutting.

1 SERVING: Calories 390 (Calories from Fat 210); Total Fat 23g (Saturated Fat 8g; Trans Fat 0g); Cholesterol 30mg; Sodium 710mg; Total Carbohydrate 38g (Dietary Fiber 3g); Protein 8g **%Daily Value:** Vitamin A 20%; Vitamin C 2%; Calcium 8%; Iron 10% **Exchanges:** 2 Starch, 1 Vegetable, 4½ Fat **Carbohydrate Choices:** 2½

Why a pie crust made with oil? While it's a bit more fragile to work with than a traditional shortening crust, and although it's not flaky, it's very, very tender.

Burrito Pot Pies

Prep Time: 15 minutes • Start to Finish: 45 minutes • 6 servings

6 **soft corn tortillas (5½ inch)**

6 **foil tart pans**

1 **can (16 oz) vegetarian refried beans**

1 **can (14.5 oz) organic diced tomatoes, drained**

2 **tablespoons pickled jalapeño slices, drained, chopped**

2 **teaspoons chili powder**

1 **teaspoon ground cumin**

1 **package (8.8 oz) microwavable Spanish rice**

1½ **cups shredded Mexican cheese blend (6 oz)**

1 **avocado, pitted, peeled and sliced**

⅓ **cup chunky-style salsa**

1 Heat oven to 375°F. Place 1 corn tortilla in each foil tart pan; place pans in 15×10×1-inch pan.

2 In medium bowl, mix beans, tomatoes, jalapeños, chili powder and cumin. Divide mixture evenly (about ½ cup) into tart pans.

3 Wipe out bowl; combine rice and cheese. Divide mixture evenly (about ½ cup) over bean mixture in pans.

4 Bake about 30 minutes or until pot pies are thoroughly heated. Top each with sliced avocado and dollop of salsa.

1 SERVING: Calories 350 (Calories from Fat 130); Total Fat 14g (Saturated Fat 6g; Trans Fat 0g); Cholesterol 30mg; Sodium 1040mg; Total Carbohydrate 41g (Dietary Fiber 8g); Protein 14g **%Daily Value:** Vitamin A 20%; Vitamin C 10%; Calcium 25%; Iron 15% **Exchanges:** 2½ Starch, ½ Vegetable, 1 Medium-Fat Meat, 1½ Fat Carbohydrate Choices: 3

Look for foil "tart" pans that are about 4½ inches in diameter by 1¼ inches high to make perfect-size pot pies. Foil pans labeled "pot pie" pans are actually wider and deeper—and are too big for this recipe. For added crunch, sprinkle pot pies with crushed corn chips.

"Chicken" Alfredo Pot Pie

Prep Time: 20 minutes • Start to Finish: 50 minutes • 6 servings

1 can (11 oz) refrigerated original breadsticks

4 frozen grilled chicken-style soy-protein patties

⅓ cup milk

1 jar (16 oz) Alfredo pasta sauce

1 bag (1 lb) frozen broccoli, cauliflower and carrots, thawed, drained

2 tablespoons grated Parmesan cheese

1 teaspoon Italian seasoning

1 Heat oven to 375°F. Unroll dough; separate at perforations into 12 breadsticks. Set aside. On small microwavable plate, microwave patties on High 30 to 45 seconds or until slightly thawed. Cut patties into cubes to make about 2 cups.

2 In 3-quart saucepan, mix patty cubes, milk, pasta sauce and vegetables. Heat to boiling, stirring occasionally. Spoon into ungreased 13×9-inch (3-quart) glass baking dish.

3 Twist each breadstick; arrange crosswise over hot patties mixture, gently stretching strips if necessary to fit. Sprinkle with cheese and Italian seasoning.

4 Bake uncovered 20 to 30 minutes or until breadsticks are deep golden brown.

1 SERVING: Calories 540 (Calories from Fat 280); Total Fat 31g (Saturated Fat 18g; Trans Fat 1g); Cholesterol 80mg; Sodium 1020mg; Total Carbohydrate 45g (Dietary Fiber 3g); Protein 20g **%Daily Value:** Vitamin A 50%; Vitamin C 20%; Calcium 25%; Iron 15% **Exchanges:** 2½ Starch, 1 Vegetable, 1½ Lean Meat, 5 Fat **Carbohydrate Choices:** 3

The pasta sauce mixture needs to be good and hot before spooning it into the baking dish so the breadsticks will bake through.

Southwestern Pot Pie

Prep Time: **15 minutes** • Start to Finish: **55 minutes** • **4 servings**

1 **tablespoon vegetable oil**

1 **large onion, chopped (1 cup)**

2 **cups cubed peeled sweet potatoes or butternut squash**

1 **jar (16 oz) chunky-style salsa (2 cups)**

½ **cup water**

¼ **teaspoon ground cinnamon**

1 **cup frozen whole kernel corn**

1 **can (15 oz) chick peas (garbanzo beans), drained**

1 **pouch (6.5 oz) cornbread & muffin mix**

½ **cup milk**

1 **tablespoon vegetable oil**

1 **tablespoon roasted sunflower nuts, if desired**

1 In 4-quart Dutch oven, heat 1 tablespoon oil over medium-high heat. Add onion; cook about 5 minutes, stirring occasionally, until crisp-tender.

2 Stir in sweet potatoes, salsa, water and cinnamon. Heat to boiling. Reduce heat; cover and simmer 20 to 25 minutes or until sweet potatoes are tender.

3 Stir in corn and beans. In medium bowl, mix cornbread mix, milk and 1 tablespoon oil; stir in nuts. Drop dough by large spoonfuls onto vegetable mixture.

4 Cover; simmer about 15 minutes or until toothpick inserted in center of dumplings comes out clean.

1 SERVING: Calories 560 (Calories from Fat 110); Total Fat 12g (Saturated Fat 2g; Trans Fat 0g); Cholesterol 0mg; Sodium 1360mg; Total Carbohydrate 96g (Dietary Fiber 10g); Protein 16g **%Daily Value:** Vitamin A 220%; Vitamin C 15%; Calcium 10%; Iron 25% **Exchanges:** 3½ Starch, 2 Other Carbohydrate, 2½ Vegetable, 2 Fat **Carbohydrate Choices:** 6½

Sweet potatoes with darker-colored skins are generally more moist and flavorful than the lighter ones. Two medium sweet potatoes or half of a small butternut squash will give you 2 cups of cubes.

"Beef" and Bean Pot Pie

Prep Time: 25 minutes • **Start to Finish:** 50 minutes • **4 servings**

2 **cups frozen soy-protein burger crumbles (from 12-oz package)**

2 **teaspoons dried minced onion**

1 **can (16 oz) vegetarian baked beans, undrained**

1 **can (8 oz) tomato sauce**

3 **tablespoons packed brown sugar**

1 **cup Original Bisquick® mix**

3 **tablespoons boiling water**

1 **tablespoon ketchup**

1 Heat oven to 375°F. Spray 1½-quart round casserole with cooking spray. In casserole, mix crumbles, onion, baked beans, tomato sauce and brown sugar; set aside.

2 In medium bowl, stir remaining ingredients until soft dough forms; beat vigorously 20 strokes. On surface dusted with Bisquick mix, gently roll dough in Bisquick mix to coat. Shape dough into ball; knead about 10 times or until smooth. Pat ball into 7½-inch round or a round the size of top of casserole; place on bean mixture in casserole.

3 Bake uncovered 20 to 25 minutes or until crust is light brown.

1 SERVING: Calories 390 (Calories from Fat 45); Total Fat 5g (Saturated Fat 1g; Trans Fat 1g); Cholesterol 0mg; Sodium 1370mg; Total Carbohydrate 64g (Dietary Fiber 9g); Protein 21g **%Daily Value:** Vitamin A 8%; Vitamin C 4%; Calcium 15%; Iron 25% **Exchanges:** 4 Starch, ½ Vegetable, 1 Lean Meat **Carbohydrate Choices:** 4

Vegetarian beans are saucy and delicious and sold right alongside regular baked beans.

Vegetarian Shepherd's Pie

Prep Time: 10 minutes • Start to Finish: 35 minutes • **6 servings**

2 cans (15 oz each) dark red kidney beans, drained, rinsed

1 jar (16 oz) chunky-style salsa (2 cups)

1 cup frozen whole kernel corn

1 medium carrot, chopped (½ cup)

1¼ cups water

¼ cup milk

2 tablespoons butter or margarine

¼ teaspoon salt

1¼ cups plain mashed potato mix (dry)

2 tablespoons grated Parmesan cheese

Chopped fresh chives or parsley, if desired

1 In 10-inch nonstick skillet, heat beans, salsa, corn and carrot to boiling. Reduce heat to low; cover and simmer about 15 minutes or until carrot is tender.

2 In 2-quart saucepan, heat water, milk, butter and salt to boiling. Remove from heat. Stir in mashed potato mix just until moistened. Let stand about 30 seconds or until liquid is absorbed. Whip mashed potatoes with fork until fluffy.

3 Spoon mashed potatoes onto bean mixture around edge of skillet. Cover; simmer 5 minutes. Sprinkle with cheese and chives before serving.

1 SERVING: Calories 340 (Calories from Fat 50); Total Fat 6g (Saturated Fat 3g; Trans Fat 0g); Cholesterol 15mg; Sodium 760mg; Total Carbohydrate 56g (Dietary Fiber 10g); Protein 15g **%Daily Value:** Vitamin A 50%; Vitamin C 2%; Calcium 10%; Iron 20% **Exchanges:** 3½ Starch, 1 Vegetable, 1 Fat **Carbohydrate Choices:** 4

Leftover mashed potatoes, instant mashed potatoes or refrigerated, prepared mashed potatoes are all quick options for topping this hearty vegetable and bean pie.

Easy Spinach Pie

Prep Time: 20 minutes • Start to Finish: 50 minutes • **4 servings**

2 **tablespoons butter or margarine**

1 **bag (10 oz) fresh spinach, finely chopped**

1 **small red bell pepper, chopped (½ cup)**

¾ **cup milk**

2 **tablespoons all-purpose flour**

½ **teaspoon salt**

⅛ **teaspoon ground nutmeg**

3 **eggs**

2 **tablespoons grated Parmesan cheese**

1 Heat oven to 350°F. Grease 9-inch pie plate with shortening. In 12-inch skillet, melt butter over medium heat. Add spinach and bell pepper; cook about 5 minutes, stirring occasionally, until spinach is wilted and bell pepper is crisp-tender.

2 In small bowl, beat remaining ingredients except cheese with whisk until smooth. Pour over vegetables in skillet; stir to mix. Pour into pie plate.

3 Bake uncovered about 30 minutes or until center is set. Sprinkle with cheese. Serve immediately.

1 SERVING: Calories 180 (Calories from Fat 110); Total Fat 12g (Saturated Fat 6g; Trans Fat 0g); Cholesterol 180mg; Sodium 490mg; Total Carbohydrate 9g (Dietary Fiber 1g); Protein 9g **%Daily Value:** Vitamin A 120%; Vitamin C 30%; Calcium 15%; Iron 10% **Exchanges:** ½ Starch, 1 Vegetable, ½ Medium-Fat Meat, 2 Fat **Carbohydrate Choices:** ½

This pie is somewhere between a spinach soufflé and crustless quiche. It makes a good main dish for casual entertaining. Serve it with your favorite pasta sauce or cheese sauce and add a salad of fresh orange and red onion slices sprinkled with toasted almonds.

Fajita Pot Pie

Prep Time: 15 minutes • Start to Finish: 45 minutes • 4 servings

4 frozen grilled chicken-style
   soy-protein patties

1 teaspoon vegetable oil

½ medium bell pepper, cut into
   ½-inch strips

1¾ cups chunky-style salsa

¼ cup water

1 cup Original Bisquick® mix

⅓ cup shredded Monterey Jack
   cheese (1⅓ oz)

½ cup milk

1 Heat oven to 400°F. On small microwavable plate, microwave patties on High 30 to 45 seconds or until slightly thawed. Cut patties into cubes to make about 2 cups; set aside.

2 In 10-inch skillet, heat oil over medium heat. Add bell pepper; cook, stirring occasionally, until crisp-tender, about 2 minutes. Stir in patty cubes, salsa and water. Cook 1 to 2 minutes, stirring occasionally, until bubbly. Pour into ungreased 1½-quart casserole; set aside.

3 In small bowl, stir remaining ingredients with fork until blended. Pour over patty mixture; carefully spread almost to edge of casserole.

4 Bake uncovered about 30 minutes or until light golden brown. If desired, with squeezable ketchup, write a message on top.

1 SERVING: Calories 300 (Calories from Fat 100); Total Fat 11g (Saturated Fat 3.5g; Trans Fat 1g); Cholesterol 10mg; Sodium 1590mg; Total Carbohydrate 36g (Dietary Fiber 6g); Protein 14g **%Daily Value:** Vitamin A 20%; Vitamin C 10%; Calcium 20%; Iron 10% **Exchanges:** 2½ Starch, 1 Lean Meat, 1 Fat **Carbohydrate Choices:** 2½

Frozen grilled chicken-style soy-protein patties offer a very tasty "chicken" patty option without breading.

chapter 4

burgers, wraps & pizzas

Samosa Patties with Mint Relish

Prep Time: 45 minutes • Start to Finish: 45 minutes • 4 servings (1 patty and 2 teaspoons relish each)

PATTIES

3 medium baking potatoes (1 lb), peeled

1 tablespoon butter or margarine

½ cup chopped onion (1 medium)

1 teaspoon finely chopped gingerroot

1 serrano chile, seeded, finely chopped

½ cup frozen sweet peas, thawed

2 tablespoons chopped cashews

1 teaspoon garam masala

½ teaspoon salt

1 egg white, slightly beaten

2 tablespoons vegetable oil

RELISH

½ cup loosely packed mint leaves, finely chopped

¼ cup loosely packed cilantro, finely chopped

1 serrano chile, seeded, finely chopped

3 tablespoons lime juice

½ teaspoon salt

1 Cut potatoes into 2-inch pieces. Place potatoes in 2-quart saucepan; add enough water just to cover potatoes. Heat to boiling. Reduce heat; cover and simmer 20 minutes or just until tender. Drain. Mash potatoes slightly with potato masher, leaving potatoes slightly lumpy; set aside.

2 Meanwhile, in small bowl, mix relish ingredients; set aside.

3 In 10-inch nonstick skillet, melt butter over medium heat. Add onion, gingerroot and 1 chile; cook and stir about 6 minutes or until onion is tender. Stir in peas, cashews, garam masala and ½ teaspoon salt; cook until thoroughly heated. Stir onion mixture into potato mixture until well combined. Stir in egg white to bind ingredients together. Shape mixture into 4 patties, about ¾ inch thick.

4 Wipe skillet clean with paper towels. In same skillet, heat oil over medium heat. Add patties; cook 10 minutes, turning once, until golden brown on each side. Serve patties with relish.

1 SERVING: Calories 230 (Calories from Fat 110); Total Fat 12g (Saturated Fat 3.5g; Trans Fat 0g); Cholesterol 10mg; Sodium 640mg; Total Carbohydrate 27g (Dietary Fiber 3g); Protein 4g **%Daily Value:** Vitamin A 15%; Vitamin C 20%; Calcium 2%; Iron 6% **Exchanges:** 1½ Starch, ½ Vegetable, 2 Fat **Carbohydrate Choices:** 2

These flavorful patties are hearty enough to stand alone without the need for buns. If you prefer them as a sandwich, burger buns work well.

Falafel Sandwiches with Yogurt Sauce

Prep Time: 1 hour • Start to Finish: 1 hour • 8 sandwiches

SANDWICHES

- ¾ **cup water**
- ¼ **cup uncooked bulgur**
- 1 **can (15 oz) garbanzo beans, drained, rinsed**
- ¼ **cup chopped fresh cilantro**
- ¼ **cup sliced green onions (4 medium)**
- 1 **tablespoon all-purpose flour**
- 3 **tablespoons water**
- 2 **teaspoons ground cumin**
- ¾ **teaspoon baking powder**
- ½ **teaspoon salt**
- 2 **cloves garlic, finely chopped**
- 2 **tablespoons vegetable oil**
- 4 **pita (pocket) breads (6 inch), cut in half to form pockets**
- 8 **slices tomato**
- 16 **slices cucumber**

SAUCE

- 1 **cup plain fat-free yogurt (from 2-lb container)**
- 2 **tablespoons chopped fresh mint leaves**
- ¼ **teaspoon ground cumin**

1 In 1-quart saucepan, heat ¾ cup water to boiling. Stir in bulgur. Remove from heat; cover and let stand 30 minutes or until tender. Drain; set aside.

2 Meanwhile, in food processor, combine beans, cilantro, onions, flour, 3 tablespoons water, the cumin, baking powder, salt and garlic. Process with on/off pulses 10 times or until well blended and coarsely chopped (mixture will be wet). Spoon mixture into large bowl.

3 Stir bulgur into bean mixture. Divide mixture into 8 equal portions, about ¼ cup each; shape each portion into ¼-inch-thick oval-shaped patty.

4 In 10-inch nonstick skillet, heat 1 tablespoon of the oil over medium heat. Place 4 patties in skillet; cook 8 minutes, turning once, until golden brown. Transfer patties to platter; cover with foil to keep warm. Repeat with remaining tablespoon oil and 4 patties.

5 Meanwhile, stir together sauce ingredients.

6 Spread 2 tablespoons sauce in each pita pocket. Fill each with tomato slices, cucumber slices and falafel patty.

1 SERVING: Calories 240 (Calories from Fat 50); Total Fat 5g (Saturated Fat 1g; Trans Fat 0g); Cholesterol 0mg; Sodium 370mg; Total Carbohydrate 39g (Dietary Fiber 5g); Protein 10g **%Daily Value:** Vitamin A 6%; Vitamin C 4%; Calcium 15%; Iron 15% **Exchanges:** 2½ Starch, ½ Vegetable, ½ Fat **Carbohydrate Choices:** 2½

> **Patties can be baked at 400°F for 20 minutes on a greased cookie sheet, turning once, but they won't have the crisp crust that comes from cooking on the stovetop. The patties can also be served in regular burger buns.**

Italian Veggie Sliders

Prep Time: 45 minutes • Start to Finish: 45 minutes • 6 servings (2 sandwiches each)

1½ **cups water**

½ **cup dried red lentils, sorted, rinsed**

½ **cup uncooked instant brown rice**

¾ **teaspoon salt**

3 **tablespoons olive or vegetable oil**

½ **chopped onion (1 medium)**

½ **cup finely chopped mushrooms**

½ **cup chopped red bell pepper**

2 **cloves garlic, finely chopped**

¼ **cup finely shredded Parmesan cheese**

¼ **cup plain bread crumbs**

1 **teaspoon Italian seasoning**

½ **teaspoon pepper**

1 **egg, slightly beaten**

12 **small burger buns (about 2½ inches in diameter), split**

¼ **cup garlic and herb mayonnaise or garlic aioli**

⅓ **cup packed baby spinach leaves**

1 In 2-quart saucepan, heat water, lentils, rice and salt to boiling. Reduce heat; cover and simmer 12 to 15 minutes, stirring occasionally, until lentils are tender but hold their shape and all water is absorbed. Spoon into large bowl; cool 15 minutes.

2 Meanwhile, in 10-inch nonstick skillet, heat 1 tablespoon of the oil over medium heat. Stir in onion, mushrooms, bell pepper and garlic; cook and stir 3 to 4 minutes or until vegetables are tender.

3 Add onion mixture to lentils and rice. Stir in cheese, bread crumbs, Italian seasoning, pepper and egg just until blended.

4 Wipe skillet clean with paper towel. In same skillet, heat 1 tablespoon of the oil over medium heat. Shape lentil mixture into 6 (2½-inch) patties, using about 2 rounded tablespoons for each; place in skillet. Cook 6 to 8 minutes, turning once, until golden brown. Repeat with remaining tablespoon oil and the lentil mixture, making 6 more patties.

5 Place patties on bottom halves of buns. Top each with 1 teaspoon mayonnaise and a few spinach leaves. Cover with top halves of buns.

1 SERVING: Calories 380 (Calories from Fat 130); Total Fat 14g (Saturated Fat 3g; Trans Fat 0g); Cholesterol 40mg; Sodium 680mg; Total Carbohydrate 51g (Dietary Fiber 5g); Protein 13g **%Daily Value:** Vitamin A 15%; Vitamin C 15%; Calcium 15%; Iron 20% **Exchanges:** 3 Starch, ½ Vegetable, 2½ Fat **Carbohydrate Choices:** 3½

If the lentil mixture is sticky, coat your hands with additional bread crumbs when shaping the patties.

Wild Rice–Pecan Burgers

Prep Time: 20 minutes • Start to Finish: 1 hour 10 minutes • 4 servings (2 burgers each)

⅔ cup uncooked wild rice

1½ cups water

1 cup soft bread crumbs
(about 1½ slices bread)

⅓ cup chopped pecans, toasted*

½ teaspoon garlic salt

2 eggs

1 jar (2.5 oz) sliced mushrooms,
drained, finely chopped

1 jar (2 oz) diced pimientos, drained

2 tablespoons vegetable oil

1 Cook wild rice in water as directed on package.

2 In medium bowl, mix rice and remaining ingredients except oil.

3 In 10-inch skillet, heat oil over medium heat. Scoop wild rice mixture by ⅓ cupfuls into skillet; flatten to ½-inch thickness. Cook about 3 minutes on each side or until light brown. Remove patties from skillet; cover to keep warm while cooking remaining patties.

*To toast pecans, sprinkle in ungreased heavy skillet. Cook over medium heat 5 to 7 minutes, stirring frequently until nuts begin to brown, then stirring constantly until nuts are light brown.

1 SERVING: Calories 390 (Calories from Fat 160); Total Fat 18g (Saturated Fat 3g; Trans Fat 0g); Cholesterol 105mg; Sodium 470mg; Total Carbohydrate 45g (Dietary Fiber 4g); Protein 12g **%Daily Value:** Vitamin A 2%; Vitamin C 0%; Calcium 8%; Iron 15% **Exchanges:** 3 Starch, 3 Fat **Carbohydrate Choices:** 3

These "burgers" are deliciously chewy with a toasted pecan crunch. We tested them in the fall and found they're really good on sandwich buns with cranberry sauce. Try serving them at Thanksgiving for those not eating turkey.

California Black Bean Burgers

Prep Time: 30 minutes • Start to Finish: 30 minutes • 5 sandwiches

1 **can (15 oz) black beans with cumin and chili, undrained**

1 **can (4.5 oz) chopped green chiles, undrained**

1 **cup plain bread crumbs**

1 **egg, beaten**

¼ **cup yellow cornmeal**

2 **tablespoons vegetable oil**

5 **burger buns, toasted**

1 **tablespoon mayonnaise or salad dressing**

1¼ **cups shredded lettuce**

3 **tablespoons chunky-style salsa**

1 Place beans in food processor or blender. Cover; process until slightly mashed. Remove from food processor to bowl; stir in chiles, bread crumbs and egg. Shape mixture into 5 patties, each about ½ inch thick. Coat each patty with cornmeal.

2 In 10-inch skillet, heat oil over medium heat. Add patties; cook 10 to 15 minutes, turning once, until crisp and thoroughly cooked on both sides.

3 Spread bottom halves of buns with mayonnaise. Top with lettuce, patties and salsa. Cover with top halves of buns.

1 SANDWICH: Calories 400 (Calories from Fat 110); Total Fat 12g (Saturated Fat 2.5g; Trans Fat 0g); Cholesterol 45mg; Sodium 850mg; Total Carbohydrate 58g (Dietary Fiber 5g); Protein 13g **%Daily Value:** Vitamin A 6%; Vitamin C 6%; Calcium 15%; Iron 20% **Exchanges:** 4 Starch, 2 Fat **Carbohydrate Choices:** 4

Coating the patties with cornmeal gives them a delicious crispy coating. If the seasoned black beans aren't available, use unseasoned black beans and add one teaspoon chili powder.

Cheesy Soy Burgers

Prep Time: 25 minutes • Start to Finish: 25 minutes • 4 sandwiches

HORSERADISH SAUCE

½ cup plain fat-free yogurt (from 2-lb container)

2 teaspoons prepared horseradish

PATTIES

1 can (15 oz) soybeans, drained, rinsed

½ cup shredded reduced-fat Cheddar cheese (2 oz)

¼ cup plain bread crumbs

2 medium green onions, finely chopped (2 tablespoons)

1 teaspoon Worcestershire sauce

¼ teaspoon pepper

⅛ teaspoon salt

2 tablespoons fat-free egg product or 1 egg white

1 tablespoon vegetable oil

BUNS

4 burger buns, split, toasted

TOPPINGS

4 slices tomato

4 lettuce leaves

1 In small bowl, mix sauce ingredients; set aside.

2 In medium bowl, mash beans with fork. Stir in all remaining patty ingredients except oil. Shape mixture into 4 patties.

3 In 10-inch nonstick skillet, heat oil over medium heat. Add patties; cook about 10 minutes, turning once, until light brown.

4 Top bottom halves of buns with patties, sauce, tomato and lettuce. Cover with top halves of buns.

1 SANDWICH: Calories 430 (Calories from Fat 150); Total Fat 16g (Saturated Fat 3g; Trans Fat 0g); Cholesterol 0mg; Sodium 480mg; Total Carbohydrate 41g (Dietary Fiber 8g); Protein 29g **%Daily Value:** Vitamin A 15%; Vitamin C 6%; Calcium 35%; Iron 40% **Exchanges:** 2½ Starch, 1 Vegetable, 2½ Lean Meat, 1½ Fat **Carbohydrate Choices:** 3

If soybeans are missing from your supermarket shelves, canned pinto beans, drained and rinsed, are a tasty bean backup for these delicious bean burgers.

Veggie and Bean Burgers

Prep Time: 25 minutes • Start to Finish: 25 minutes • 4 sandwiches

¼ cup uncooked instant rice

¼ cup boiling water

½ cup fresh broccoli florets

2 oz fresh mushrooms (about 4 medium)

½ small red bell pepper, cut up

1 can (15 oz) garbanzo beans, drained, rinsed

1 egg

1 clove garlic

½ teaspoon seasoned salt

1 teaspoon dried chopped onion

⅓ cup Italian style bread crumbs

3 tablespoons vegetable oil

4 whole wheat burger buns, split

Toppings (Cheddar cheese slices, lettuce, sliced tomato, sliced onion and mayonnaise), if desired

1 In medium bowl, stir rice and boiling water. Cover; let stand 5 minutes. Drain if necessary.

2 Meanwhile, in food processor, place broccoli, mushrooms and bell pepper. Cover; process with quick on-and-off pulses to finely chop vegetables (do not puree). Stir vegetables into rice.

3 Add beans, egg, garlic and seasoned salt to food processor. Cover; process until smooth. Stir bean mixture, onion and bread crumbs into vegetable mixture.

4 Using about ½ cup vegetable mixture for each, shape into 4 patties, each about ½ inch thick.

5 In 10-inch nonstick skillet, heat oil over medium-high heat. Add patties; cook 8 to 10 minutes, turning once, until brown and crisp. Top bottom halves of buns with patties and desired toppings. Cover with top halves of buns.

1 SANDWICH: Calories 450 (Calories from Fat 150); Total Fat 16g (Saturated Fat 2.5g; Trans Fat 0g); Cholesterol 55mg; Sodium 520mg; Total Carbohydrate 58g (Dietary Fiber 10g); Protein 18g **%Daily Value:** Vitamin A 10%; Vitamin C 20%; Calcium 10%; Iron 30% **Exchanges:** 3½ Starch, 1 Vegetable, 1 Very Lean Meat, 2½ Fat **Carbohydrate Choices:** 4

Want to make Veggie and Bean "Meatballs"? Heat oven to 400°F. Generously spray 15×10×1-inch pan with cooking spray. Shape vegetable mixture into 16 balls; place in pan. Generously spray tops of balls with cooking spray. Bake about 20 minutes or until crisp. Serve with pasta sauce (any flavor) or cheese sauce.

Portabella Mushroom Burgers

Prep Time: 20 minutes • Start to Finish: 35 minutes • **4 sandwiches**

4 **portabella mushroom caps (about ¾ lb)**

¼ **cup balsamic vinegar**

2 **tablespoons olive or vegetable oil**

1 **teaspoon dried basil leaves**

1 **teaspoon dried oregano leaves**

1 **tablespoon finely chopped garlic**

½ **teaspoon salt**

¼ **teaspoon pepper**

4 **slices provolone cheese**

4 **burger buns, split**

1 Heat gas or charcoal grill.

2 In resealable food-storage plastic bag, place mushroom caps. In small bowl, mix vinegar, oil, basil, oregano, garlic, salt and pepper with whisk. Pour over mushrooms; seal bag. Let stand 15 minutes, turning twice.

3 Place mushrooms on grill over medium heat; reserve marinade for basting. Cook uncovered, brushing with marinade frequently, 5 to 8 minutes. Turn mushrooms over; cook 3 to 6 minutes longer.

4 Top mushrooms with cheese and place burger buns, cut side down, on grill rack. Cook 2 minutes more or until mushrooms are tender and cheese is melted. Serve mushrooms in buns.

1 SANDWICH: Calories 320 (Calories from Fat 150); Total Fat 16g (Saturated Fat 6g; Trans Fat 0g); Cholesterol 20mg; Sodium 760mg; Total Carbohydrate 29g (Dietary Fiber 2g); Protein 13g **%Daily Value:** Vitamin A 6%; Vitamin C 0%; Calcium 30%; Iron 10% **Exchanges:** 1½ Starch, 1 Vegetable, 1 Medium-Fat Meat, 2 Fat **Carbohydrate Choices:** 2

Recipe submitted by **Shreya Sasaki,** *San Diego CA* { *www.recipematcher.com* }

Fontina Panini with Spinach

Prep Time: 15 minutes • **Start to Finish:** 15 minutes • **4 sandwiches**

8 **slices crusty Italian bread (½ inch thick)**

2 **tablespoons honey mustard**

2 **tablespoons sliced green onions (2 medium)**

1 **cup loosely packed fresh spinach leaves**

½ **cup roasted red bell peppers (from a jar), drained, cut into strips**

4 **oz fontina cheese, cut into ⅛-inch-thick slices**

1 Heat closed contact grill or panini maker for 5 minutes.

2 Meanwhile, spread 1 side of each bread slice with honey mustard; sprinkle onions over 4 slices of bread. Top onions with spinach leaves, roasted red peppers and sliced cheese. Place remaining slices of bread over cheese.

3 When grill is heated, place sandwiches on grill. Close grill; cook 2 to 3 minutes or until bread is toasted and cheese is melted. Cut each sandwich in half to serve.

1 SERVING: Calories 260 (Calories from Fat 110); Total Fat 13g (Saturated Fat 6g; Trans Fat 0.5g); Cholesterol 35mg; Sodium 570mg; Total Carbohydrate 25g (Dietary Fiber 2g); Protein 11g **%Daily Value:** Vitamin A 20%; Vitamin C 2%; Calcium 20%; Iron 8% **Exchanges:** 1½ Starch, 1 Medium-Fat Meat, 1½ Fat **Carbohydrate Choices:** 1½

For great flavor and crunch, add a few chopped pecans with the green onions.

Pesto, Mozzarella and Tomato Panini

Prep Time: 20 minutes • Start to Finish: 20 minutes • 4 sandwiches

4 ciabatta sandwich rolls

2 tablespoons olive oil

½ cup basil pesto

8 slices mozzarella cheese

1 medium tomato, cut into 8 thin slices

½ teaspoon salt

¼ teaspoon pepper

1 Heat closed contact grill 5 minutes.

2 Cut each roll in half horizontally; brush outside of each half with oil. Spread pesto on inside of both halves. Layer each sandwich with cheese and tomato. Sprinkle with salt and pepper.

3 When grill is heated, place sandwiches on grill. Close grill; grill 4 minutes or until bread is toasty and cheese is melted. Cut sandwiches diagonally; serve warm.

1 SANDWICH: Calories 530 (Calories from Fat 300); Total Fat 33g (Saturated Fat 10g; Trans Fat 0g); Cholesterol 40mg; Sodium 1200mg; Total Carbohydrate 36g (Dietary Fiber 1g); Protein 22g **%Daily Value:** Vitamin A 25%; Vitamin C 10%; Calcium 50%; Iron 15% **Exchanges:** 2½ Starch, 2 Medium-Fat Meat, 4 Fat **Carbohydrate Choices:** 2½

If you can't find ciabatta rolls, substitute focaccia or 8 slices of country bread. Also, you can use fresh mozzarella instead of the slices.

Poblano and Mushroom Quesadillas

Prep Time: 30 minutes • Start to Finish: 30 minutes • **4 quesadillas**

1 **tablespoon vegetable oil**

2 **poblano chiles, seeded, finely chopped**

1 **large onion, finely chopped (1 cup)**

1 **package (8 oz) sliced fresh mushrooms (about 3 cups)**

8 **flour tortillas for soft tacos & fajitas (6 inch; from 8.2-oz package)**

1⅓ **cups shredded Mexican cheese blend (5⅓ oz)**

1 In 10-inch skillet, heat oil over medium heat. Add chiles, onion and mushrooms; cook 10 minutes, stirring frequently, until vegetables are tender.

2 Divide vegetable mixture evenly onto 4 tortillas. Sprinkle each with 3 tablespoons cheese. Top with remaining tortillas.

3 Wipe skillet clean with paper towels. Spray skillet with cooking spray; heat over medium heat. Place 1 quesadilla in skillet; cook 1 to 2 minutes or until golden brown on bottom. Turn; cook 1 to 2 minutes longer or until golden brown on bottom and cheese is melted. Remove from skillet to serving platter; cover with foil to keep warm. Repeat with remaining quesadillas.

1 SERVING: Calories 370 (Calories from Fat 170); Total Fat 19g (Saturated Fat 9g; Trans Fat 2g); Cholesterol 40mg; Sodium 610mg; Total Carbohydrate 34g (Dietary Fiber 2g); Protein 15g **%Daily Value:** Vitamin A 10%; Vitamin C 50%; Calcium 30%; Iron 10% **Exchanges:** 2½ Starch, 1 Lean Meat, 3 Fat **Carbohydrate Choices:** 2

For a spicier flavor, spread each tortilla lightly with salsa. Then top with the vegetables and cheese. If you want to walk on the mild side, 1 green bell pepper can be substituted for the poblano chiles.

Cheesy Green Chile Quesadillas

Prep Time: **10 minutes** • Start to Finish: **15 minutes** • **6 quesadillas**

2 cups shredded Cheddar or
   Monterey Jack cheese (8 oz)

6 flour tortillas for burritos
   (8 inch; from 11-oz package)

1 small tomato, seeded, chopped
   (½ cup)

4 medium green onions, chopped
   (¼ cup)

1 can (4.5 oz) chopped green chiles,
   drained

   Chopped fresh cilantro, if desired

1 Heat oven to 350°F. Sprinkle ⅓ cup cheese evenly over half of each tortilla. Sprinkle tomato, onions, chiles and cilantro over cheese. Fold tortillas over filling; sprinkle with additional cilantro. Place on ungreased cookie sheet.

2 Bake about 5 minutes or just until cheese is melted. Serve quesadillas whole, or cut each into 3 wedges, beginning cuts from center of folded sides.

1 QUESADILLA: Calories 290 (Calories from Fat 140); Total Fat 16g (Saturated Fat 9g; Trans Fat 1.5g); Cholesterol 40mg; Sodium 610mg; Total Carbohydrate 23g (Dietary Fiber 0g); Protein 12g **%Daily Value:** Vitamin A 10%; Vitamin C 8%; Calcium 25%; Iron 8% **Exchanges:** 1½ Starch, 1 Medium-Fat Meat, 2 Fat **Carbohydrate Choices:** 1½

Tortillas are handy wrappers to keep on hand! They can be stuffed, rolled and folded for a super-easy meal. Look for regular, whole wheat, fat-free and flavored varieties.

Vegetarian Cobb Salad Wraps

Prep Time: 15 minutes • **Start to Finish:** 15 minutes • **2 sandwiches**

2 cups torn romaine lettuce

2 tablespoons red wine vinaigrette or Italian dressing

2 flour tortillas for wraps (11 to 12 inch)

½ cup chopped tomato (1 small)

4 teaspoons crumbled blue cheese

1 tablespoon chopped green onion (1 medium)

2 slices vegetarian bacon, cut into small pieces

1 hard-cooked egg, sliced

½ avocado, pitted, peeled and sliced

1 In large bowl, toss lettuce with vinaigrette to coat. Spoon lettuce evenly down center of each tortilla. Top each evenly with tomato, cheese, onion, bacon, egg and avocado.

2 Fold opposite sides of each tortilla up toward center about 1 inch over filling (sides will not meet in center). Beginning at one open end, roll up each tortilla. Cut diagonally in half; if desired, secure with toothpick. Serve immediately.

1 SERVING: Calories 400 (Calories from Fat 180); Total Fat 20g (Saturated Fat 4.5g; Trans Fat 1g); Cholesterol 110mg; Sodium 770mg; Total Carbohydrate 42g (Dietary Fiber 5g); Protein 14g **%Daily Value:** Vitamin A 90%; Vitamin C 35%; Calcium 20%; Iron 20% **Exchanges:** 2½ Starch, ½ Vegetable, ½ Medium-Fat Meat, 3 Fat **Carbohydrate Choices:** 3

Instead of a traditional wrap, try a flatbread wrap. You can find flatbread wraps near other breads at your grocery store.

Mexican Potato Tacos

Prep Time: 35 minutes • Start to Finish: 35 minutes • 4 tacos

2 large Yukon Gold or 3 to 4 medium red potatoes (½ lb), unpeeled, cut into ¼- to ½-inch pieces

2 tablespoons vegetable oil

½ cup chopped onion (1 medium)

½ medium green bell pepper, finely chopped (½ cup)

½ cup salsa verde

2½ teaspoons taco seasoning mix (from 1-oz package)

4 taco shells that stand on their own (from 4.7-oz box)

1 cup shredded lettuce

1 medium tomato, seeded, chopped

½ cup taco sauce

½ cup queso fresco cheese or Mexican cheese blend (2 oz)

1 Place potatoes in microwavable bowl; cover with microwavable plastic wrap. Microwave on High 5 minutes or until tender.

2 In 10-inch skillet, heat oil over medium-high heat. Add potatoes, onion and bell pepper; cook 5 to 7 minutes, stirring frequently, until onion and bell pepper are crisp-tender. Reduce heat to medium-low. Stir in salsa verde and seasoning mix; cook 3 to 5 minutes, stirring occasionally.

3 Divide filling evenly into taco shells. Top each with lettuce, tomato, taco sauce and cheese.

1 SERVING: Calories 200 (Calories from Fat 90); Total Fat 11g (Saturated Fat 3.5g; Trans Fat 0g); Cholesterol 10mg; Sodium 700mg; Total Carbohydrate 20g (Dietary Fiber 2g); Protein 5g **%Daily Value:** Vitamin A 15%; Vitamin C 20%; Calcium 10%; Iron 6% **Exchanges:** 1 Starch, 1 Vegetable, 2 Fat **Carbohydrate Choices:** 1

Salsa verde is a green salsa, often made of tomatillos, cilantro and green chiles. It is now commonly available at the grocery store. Feel free to substitute other types of salsas in this recipe.

Veggie Burritos

Prep Time: 45 minutes • Start to Finish: 1 hour 10 minutes • 8 servings

2 tablespoons vegetable oil

½ cup chopped onion (1 medium)

2 medium red or green bell peppers, seeded, chopped (about 2 cups)

1½ cups shredded carrots (2 medium)

2 cloves garlic, finely chopped

1 jalapeño chile, seeded, finely chopped

1 teaspoon dried oregano leaves

1 teaspoon ground cumin

½ teaspoon salt

2 tablespoons water

1 can (16 oz) vegetarian refried beans

8 flour tortillas (about 10 inch)

2 cups shredded Cheddar, Colby–Monterey Jack cheese blend or Mexican cheese blend (8 oz)

⅓ cup chunky-style salsa

1 Heat oven to 350°F. In 12-inch skillet, heat oil over medium-high heat. Add onion; cook about 5 minutes, stirring frequently, until onion is tender. Stir in bell peppers, carrots, garlic, chile, oregano, cumin and salt. Cook 5 minutes, stirring frequently. Stir in water. Reduce heat to low; cover and steam 5 to 10 minutes or until vegetables are crisp-tender.

2 Meanwhile, spread about 3 tablespoons refried beans on each tortilla.

3 Spoon about ⅓ cup vegetable mixture and ¼ cup cheese onto each tortilla. Fold sides up over filling; roll up tortilla. On ungreased large cookie sheet, place burritos seam side down about 1 inch apart. Brush tops and sides with salsa.

4 Bake 18 to 22 minutes or until thoroughly heated. Serve topped with additional salsa and sour cream, if desired.

1 SERVING: Calories 220 (Calories from Fat 120); Total Fat 13g (Saturated Fat 7g; Trans Fat 0g); Cholesterol 30mg; Sodium 660mg; Total Carbohydrate 14g (Dietary Fiber 4g); Protein 10g **%Daily Value:** Vitamin A 90%; Vitamin C 35%; Calcium 20%; Iron 8% **Exchanges:** ½ Starch, ½ Vegetable, 1 Medium-Fat Meat, 1½ Fat **Carbohydrate Choices:** 1

Make these ahead to eat for lunch or quick dinners on-the-go. Prepare burritos as directed but do not bake. Wrap each burrito in plastic wrap and refrigerate for up to 5 days. When ready to serve, remove plastic wrap and wrap burrito in paper towel. Microwave 1 burrito on High for 45 to 60 seconds or until hot and cheese is melted.

For this recipe, use packaged shredded carrots to make it especially quick to prepare.

Hot "Chicken" Sub

Prep Time: 30 minutes • **Start to Finish:** 30 minutes • **6 servings**

6 **frozen chicken-style breaded soy-protein patties (from two 10-oz packages)**

1 **loaf (1 lb) French bread, cut in half horizontally**

½ **cup creamy Italian dressing**
Lettuce

1 **large tomato, thinly sliced**

1 Heat patties as directed on package.

2 Spread cut sides of bread with dressing. Layer lettuce, patties and tomato on bottom half of bread. Cover with top half of bread. Cut into slices to serve.

1 SERVING: Calories 460 (Calories from Fat 130); Total Fat 15g (Saturated Fat 2.5g; Trans Fat 0g); Cholesterol 0mg; Sodium 1120mg; Total Carbohydrate 61g (Dietary Fiber 4g); Protein 20g **%Daily Value:** Vitamin A 15%; Vitamin C 4%; Calcium 8%; Iron 25% **Exchanges:** 4 Starch, ½ Vegetable, 1 Lean Meat, 2 Fat **Carbohydrate Choices:** 4

Chicken-style breaded soy-protein patties cook up crispy on the outside just like their real chicken counterparts, but the patty itself has a slightly softer texture. Look for regular and spicy varieties.

Pesto-Eggplant Sandwiches

Prep Time: 20 minutes • Start to Finish: 20 minutes • **4 open-face sandwiches**

4 **slices (½ inch thick) unpeeled eggplant**

1 **egg, beaten**

⅓ **cup Italian style bread crumbs**

2 **tablespoons olive or vegetable oil**

4 **thin slices red onion**

4 **slices (1 oz each) provolone cheese**

2 **tablespoons basil pesto**

4 **slices (½ inch thick) Italian bread, toasted**

8 **thin slices cucumber**

4 **thin slices tomato**

1 Dip eggplant slices into egg, then coat with bread crumbs. In 10-inch skillet, heat oil over medium heat. Add eggplant; cook 3 to 4 minutes, turning once, until golden brown and crisp.

2 Top each eggplant slice with onion and cheese. Cover; cook 1 to 2 minutes or until cheese is melted.

3 Spread pesto on bread. Top with cucumber, tomato and eggplant.

1 OPEN-FACE SANDWICH: Calories 310 (Calories from Fat 180); Total Fat 20g (Saturated Fat 7g; Trans Fat 0g); Cholesterol 75mg; Sodium 540mg; Total Carbohydrate 18g (Dietary Fiber 3g); Protein 12g **%Daily Value:** Vitamin A 15%; Vitamin C 4%; Calcium 25%; Iron 8% **Exchanges:** 1 Starch, 1 Vegetable, 1 Medium-Fat Meat, 3 Fat **Carbohydrate Choices:** 1

The peak season for eggplant is generally August and September, but they usually are available all year. Choose eggplants that are firm and smooth skinned with no soft or wrinkled spots.

Italian Grinders

Prep Time: 25 minutes • Start to Finish: 25 minutes • **4 sandwiches**

4 frozen soy-protein burgers or soy-protein vegetable burgers

3 tablespoons grated Parmesan cheese

1 teaspoon Italian seasoning

4 teaspoons olive or vegetable oil

1 small onion, cut in half, sliced

1 small red bell pepper, cut into ¼-inch strips

1 small green bell pepper, cut into ¼-inch strips

4 hot dog buns, split

½ cup organic tomato pasta sauce (any variety), heated

1 On large microwavable plate, microwave burgers uncovered on High 2 to 3 minutes, turning once, until thawed. In medium bowl, mix thawed burgers, cheese and Italian seasoning. Shape mixture into 16 balls.

2 In 10-inch nonstick skillet, heat 2 teaspoons of the oil over medium heat. Add burger balls; cook, turning frequently, until brown. Remove from skillet; keep warm.

3 In same skillet, heat remaining 2 teaspoons oil over medium heat. Add onion and bell peppers; cook, stirring frequently, until crisp-tender.

4 Place 4 burger balls in each bun. Top with vegetable mixture. Serve with pasta sauce.

1 SANDWICH: Calories 330 (Calories from Fat 100); Total Fat 11g (Saturated Fat 3g; Trans Fat 0g); Cholesterol 0mg; Sodium 780mg; Total Carbohydrate 46g (Dietary Fiber 7g); Protein 12g **%Daily Value:** Vitamin A 20%; Vitamin C 35%; Calcium 15%; Iron 10% **Exchanges:** 3 Starch, ½ Vegetable, 2 Fat **Carbohydrate Choices:** 3

Can't resist the aroma and flavor of a meatball sandwich slathered in spaghetti sauce and adorned with peppers and onions? The solution is at hand. Frozen soy-protein burgers mixed with just a few ingredients create memorable "meatless" meatballs.

Cajun Muffulettas

Prep Time: 25 minutes • **Start to Finish:** 1 hour 25 minutes • **4 sandwiches**

OLIVE SALAD

¼ cup chopped pimiento-stuffed olives

¼ cup chopped kalamata or ripe olives

¼ cup sliced hot pickled okra (from 16-oz jar)

1 tablespoon chopped fresh parsley

1 tablespoon olive or vegetable oil

¼ teaspoon dried oregano leaves, crumbled

⅛ teaspoon pepper

1 small clove garlic, finely chopped

SANDWICHES

1 can (15 to 16 oz) black-eyed peas, drained, rinsed

¼ cup water

1 teaspoon red pepper sauce

4 large kaiser rolls, split

4 slices (1 oz each) provolone cheese

4 slices tomato

1 In small bowl, mix salad ingredients. Cover; refrigerate at least 1 hour to blend flavors.

2 In blender or food processor, place peas, water and pepper sauce. Cover; blend or process until smooth.

3 Cut ½-inch slice from top of each roll; set aside. Remove soft bread from inside of each roll to within ½ inch of edge; reserve bread trimmings for another use.

4 Spread about ¼ cup pea mixture in each roll. Top pea mixture in each with cheese slice, tomato slice and scant 2 tablespoons salad. Spoon remaining pea mixture and salad evenly into each. Cover with tops of rolls.

1 SANDWICH: Calories 470 (Calories from Fat 150); Total Fat 16g (Saturated Fat 6g; Trans Fat 1g); Cholesterol 20mg; Sodium 1100mg; Total Carbohydrate 57g (Dietary Fiber 7g); Protein 22g **%Daily Value:** Vitamin A 10%; Vitamin C 6%; Calcium 30%; Iron 30% **Exchanges:** 3½ Starch, 1 Vegetable, 1 Very Lean Meat, 2½ Fat **Carbohydrate Choices:** 4

In 1906, the Central Grocery in New Orleans created the muffuletta, a wonderful specialty sandwich. It combines meats and cheeses, but it's the olive salad that makes it unique. Our vegetarian version keeps the olive salad but replaces the meat with a spicy, mashed black-eyed pea mixture.

The Great Greek Sandwiches

Prep Time: 25 minutes • Start to Finish: 25 minutes • **4 sandwiches**

4 slices eggplant, 3 inches in diameter, ½ inch thick

2 teaspoons olive oil

⅛ teaspoon salt

4 ciabatta rolls (about 3 inches in diameter), split

4 slices provolone cheese

4 thin slices red onion

4 slices tomato

4 teaspoons Greek vinaigrette dressing

¼ cup sliced kalamata olives

½ cup packed spinach leaves

1 Heat gas or charcoal grill. Brush both sides of eggplant slices with oil; sprinkle with salt. Place on gas grill over medium heat. Cover grill; cook 8 to 10 minutes, turning once, until tender. During last minute of cooking, add rolls to grill, cut sides down; cook about 1 minute or until toasted.

2 Place eggplant slices on bottom halves of buns. Top each with cheese, onion, tomato, dressing, olives and spinach. Cover with top halves of buns.

1 SERVING: Calories 320 (Calories from Fat 120); Total Fat 14g (Saturated Fat 6g; Trans Fat 0g); Cholesterol 20mg; Sodium 800mg; Total Carbohydrate 37g (Dietary Fiber 2g); Protein 12g **%Daily Value:** Vitamin A 15%; Vitamin C 10%; Calcium 25%; Iron 15% **Exchanges:** 2 Starch, 1 Vegetable, ½ Medium-Fat Meat, 2 Fat **Carbohydrate Choices:** 2½

If your store offers only large ciabatta rolls, look for smaller take-and-bake ciabatta rolls in the bakery section of your supermarket.

Toasted Cheese, Avocado and Tomato Sandwiches

Prep Time: 15 minutes • Start to Finish: 15 minutes • **4 sandwiches**

8 slices pumpernickel bread

2 to 3 tablespoons creamy Dijon mustard-mayonnaise spread

1 medium avocado, pitted, peeled and thinly sliced

1 medium tomato, thinly sliced

4 slices (1 oz each) Colby–Monterey Jack cheese blend

2 tablespoons butter or margarine

1 Spread each slice of bread with mustard-mayonnaise spread. Top 4 slices with avocado, tomato and cheese. Top with remaining bread slices, spread side down.

2 In 12-inch skillet, melt butter over medium heat. Add sandwiches; cover and cook 4 to 5 minutes, turning once, until both sides are crisp and cheese is melted.

1 SANDWICH: Calories 370 (Calories from Fat 190); Total Fat 22g (Saturated Fat 10g; Trans Fat 0.5g); Cholesterol 40mg; Sodium 650mg; Total Carbohydrate 31g (Dietary Fiber 5g); Protein 12g **%Daily Value:** Vitamin A 15%; Vitamin C 6%; Calcium 25%; Iron 10% **Exchanges:** 2 Starch, 1 Medium-Fat Meat, 3 Fat **Carbohydrate Choices:** 2

Colby–Monterey Jack cheese is also known as marble cheese or Co-Jack; it has a fairly mild flavor. For an all-American favorite, use American cheese slices instead of the Colby–Monterey Jack.

Pear–Caramelized Onion Grilled Cheese Sandwiches

Prep Time: 30 minutes • Start to Finish: 30 minutes • **4 sandwiches**

2   **teaspoons olive oil**

1   **large red onion, thinly sliced**

1   **teaspoon sugar**

½   **teaspoon dried rosemary leaves**

2   **tablespoons butter, softened**

8   **slices firm pumpernickel or rye bread (not soft sandwich-style bread)**

8   **slices (¾ oz each) Cheddar cheese**

1   **medium Bosc or Anjou pear, cut into 16 slices**

1 In 12-inch skillet, heat oil over medium-high heat. Add onion; cook 10 to 12 minutes, tossing frequently, until soft, translucent and beginning to turn golden brown. Reduce heat to medium. Stir in sugar and rosemary. Cook about 4 minutes longer or until onion is deep golden brown (onion will shrink during cooking). Remove onion from skillet to heatproof bowl; cover to keep warm.

2 Wash skillet. Heat same skillet over medium heat. Meanwhile, spread butter on one side of each slice of bread. Place 1 slice of cheese on unbuttered side of 4 slices of bread. Arrange pear and onion over cheese; top with remaining slices of cheese. Place remaining slices of bread, buttered side up, over cheese.

3 Place sandwiches in skillet; cook 2 to 3 minutes on each side or until bread is toasted and cheese is melted. Serve immediately.

1 SERVING: Calories 430 (Calories from Fat 220); Total Fat 24g (Saturated Fat 13g; Trans Fat 0.5g); Cholesterol 60mg; Sodium 650mg; Total Carbohydrate 37g (Dietary Fiber 4g); Protein 15g **%Daily Value:** Vitamin A 10%; Vitamin C 4%; Calcium 30%; Iron 10% **Exchanges:** 2½ Starch, 1 Medium-Fat Meat, 3½ Fat **Carbohydrate Choices:** 2½

Firm, dense bread adds a nice variation in texture from the soft fillings. Look in the bakery section of your grocery store for this kind of bread. How do you know it's firm? Give it a little squeeze—you want a bread that won't squeeze as easily as sandwich bread.

Flavor It Up!

Taste buds, take notice! Plain dishes, such as pasta, rice, soy-protein products or vegetables need never be boring again when you turn up the flavor with one of these delicious sauces. Or create your own by stirring appetizing ingredients into sour cream, mustard or mayonnaise, combining fruits or veggies into salsas or mixing salad dressings together to make brand new tasty toppings.

Chipotle Mayonnaise `easy`

Prep Time: 5 minutes • **Start to Finish:** 1 hour 5 minutes
1 cup; 16 servings (1 tablespoon each)

- 2 canned chipotle chiles in adobo sauce, finely chopped
- ½ cup mayonnaise or salad dressing
- ½ cup sour cream
- ⅛ teaspoon dried oregano leaves, if desired

1 In small bowl, mix all ingredients. Cover; refrigerate at least 1 hour to blend flavors.

2 Serve with soy-protein burgers, chicken-style breaded soy-protein patties and nuggets, grilled chicken-style soy-protein patties, bean burgers and vegetable burgers.

1 SERVING: Calories 70 (Calories from Fat 60); Total Fat 7g (Saturated Fat 1.5g; Trans Fat 0g); Cholesterol 5mg; Sodium 55mg; Total Carbohydrate 0g (Dietary Fiber 0g); Protein 0g **%Daily Value:** Vitamin A 0%; Vitamin C 0%; Calcium 0%; Iron 0% **Exchanges:** 1½ Fat **Carbohydrate Choices:** 0

Peanut Sauce `easy` `quick`

Prep Time: 5 minutes • **Start to Finish:** 10 minutes
About 1 cup sauce; 8 servings (2 tablespoons each)

- ½ cup creamy peanut butter
- ½ cup water
- 2 tablespoons lime juice
- ½ teaspoon ground coriander
- ½ teaspoon ground cumin
- ⅛ teaspoon salt
- ⅛ teaspoon ground red pepper (cayenne), if desired
- 2 cloves garlic, finely chopped

1 In 1-quart saucepan, mix all ingredients with whisk. Heat over medium heat, stirring occasionally, until smooth and warm.

2 Use sauce immediately, or cover and refrigerate up to 3 days or freeze up to 2 months.

1 SERVING: Calories 110 (Calories from Fat 70); Total Fat 8g (Saturated Fat 1.5g; Trans Fat 0g); Cholesterol 0mg; Sodium 110mg; Total Carbohydrate 4g (Dietary Fiber 1g); Protein 4g **%Daily Value:** Vitamin A 0%; Vitamin C 0%; Calcium 0%; Iron 2% **Exchanges:** ½ Other Carbohydrate, ½ High-Fat Meat, 1 Fat **Carbohydrate Choices:** 0

Basil Pesto

`easy` `quick`

Prep Time: 10 minutes • **Start to Finish:** 10 minutes
About 1¼ cups pesto; 10 servings (2 tablespoons each)

  2 **cups firmly packed fresh basil leaves**
  ¾ **cup grated Parmesan cheese**
  ¼ **cup pine nuts, toasted if desired**
  ½ **cup olive or vegetable oil**
  3 **cloves garlic**

1 In blender or food processor, place all ingredients. Cover; blend on medium speed, stopping occasionally to scrape sides, about 3 minutes until smooth.

2 Use pesto immediately, or cover tightly and refrigerate up to 5 days or freeze up to 1 month (color of pesto will darken as it stands).

3 Toss over hot cooked pasta or rice. Serve over soy-protein burgers, bean or vegetable burgers or hot cooked vegetables.

1 SERVING: Calories 160 (Calories from Fat 135); Total Fat 15g (Saturated Fat 3g; Trans Fat 0g); Cholesterol 5mg; Sodium 140mg; Total Carbohydrate 1g (Dietary Fiber 0g); Protein 4g **% Daily Value:** Vitamin A 6%; Vitamin C 2%; Calcium 11%; Iron 2% **Exchanges:** ½ Vegetable, 3 Fat **Carbohydrate Choices:** 0

Cilantro Pesto: Substitute 1½ cups firmly packed fresh cilantro and ½ cup firmly packed fresh parsley for the basil.

Spinach Pesto: Substitute 2 cups firmly packed fresh spinach leaves for the basil.

Sun-Dried Tomato Pesto: Use food processor. Omit basil. Decrease oil to ⅓ cup; add ½ cup oil-packed sun-dried tomatoes (undrained).

Spicy Chimichurri Sauce

`easy` `quick`

Prep Time: 5 minutes • **Start to Finish:** 5 minutes
⅔ cup; about 10 servings (1 tablespoon each)

  ¼ **cup olive or vegetable oil**
  2 **tablespoons chopped fresh parsley**
  3 **tablespoons red wine vinegar**
  1 **tablespoon lemon juice**
  1 **teaspoon chopped fresh or ½ teaspoon dried oregano leaves**
  ½ **teaspoon crushed red pepper flakes**
  2 **cloves garlic, finely chopped**

1 In tightly covered container, shake all ingredients.

2 Serve with grilled or steamed vegetables, soy-protein burgers or bean burgers or use as a dipping sauce for bread and raw vegetables.

1 SERVING: Calories 50 (Calories from Fat 50); Total Fat 5g (Saturated Fat 1g; Trans Fat 0g); Cholesterol 0mg; Sodium 0mg; Total Carbohydrate 0g (Dietary Fiber 0g); Protein 0g **%Daily Value:** Vitamin A 0%; Vitamin C 0%; Calcium 0%; Iron 0% **Exchanges:** 1 Fat **Carbohydrate Choices:** 0

Veggie Melts

Prep Time: 25 minutes • Start to Finish: 25 minutes • 4 sandwiches

4 slices hearty multigrain bread

4 tablespoons chives-and-onion
   cream cheese spread
   (from 8-oz container)

½ cup packed fresh spinach
   or arugula leaves

1 medium zucchini, shaved
   lengthwise into 16 thin strips

4 slices provolone cheese
   (1 oz each)

4 slices tomato (from 1 large)

2 slices red onion, thinly sliced,
   separated into rings

1 Place oven rack 5 to 6 inches from broiler; set oven control to broil. Place bread on ungreased large cookie sheet. Broil 1 to 2 minutes or until golden brown and toasted. Turn bread; toast other side.

2 Spread 1 tablespoon cheese spread on each slice of toasted bread. Top each with spinach, zucchini, cheese, tomato and onion.

3 Broil about 3 minutes or until cheese is melted and bubbly. Serve immediately.

1 SERVING: Calories 210 (Calories from Fat 100); Total Fat 11g (Saturated Fat 7g; Trans Fat 0g); Cholesterol 30mg; Sodium 460mg; Total Carbohydrate 15g (Dietary Fiber 2g); Protein 12g **%Daily Value:** Vitamin A 20%; Vitamin C 10%; Calcium 30%; Iron 6% **Exchanges:** 1 Starch, ½ Vegetable, 1 Medium-Fat Meat, 1 Fat **Carbohydrate Choices:** 1

Use a vegetable peeler to "shave" the zucchini.

Garbanzo Bean Sandwiches

Prep Time: 15 minutes • **Start to Finish:** 15 minutes • **8 servings**

1 **can (15 oz) garbanzo beans, drained, rinsed**

½ **cup water**

2 **tablespoons chopped fresh parsley**

2 **tablespoons chopped walnuts**

1 **tablespoon chopped onion**

1 **clove garlic, chopped**

4 **whole wheat pita breads (6 inches in diameter)**

Lettuce leaves

1 **medium tomato, seeded, chopped (¾ cup)**

½ **medium cucumber, sliced**

½ **cup cucumber ranch dressing**

1 In food processor or blender, place beans, water, parsley, walnuts, onion and garlic. Cover; process until smooth.

2 Cut each pita bread in half to form 2 pockets; line with lettuce leaves. Spoon 2 tablespoons bean spread into each pita half. Add tomato, cucumber and dressing.

1 SERVING: Calories 260 (Calories from Fat 100); Total Fat 11g (Saturated Fat 1.5g; Trans Fat 0g); Cholesterol 0mg; Sodium 340mg; Total Carbohydrate 32g (Dietary Fiber 6g); Protein 8g **%Daily Value:** Vitamin A 8%; Vitamin C 6%; Calcium 4%; Iron 15% **Exchanges:** 2 Starch, ½ Lean Meat, 1 Fat **Carbohydrate Choices:** 2

> Nuts and seeds are great little nuggets of nutrients, but adding them in moderation is best because they can be high in fat. Fortunately, a little goes a long way in terms of flavor, and when nuts and seeds are lightly toasted, they become flavor giants!

Asian Sloppy Joes

Prep Time: **15 minutes** • Start to Finish: **15 minutes** • **6 sandwiches**

1 tablespoon vegetable oil

¼ cup chopped onion

¼ cup chopped green bell pepper

1 tablespoon finely chopped gingerroot

1 package (12 oz) frozen soy-protein burger crumbles

½ cup barbecue sauce

2 tablespoons reduced-sodium soy sauce

6 whole wheat burger buns, split

1 In 10-inch skillet, heat oil over medium heat. Add onion, bell pepper and gingerroot; cook 3 to 4 minutes or until onion is softened.

2 Stir in crumbles, barbecue sauce and soy sauce. Heat to boiling. Reduce heat to low; simmer uncovered 2 minutes or until thoroughly heated.

3 Spoon about ⅓ cup mixture into each bun.

1 SERVING: Calories 300 (Calories from Fat 50); Total Fat 5g (Saturated Fat 1g; Trans Fat 0g); Cholesterol 0mg; Sodium 940mg; Total Carbohydrate 45g (Dietary Fiber 4g); Protein 19g **%Daily Value:** Vitamin A 0%; Vitamin C 6%; Calcium 15%; Iron 25% **Exchanges:** 2½ Starch, ½ Other Carbohydrate, 1½ Lean Meat **Carbohydrate Choices:** 3

Soy-protein crumbles come both frozen and refrigerated. When frozen, the crumbles do not require thawing.

Sharp Cheddar, Artichoke and Red Onion Pizza

Prep Time: 10 minutes • Start to Finish: 20 minutes • **4 servings**

2 teaspoons butter or margarine

1 large red onion, sliced (2 cups)

1 package (14 oz) prebaked original Italian pizza crust or other 12-inch prebaked pizza crust

½ cup marinated artichoke hearts (from 6-oz jar), drained, sliced

3 tablespoons sliced drained roasted red bell peppers (from a jar)

1 cup shredded sharp Cheddar cheese (4 oz)

1 Heat oven to 400°F. In 8-inch skillet, melt butter over medium heat. Add onion; cook 3 to 5 minutes, stirring occasionally, until crisp-tender.

2 Spread onion over pizza crust. Top with artichokes, roasted peppers and cheese.

3 Bake 8 to 10 minutes or until cheese is melted. Cut into wedges to serve.

1 SERVING: Calories 440 (Calories from Fat 160); Total Fat 18g (Saturated Fat 8g; Trans Fat 0g); Cholesterol 35mg; Sodium 740mg; Total Carbohydrate 55g (Dietary Fiber 5g); Protein 15g **%Daily Value:** Vitamin A 10%; Vitamin C 10%; Calcium 15%; Iron 20% **Exchanges:** 1½ Starch, 2 Other Carbohydrate, 1 Vegetable, 1 High-Fat Meat, 2 Fat **Carbohydrate Choices:** 3½

Artichoke hearts add distinctive flavor to this easy pizza. Serve the pizza for a light supper, or cut it into small squares for a great meatless appetizer. If roasted red bell peppers aren't available, use jarred pimiento.

Caramelized Onion–Potato-Polenta Pizza

Prep Time: 50 minutes • Start to Finish: 2 hours 20 minutes • 6 servings

CRUST

1 cup plus 1 tablespoon
   yellow cornmeal

¾ cup water

3¼ cups boiling water

1½ teaspoons salt

1 tablespoon olive oil

TOPPING

2 tablespoons butter

1 large sweet onion (Maui
   or Walla Walla), cut in half,
   thinly sliced (3 cups)

1 tablespoon sugar

1 cup refrigerated home-style
   potato slices (from 20-oz bag)

1 tablespoon vegetable oil

⅛ teaspoon salt

⅛ teaspoon pepper

½ cup pizza sauce

1 cup shredded fontina cheese
   (4 oz)

1 tablespoon chopped
   fresh oregano leaves

1 Spray large cookie sheet with cooking spray; sprinkle with 1 tablespoon cornmeal. In 2-quart saucepan, mix 1 cup cornmeal and ¾ cup water. Stir in 3¼ cups boiling water and 1½ teaspoons salt. Cook over medium heat about 4 minutes, stirring constantly, until mixture thickens and boils.

2 Reduce heat; cover and simmer about 10 minutes, stirring occasionally, until very thick. Remove from heat. Stir in olive oil until smooth. Spread hot polenta in 11-inch round on cookie sheet. Cover with plastic wrap; refrigerate at least 1 hour or until very firm.

3 Meanwhile, in 10-inch nonstick skillet, melt butter over medium heat. Add onion and sugar; cook 15 to 20 minutes, stirring frequently, until deep golden brown and caramelized. In 7-inch skillet, cook potatoes in hot vegetable oil as directed on package; season with ⅛ teaspoon salt and the pepper.

4 Heat oven to 450°F. Bake crust 20 minutes. Remove from oven. Spread pizza sauce over crust; spoon onions evenly over sauce. Top with potatoes and cheese. Return to oven; bake 8 to 10 minutes longer or until cheese is melted and potatoes are tender. Sprinkle with oregano before serving.

1 SERVING: Calories 310 (Calories from Fat 130); Total Fat 15g (Saturated Fat 7g; Trans Fat 0g); Cholesterol 30mg; Sodium 880mg; Total Carbohydrate 36g (Dietary Fiber 3g); Protein 8g **%Daily Value:** Vitamin A 10%; Vitamin C 6%; Calcium 15%; Iron 10% **Exchanges:** 2 Starch, ½ Vegetable, 3 Fat **Carbohydrate Choices:** 2½

Polenta as a crust adds flavor and texture to this great pizza. If you like, you can make the crust as directed up to 24 hours before you plan to bake it. This pizza topping works well on a traditional pizza crust, too.

Cheesy Tomato and Bell Pepper Pizzas

Prep Time: **10 minutes** • Start to Finish: **25 minutes** • **6 pizzas**

3 packages (10 oz each) prebaked Italian pizza crusts (6 inch) or 6 pita breads (6 inch)

6 oz ⅓-less-fat cream cheese (Neufchâtel) or regular cream cheese, softened (from 8-oz package)

6 tablespoons basil pesto

4 plum (Roma) tomatoes, sliced

¾ cup ½-inch pieces yellow bell pepper

4 medium green onions, sliced (¼ cup)

1 tablespoon chopped fresh or ½ teaspoon dried basil leaves

1 cup shredded mozzarella cheese (4 oz)

2 tablespoons freshly grated Parmesan cheese

1 Heat oven to 450°F. On ungreased large cookie sheet, place pizza crusts.

2 Spread cream cheese on pizza crusts to within ¼ inch of edges. Gently spread pesto over cream cheese. Top with tomatoes, bell pepper and onions. Sprinkle with basil and both cheeses.

3 Bake 7 to 12 minutes or until cheeses are melted.

1 PIZZA: Calories 620 (Calories from Fat 240); Total Fat 27g (Saturated Fat 9g; Trans Fat 0g); Cholesterol 30mg; Sodium 1200mg; Total Carbohydrate 71g (Dietary Fiber 3g); Protein 24g **%Daily Value:** Vitamin A 20%; Vitamin C 25%; Calcium 45%; Iron 20% **Exchanges:** 4½ Starch, 1 Vegetable, ½ Medium-Fat Meat, ½ High-Fat Meat, 3½ Fat **Carbohydrate Choices:** 5

Keep prebaked pizza crusts or pita bread on hand for impromptu meals and snacks. You can top them a thousand ways to satisfy even the pickiest eaters.

Thai Vegetable Pizza

easy   quick

Prep Time: **15 minutes** • Start to Finish: **30 minutes** • **6 pizzas**

6 fat-free flour tortillas (8 to 10 inch)

⅔ cup reduced-fat peanut butter spread

¼ cup soy sauce

2 tablespoons seasoned rice vinegar

2 teaspoons sugar

2 cups shredded mozzarella cheese (8 oz)

1 bag (1 lb) frozen stir-fry vegetables, thawed, drained

1 Heat oven to 400°F. On ungreased large cookie sheet, place tortillas. Bake 5 minutes.

2 Meanwhile, in small bowl, mix peanut butter spread, soy sauce, vinegar and sugar.

3 Spread peanut butter mixture on warm tortillas. Top each with ¼ cup cheese. Spread stir-fry vegetables evenly on tortillas. Sprinkle with remaining ½ cup cheese.

4 Bake 10 to 15 minutes or until cheese is melted.

1 PIZZA: Calories 500 (Calories from Fat 210); Total Fat 23g (Saturated Fat 8g; Trans Fat 0.5g); Cholesterol 20mg; Sodium 1270mg; Total Carbohydrate 45g (Dietary Fiber 4g); Protein 26g **%Daily Value:** Vitamin A 8%; Vitamin C 10%; Calcium 35%; Iron 15% **Exchanges:** 2½ Starch, ½ Other Carbohydrate, ½ Vegetable, 1½ Lean Meat, 1 Medium-Fat Meat, 2½ Fat **Carbohydrate Choices:** 3

Purchased peanut sauce, found in the ethnic-foods section of your grocery store, can be used in place of the peanut butter spread, soy sauce, vinegar and sugar. Use a scant 1 cup of purchased sauce.

Mediterranean Pizza

Prep Time: 15 minutes • Start to Finish: 25 minutes • 6 servings

1   package (14 oz) prebaked original
    Italian pizza crust or other
    12-inch prebaked pizza crust

1½ cups shredded mozzarella cheese
    (6 oz)

1   jar (7 or 7.25 oz) roasted red bell
    peppers, drained, diced (¾ cup)

1   jar (7 oz) sun-dried tomatoes
    in oil, drained, chopped

2   plum (Roma) tomatoes, sliced

1   small red onion, sliced

2   pepperoncini peppers (bottled
    Italian peppers), drained, sliced

2   tablespoons sliced pimiento-
    stuffed olives

2   tablespoons sliced ripe olives

1   tablespoon chopped fresh or
    1 teaspoon dried basil leaves

1 Heat oven to 450°F. On ungreased cookie sheet, place pizza crust.

2 Sprinkle 1 cup of the cheese over crust. Top with remaining ingredients except basil. Sprinkle with remaining ½ cup cheese and the basil.

3 Bake about 10 minutes or until cheese is melted. Cut into wedges to serve.

1 SERVING: Calories 360 (Calories from Fat 130); Total Fat 15g (Saturated Fat 5g; Trans Fat 0g); Cholesterol 15mg; Sodium 660mg; Total Carbohydrate 43g (Dietary Fiber 4g); Protein 13g **%Daily Value:** Vitamin A 25%; Vitamin C 50%; Calcium 25%; Iron 15% **Exchanges:** 1½ Starch, 1 Other Carbohydrate, 1 Vegetable, 1 Medium-Fat Meat, 2 Fat **Carbohydrate Choices:** 3

Pepperoncini peppers, also called Tuscan peppers, are a pickled variety of chile pepper; they give a slightly sweet and spicy-hot flavor to this pizza. They are most often sold next to pickles or specialty pickled items.

Layered Pizza Pie

Prep Time: **10 minutes** • Start to Finish: **50 minutes** • **6 servings**

2 **cans (13.8 oz each) refrigerated pizza crust**

1 **can (8 oz) pizza sauce (1 cup)**

1 **jar (4.5 oz) sliced mushrooms, drained**

¼ **cup sliced ripe olives**

1½ **cups shredded mozzarella cheese (6 oz)**

2 **boxes (9 oz each) frozen chopped spinach, thawed, squeezed to drain**

1 **teaspoon olive or vegetable oil**

1 **tablespoon grated Parmesan cheese**

1 Heat oven to 400°F. Lightly grease 9-inch pie plate. Unroll 1 can of dough; place in pie plate. Starting at center, press dough in bottom and up side of pie plate to form crust.

2 In small bowl, mix pizza sauce and mushrooms; spoon onto dough. Layer with olives, ¾ cup of the mozzarella cheese, the spinach and remaining ¾ cup mozzarella cheese.

3 Unroll remaining can of dough on work surface. Starting at center, press dough into 9-inch round; place dough over filling. Pinch edges of dough together to seal; roll up edge of dough or flute to form rim. Cut several slits in dough. Brush with oil; sprinkle with Parmesan cheese.

4 Bake 35 to 40 minutes or until deep golden brown.

1 SERVING: Calories 470 (Calories from Fat 110); Total Fat 12g (Saturated Fat 5g; Trans Fat 0g); Cholesterol 15mg; Sodium 1340mg; Total Carbohydrate 70g (Dietary Fiber 5g); Protein 20g **%Daily Value:** Vitamin A 110%; Vitamin C 4%; Calcium 30%; Iron 30% **Exchanges:** 3½ Starch, 1 Other Carbohydrate, 1 Vegetable, 1 Medium-Fat Meat, 1 Fat **Carbohydrate Choices:** 4½

Eat your spinach! Mom was right, spinach is very good for you. It's rich in iron, calcium and vitamin A. Look for prewashed spinach leaves to save time.

Calzone Rustica

Prep Time: 25 minutes • Start to Finish: 35 minutes • **4 calzones**

1 **can (11 oz) refrigerated thin pizza crust**

¾ **cup pizza sauce**

¾ **cup sliced frozen (thawed) Italian-style soy-protein sausage links**

¼ **cup chopped green bell pepper**

2 **tablespoons finely chopped onion**

1⅓ **cups shredded mozzarella cheese (5⅓ oz)**

4 **teaspoons finely shredded Parmesan cheese**

1 Heat oven to 400°F. Unroll dough onto ungreased large dark or nonstick cookie sheet. Starting at center, press out dough into 14×10-inch rectangle; cut into 4 (7×5-inch) rectangles.

2 Spread 1 tablespoon pizza sauce on half of each rectangle to within ½ inch of edges. Top each with sausage, bell pepper, onion and mozzarella cheese. Fold dough in half over filling; press edges firmly with fork to seal. Prick tops with fork to vent. Sprinkle tops with Parmesan cheese.

3 Bake 8 to 10 minutes or until golden brown. Serve calzones with remaining warmed ½ cup pizza sauce.

1 SERVING: Calories 410 (Calories from Fat 140); Total Fat 16g (Saturated Fat 6g; Trans Fat 0g); Cholesterol 20mg; Sodium 910mg; Total Carbohydrate 46g (Dietary Fiber 3g); Protein 21g **%Daily Value:** Vitamin A 15%; Vitamin C 15%; Calcium 35%; Iron 15% **Exchanges:** 3 Starch, ½ Vegetable, 1½ Medium-Fat Meat, 1 Fat **Carbohydrate Choices:** 3

Customize your calzone by adding other favorite ingredients, such as mushrooms and olives. If you don't have a nonstick cookie sheet, use a regular cookie sheet and bake about 3 minutes longer.

Broccoli-Cheese Calzones

Prep Time: 15 minutes • **Start to Finish:** 35 minutes • **6 servings**

1 container (15 oz) fat-free
  ricotta cheese

1 box (9 oz) frozen cut broccoli,
  thawed

⅓ cup grated Parmesan cheese

¼ cup fat-free egg product
  or 2 egg whites

1 tablespoon chopped fresh or
  1 teaspoon dried basil leaves

¼ teaspoon garlic powder

1 loaf (1 lb) frozen wheat or
  white bread dough, thawed

1 can (8 oz) pizza sauce

1 Heat oven to 375°F. Grease 2 cookie sheets with shortening. In medium bowl, mix all ingredients except bread dough and pizza sauce.

2 Divide bread dough into 6 equal pieces. On lightly floured surface using floured rolling pin, roll each piece into 7-inch round.

3 Top half of each dough round with cheese mixture to within 1 inch of edge. Carefully fold dough over filling; pinch edge or press with fork to seal securely. Place calzones on cookie sheets.

4 Bake about 20 minutes or until golden brown. Cool 5 minutes. Meanwhile, in 1-quart saucepan, heat pizza sauce over medium heat about 2 minutes, stirring occasionally, until hot.

5 Serve warm sauce over calzones.

1 SERVING: Calories 310 (Calories from Fat 40); Total Fat 4.5g (Saturated Fat 1.5g; Trans Fat 0g); Cholesterol 10mg; Sodium 610mg; Total Carbohydrate 47g (Dietary Fiber 3g); Protein 20g **%Daily Value:** Vitamin A 15%; Vitamin C 15%; Calcium 25%; Iron 15% **Exchanges:** 2 Starch, 1 Other Carbohydrate, 1 Vegetable, 1½ Very Lean Meat, ½ Fat **Carbohydrate Choices:** 3

A calzone is a stuffed pizza that looks like a big turnover. To give these calzones a shiny top, brush them with a slightly beaten egg white before baking.

Garden Vegetable Calzones

Prep Time: 20 minutes • Start to Finish: 35 minutes • 4 calzones

¾ **cup sliced fresh mushrooms (about 2 oz)**

1 **small zucchini, cut in half lengthwise, thinly sliced (¾ cup)**

½ **cup coarsely chopped red or yellow bell pepper**

¼ **cup sliced green onions (4 medium)**

¼ **teaspoon garlic salt**

¼ **teaspoon dried basil leaves**

1 **can (13.8 oz) refrigerated classic pizza crust**

4 **oz shredded mozzarella or provolone cheese (1 cup)**

1 **egg white, beaten**

1 Heat oven to 425°F. Spray cookie sheet with cooking spray. In medium bowl, mix mushrooms, zucchini, bell pepper and onions. Sprinkle with garlic salt and basil; mix well.

2 Unroll dough; place on cookie sheet. Starting at center, press out dough to form 14-inch square; cut into four 7-inch squares. Place ¼ cup cheese on half of each square; spread to within ½ inch of edge. Top each with one-fourth of vegetable mixture.

3 Fold dough in half over filling; press edges firmly with fork to seal. Brush each with beaten egg white. With sharp knife, cut 2 or 3 slits in top of each for steam to escape.

4 Bake 12 to 15 minutes or until golden brown.

1 CALZONE: Calories 350 (Calories from Fat 80); Total Fat 9g (Saturated Fat 4.5g; Trans Fat 0g); Cholesterol 15mg; Sodium 930mg; Total Carbohydrate 51g (Dietary Fiber 0g); Protein 17g **%Daily Value:** Vitamin A 15%; Vitamin C 30%; Calcium 20%; Iron 15% **Exchanges:** 1½ Starch, 1½ Other Carbohydrate, 1 Vegetable, 1½ Medium-Fat Meat **Carbohydrate Choices:** 3½

Calzones are portable and easy to reheat in the microwave. Place 1 calzone on a microwavable paper towel and microwave on Medium (50%) for 1 to 1½ minutes or until cheese is melted and calzone is hot, turning once halfway through cooking.

chapter 5

slow cooker

Slow Cooker Lasagna

Prep Time: 35 minutes • Start to Finish: 6 hours 45 minutes • **6 servings**

1 **medium onion, chopped (½ cup)**

2 **cups frozen sausage-style soy-protein crumbles (from 12-oz package)**

2 **cans (15 oz each) Italian-style tomato sauce**

2 **teaspoons dried basil leaves**

½ **teaspoon salt**

3 **cups shredded mozzarella cheese (12 oz)**

1 **container (15 oz) part-skim ricotta cheese**

1 **cup grated Parmesan cheese**

12 **uncooked lasagna noodles**

1 Spray 10-inch skillet with cooking spray. Add onion; cook over medium heat about 3 minutes, stirring occasionally, until crisp-tender. Stir in crumbles, tomato sauce, basil and salt.

2 In medium bowl, mix 2 cups of the mozzarella cheese, the ricotta cheese and Parmesan cheese.

3 Spray 3½- to 4-quart slow cooker with cooking spray. Into slow cooker, spoon one-fourth of the crumbles mixture; top with 4 noodles, broken into pieces to fit. Top with half of the cheese mixture and one-fourth of the crumbles mixture. Top with 4 noodles, remaining cheese mixture and one-fourth of the crumbles mixture. Top with remaining 4 noodles and remaining crumbles mixture.

4 Cover; cook on Low heat setting 6 to 8 hours. (If slow cooker has black liner, do not cook longer than 8 hours or mixture may burn around edge.)

5 Sprinkle top of lasagna with remaining 1 cup mozzarella cheese. Cover; let stand about 10 minutes or until cheese is melted. Cut into pieces to serve.

1 SERVING: Calories 800 (Calories from Fat 260); Total Fat 29g (Saturated Fat 15g; Trans Fat 0.5g); Cholesterol 65mg; Sodium 1590mg; Total Carbohydrate 69g (Dietary Fiber 5g); Protein 66g **%Daily Value:** Vitamin A 25%; Vitamin C 10%; Calcium 90%; Iron 45% **Exchanges:** 1 Starch, 3½ Other Carbohydrate, 1 Vegetable, 5 Very Lean Meat, 3½ Lean Meat, 3 Fat **Carbohydrate Choices:** 4½

How wonderful to come home to delicious lasagna! This hearty meat-free version will please everyone. It's great for casual entertaining—just add a green salad and some garlic bread. *Mangia!*

Cheesy Ravioli Casserole

Prep Time: 15 minutes • Start to Finish: 5 hours 45 minutes • **10 servings**

1 **tablespoon olive or vegetable oil**

1 **medium onion, chopped (½ cup)**

1 **large clove garlic, finely chopped**

2 **jars (25.5 oz each) four cheese pasta sauce**

1 **can (15 oz) tomato sauce**

1 **teaspoon Italian seasoning**

2 **bags (25 oz each) frozen cheese-filled ravioli**

2 **cups shredded mozzarella cheese (8 oz)**

¼ **cup chopped fresh parsley, if desired**

1 In 4-quart Dutch oven or 12-inch skillet, heat oil over medium heat. Add onion and garlic; cook about 4 minutes, stirring occasionally, until onion is tender. Stir in pasta sauce, tomato sauce and Italian seasoning.

2 Spray 5- to 6-quart slow cooker with cooking spray. Place 1 cup of the sauce mixture in cooker. Add 1 bag frozen ravioli; top with 1 cup of the cheese. Top with remaining bag of ravioli and 1 cup cheese. Pour remaining sauce mixture over top.

3 Cover; cook on Low heat setting 5 hours 30 minutes to 6 hours 30 minutes.

4 Before serving, sprinkle with parsley. Ravioli will hold on Low heat setting up to 30 minutes.

1 SERVING: Calories 430 (Calories from Fat 120); Total Fat 13g (Saturated Fat 6g; Trans Fat 0g); Cholesterol 35mg; Sodium 1100mg; Total Carbohydrate 57g (Dietary Fiber 5g); Protein 22g **%Daily Value:** Vitamin A 25%; Vitamin C 10%; Calcium 25%; Iron 15% **Exchanges:** 3 Starch, ½ Other Carbohydrate, ½ Vegetable, ½ Lean Meat, 1 Medium-Fat Meat, 1 Fat **Carbohydrate Choices:** 4

Watching your fat? Be sure to compare the nutrition labels on various brands of cheese-filled ravioli; some are higher in fat than others—and lower-fat varieties are just as tasty.

Taco Casserole

Prep Time: 15 minutes • Start to Finish: 4 hours 20 minutes • **4 servings**

3 cups frozen soy-protein burger crumbles (from 12-oz package)

1 can (14.5 oz) diced tomatoes with green chiles, undrained

1 can (10¾ oz) condensed tomato soup

1 package (1 oz) taco seasoning mix

½ cup water

6 corn tortillas (5 or 6 inch), cut into ½-inch strips

½ cup sour cream

1 cup shredded Cheddar cheese (4 oz)

3 medium green onions, sliced (3 tablespoons)

1 Spray 3- to 3½-quart slow cooker with cooking spray. In slow cooker, mix crumbles, tomatoes, soup, seasoning mix (dry) and water. Gently stir in tortilla strips.

2 Cover; cook on Low heat setting 4 to 5 hours. (If slow cooker has black liner, do not cook longer than 5 hours or mixture may burn around edge.)

3 Spread sour cream over casserole; sprinkle with cheese. Cover; let stand about 5 minutes or until cheese is melted. Sprinkle with onions.

1 SERVING: Calories 470 (Calories from Fat 160); Total Fat 18g (Saturated Fat 10g; Trans Fat 0g); Cholesterol 45mg; Sodium 2020mg; Total Carbohydrate 46g (Dietary Fiber 8g); Protein 31g **%Daily Value:** Vitamin A 25%; Vitamin C 20%; Calcium 35%; Iron 25% **Exchanges:** 2½ Starch, ½ Other Carbohydrate, ½ Vegetable, 3 Very Lean Meat, 3 Fat **Carbohydrate Choices:** 3

Can't find diced tomatoes with green chiles? Mix a 14.5-ounce can of plain diced tomatoes with an undrained 4.5-ounce can of chopped green chiles.

Tamale Pie

Prep Time: 15 minutes • **Start to Finish:** 4 hours 45 minutes • **4 servings**

1 medium onion, chopped (½ cup)

2 cups frozen soy-protein burger crumbles (from 12-oz package)

1 can (15 oz) dark red kidney beans, drained, rinsed

1 can (10 oz) enchilada sauce

1 pouch (6.5 oz) cornbread & muffin mix

⅓ cup milk

2 tablespoons butter or margarine, melted

1 egg

½ cup shredded Colby–Monterey Jack cheese blend (2 oz)

1 can (4.5 oz) chopped green chiles, undrained

¼ cup sour cream

4 medium green onions, chopped (¼ cup)

1 Generously spray 8-inch skillet with cooking spray. Add onion; cook over medium heat about 3 minutes, stirring occasionally, until crisp-tender. Spray 3- to 3½-quart slow cooker with cooking spray. In slow cooker, mix crumbles, onion, beans and enchilada sauce.

2 In medium bowl, stir muffin mix, milk, butter and egg just until moistened (batter will be lumpy). Stir in cheese and chiles. Spoon over mixture in slow cooker.

3 Cover; cook on Low heat setting 4 hours 30 minutes to 5 hours 30 minutes or until toothpick inserted in center of cornbread comes out clean. (If slow cooker has black liner, do not cook longer than 5 hours 30 minutes or mixture may burn around edge.)

4 Serve tamale pie with sour cream and green onions.

1 SERVING: Calories 580 (Calories from Fat 170); Total Fat 19g (Saturated Fat 9g; Trans Fat 0g); Cholesterol 90mg; Sodium 1380mg; Total Carbohydrate 72g (Dietary Fiber 9g); Protein 29g **%Daily Value:** Vitamin A 15%; Vitamin C 15%; Calcium 25%; Iron 30% **Exchanges:** 3½ Starch, 1 Other Carbohydrate, 1½ Vegetable, 1½ Very Lean Meat, ½ High-Fat Meat, 2½ Fat **Carbohydrate Choices:** 5

Sweet and crunchy jicama that has been cut into thin strips, drizzled with lime juice and sprinkled with a little salt and paprika would make a nice side dish for this hearty meatless meal.

Picadillo

Prep Time: 20 minutes • Start to Finish: 3 hours 20 minutes • **12 servings**

4 cups frozen soy-protein burger crumbles (from two 12-oz packages)

1 large onion, chopped (1 cup)

1 cup raisins

2 teaspoons chili powder

1 teaspoon salt

¾ teaspoon ground cinnamon

½ teaspoon ground cumin

½ teaspoon pepper

2 cloves garlic, finely chopped

2 medium apples, peeled, chopped (2 cups)

2 cans (10 oz each) diced tomatoes with green chiles, undrained

½ cup slivered almonds, toasted*

1 Spray 3- to 4-quart slow cooker with cooking spray. In slow cooker, mix all ingredients except almonds.

2 Cover; cook on Low heat setting 3 to 4 hours. (If slow cooker has black liner, do not cook longer than 4 hours or mixture may burn around edge.)

3 Before serving, stir in almonds.

*To toast almonds, bake uncovered in ungreased shallow pan in 350°F oven 6 to 10 minutes, stirring occasionally, until golden brown. Or cook in ungreased heavy skillet over medium-low heat 5 to 7 minutes, stirring frequently until browning begins, then stirring constantly until golden brown.

1 SERVING: Calories 150 (Calories from Fat 25); Total Fat 3g (Saturated Fat 0g; Trans Fat 0g); Cholesterol 0mg; Sodium 500mg; Total Carbohydrate 22g (Dietary Fiber 4g); Protein 10g **%Daily Value:** Vitamin A 6%; Vitamin C 8%; Calcium 8%; Iron 10% **Exchanges:** ½ Starch, ½ Fruit, ½ Other Carbohydrate, 1 Very Lean Meat, ½ Fat **Carbohydrate Choices:** 1½

This Mexican version of hash is great on its own and is also terrific as a filling for tacos, enchiladas and tostadas.

Baked Potato Bar

Prep Time: 10 minutes • **Start to Finish:** 6 hours 10 minutes • **12 servings**

12 unpeeled russet potatoes
(6 to 8 oz each)

2 tablespoons olive or vegetable oil

1½ teaspoons salt

1 teaspoon coarse ground
black pepper

1 cup sour cream

¼ cup bacon flavor bits

1½ cups shredded cheese (6 oz)

4 medium green onions, sliced
(¼ cup)

1 Pierce potatoes with fork. In large resealable food-storage plastic bag, place potatoes and oil; toss to coat potatoes with oil. Sprinkle with salt and pepper. Wrap potatoes individually in foil. In 5- to 6-quart slow cooker, place wrapped potatoes.

2 Cover; cook on Low heat setting 6 to 8 hours.

3 Serve potatoes with remaining ingredients as toppings. Potatoes will hold on Low heat setting up to 2 hours.

1 SERVING: Calories 260 (Calories from Fat 100); Total Fat 11g (Saturated Fat 6g; Trans Fat 0g); Cholesterol 25mg; Sodium 440mg; Total Carbohydrate 31g (Dietary Fiber 3g); Protein 8g **%Daily Value:** Vitamin A 6%; Vitamin C 10%; Calcium 10%; Iron 10% **Exchanges:** 1 Starch, ½ Other Carbohydrate, 1 Vegetable, ½ High-Fat Meat, 1½ Fat **Carbohydrate Choices:** 2

Set out the cooked potatoes and toppings and let your family or guests top their own, just the way they like them.

Great Northern Bean and Veggie Sausage Cassoulet

Prep Time: 20 minutes • Start to Finish: 7 hours 50 minutes • 6 servings (1½ cups each)

3 carrots, sliced (1½ cups)

1 large onion, finely chopped (1 cup)

3 cans (15.5 oz each) great northern beans, drained, rinsed

¾ cup dry white wine or vegetable broth

¼ cup chopped dry-pack sun-dried tomatoes

2 teaspoons dried minced garlic

1 teaspoon dried thyme leaves

1 dried bay leaf

½ teaspoon salt

¼ teaspoon pepper

1 package (14 oz) frozen Italian-style soy-protein sausages with sun-dried tomatoes & basil, each cut into 3 pieces

1 can (14.5 oz) organic diced tomatoes, undrained

2 tablespoons finely chopped fresh Italian (flat-leaf) parsley

1 tablespoon finely chopped fresh thyme leaves

1 Spray 3- to 4-quart slow cooker with cooking spray. In cooker, gently mix carrots, onion, beans, wine, sun-dried tomatoes, garlic, dried thyme, bay leaf, salt and pepper. Arrange soy-protein sausage pieces on top of beans. Pour tomatoes over all.

2 Cover; cook on Low heat setting 7 hours 30 minutes to 8 hours 30 minutes or on High heat setting 3 hours 30 minutes to 4 hours 30 minutes.

3 Just before serving, remove bay leaf. Sprinkle with parsley and fresh thyme.

1 SERVING: Calories 580 (Calories from Fat 90); Total Fat 10g (Saturated Fat 1.5g; Trans Fat 0g); Cholesterol 0mg; Sodium 850mg; Total Carbohydrate 76g (Dietary Fiber 22g); Protein 42g **%Daily Value:** Vitamin A 120%; Vitamin C 15%; Calcium 30%; Iron 70% **Exchanges:** 4½ Starch, 2 Vegetable, 3½ Very Lean Meat, 1 Fat **Carbohydrate Choices:** 5

> Be sure to keep the soy-protein links frozen until ready to add to the cassoulet. They will thaw and cook without overcooking while the cassoulet cooks. If you have a veggie sausage that is not frozen, cut it into 1- to 2-inch chunks and add it during the last hour of cooking.

Cuban Black Beans and Rice

Prep Time: 20 minutes • Start to Finish: 6 hours 20 minutes • **6 servings**

1 **bag (16 oz) dried black beans (2 cups), sorted, rinsed**

1 **large onion, chopped (1 cup)**

1 **large bell pepper, chopped (1½ cups)**

5 **cloves garlic, finely chopped**

2 **dried bay leaves**

1 **can (14.5 oz) organic diced tomatoes, undrained**

5 **cups water**

2 **tablespoons olive or vegetable oil**

4 **teaspoons ground cumin**

2 **teaspoons finely chopped jalapeño chile**

1 **teaspoon salt**

3 **cups hot cooked rice**

1 In 3- to 4-quart slow cooker, mix all ingredients except rice.

2 Cover; cook on High heat setting 6 to 8 hours.

3 Remove bay leaves. Serve beans over rice.

1 SERVING: Calories 430 (Calories from Fat 50); Total Fat 6g (Saturated Fat 1g; Trans Fat 0g); Cholesterol 0mg; Sodium 560mg; Total Carbohydrate 73g (Dietary Fiber 17g); Protein 19g **%Daily Value:** Vitamin A 10%; Vitamin C 30%; Calcium 10%; Iron 35% **Exchanges:** 2½ Starch, 1½ Other Carbohydrate, 2½ Vegetable, 1 Very Lean Meat, 1 Fat **Carbohydrate Choices:** 5

Serve with bowls of chopped red onion and hard-cooked eggs to sprinkle on top for traditional black beans and rice. Or instead of rice, top each serving of beans with a poached egg and sprinkle with shredded Cheddar cheese and chopped fresh cilantro.

Red Beans and Rice

Prep Time: 20 minutes • Start to Finish: 4 hours 40 minutes • **8 servings**

1 **bag (16 oz) dried kidney beans (2 cups), sorted, rinsed**

1 **large green bell pepper, chopped (1½ cups)**

1 **large onion, chopped (1 cup)**

2 **cloves garlic, finely chopped**

7 **cups water**

1½ **teaspoons salt**

¼ **teaspoon pepper**

2 **cups uncooked instant rice**

Red pepper sauce

1 In 4- to 5-quart slow cooker, mix all ingredients except rice and pepper sauce.

2 Cover; cook on High heat setting 4 to 5 hours.

3 Stir in rice. Cover; cook on High heat setting 15 to 20 minutes longer or until rice is tender. Serve with pepper sauce.

1 SERVING: Calories 280 (Calories from Fat 10); Total Fat 1g (Saturated Fat 0g; Trans Fat 0g); Cholesterol 0mg; Sodium 460mg; Total Carbohydrate 55g (Dietary Fiber 10g); Protein 14g **%Daily Value:** Vitamin A 0%; Vitamin C 15%; Calcium 6%; Iron 25% **Exchanges:** 2½ Starch, ½ Other Carbohydrate, 1½ Vegetable, ½ Very Lean Meat **Carbohydrate Choices:** 3½

Our test kitchen had good results using instant rice in slow cooker recipes. Instant rice is fully or partially cooked before dehydration and packaging. It produces less starch, so the finished dish is not as sticky as in some dishes using regular long-grain rice. And it's easier to cook everything all in one pot! The beans are great topped with chopped avocado and sliced green onion.

White Beans with Sun-Dried Tomatoes

Prep Time: 10 minutes • **Start to Finish:** 4 hours 10 minutes • **5 servings**

- 1 **bag (16 oz) dried great northern beans (2 cups), sorted, rinsed**
- 2 **cloves garlic, crushed**
- 6 **cups water**
- 1½ **teaspoons dried basil leaves**
- 1 **teaspoon salt**
- ¼ **teaspoon pepper**
- ¾ **cup finely chopped sun-dried tomatoes in olive oil**
- 1 **can (2¼ oz) sliced ripe olives, drained**

1 In 3½- to 6-quart slow cooker, mix all ingredients except tomatoes and olives.

2 Cover; cook on High heat setting 4 to 5 hours.

3 Before serving, stir in tomatoes and olives.

1 SERVING: Calories 380 (Calories from Fat 35); Total Fat 4g (Saturated Fat 0.5g; Trans Fat 0g); Cholesterol 0mg; Sodium 620mg; Total Carbohydrate 61g (Dietary Fiber 15g); Protein 23g **%Daily Value:** Vitamin A 6%; Vitamin C 15%; Calcium 25%; Iron 50% **Exchanges:** 3½ Starch, 1½ Vegetable, 1½ Very Lean Meat, ½ Fat **Carbohydrate Choices:** 4

Sun-dried tomatoes add a robust meaty flavor and a bit of chewiness to this dish. You can add a cup of finely chopped seeded fresh tomatoes instead of the sun-dried tomatoes if you want.

Spicy Black-Eyed Peas

Prep Time: 5 minutes • **Start to Finish:** 3 hours 15 minutes • **8 servings**

1 bag (16 oz) dried black-eyed peas (2 cups), sorted, rinsed

1 medium onion, chopped (½ cup)

6 cups water

1 teaspoon salt

½ teaspoon pepper

¾ cup chunky-style salsa

1 In 3- to 4-quart slow cooker, mix all ingredients except salsa.

2 Cover; cook on High heat setting 3 to 4 hours.

3 Stir in salsa. Cover; cook on High heat setting about 10 minutes longer or until hot.

1 SERVING: Calories 200 (Calories from Fat 10); Total Fat 1g (Saturated Fat 0g; Trans Fat 0g); Cholesterol 0mg; Sodium 480mg; Total Carbohydrate 36g (Dietary Fiber 10g); Protein 12g **%Daily Value:** Vitamin A 4%; Vitamin C 0%; Calcium 4%; Iron 20% **Exchanges:** 2 Starch, 1 Vegetable, ½ Very Lean Meat **Carbohydrate Choices:** 2½

Cooked greens, like spinach, mustard or collards, are perfect mates for black-eyed peas. Serve the greens with red wine vinegar to splash on top. Add a special touch by topping each serving of beans with sour cream and salsa.

Savory Garbanzo Beans with Vegetables

Prep Time: 15 minutes • Start to Finish: 4 hours 30 minutes • 8 servings

1 bag (16 oz) dried garbanzo beans (2 cups), sorted, rinsed

5½ cups water

1 teaspoon salt

½ teaspoon pepper

2 tablespoons olive or vegetable oil

2 cups sliced fresh mushrooms

1 cup shredded carrots (1½ medium)

4 medium green onions, thinly sliced (¼ cup)

2 cloves garlic, finely chopped

2 tablespoons lemon juice

1 to 2 tablespoons prepared horseradish

2 teaspoons yellow mustard

1 In 4- to 5-quart slow cooker, place beans, water, salt and pepper.

2 Cover; cook on High heat setting 4 to 5 hours.

3 In 12-inch skillet, heat oil over medium heat. Add mushrooms, carrots, onions and garlic; cook about 5 minutes, stirring occasionally, until vegetables are tender. Stir vegetables into beans. Stir in remaining ingredients.

4 Cover; cook on High heat setting 15 minutes longer to blend flavors.

1 SERVING: Calories 250 (Calories from Fat 60); Total Fat 7g (Saturated Fat 1g; Trans Fat 0g); Cholesterol 0mg; Sodium 350mg; Total Carbohydrate 37g (Dietary Fiber 10g); Protein 11g **%Daily Value:** Vitamin A 110%; Vitamin C 6%; Calcium 8%; Iron 20% **Exchanges:** 2 Starch, 1½ Vegetable, ½ Very Lean Meat, 1 Fat **Carbohydrate Choices:** 2½

Want to make this even easier? Use a drained 8-ounce can of sliced mushrooms instead of the fresh mushrooms. Skip the sautéing in step 3 and just add the canned mushrooms, carrots, onions and garlic to the cooked beans. Stir in a tablespoon of olive oil for added flavor.

Mediterranean Bulgur and Lentils

Prep Time: 15 minutes • Start to Finish: 3 hours 30 minutes • **8 servings**

1 **cup uncooked bulgur or cracked wheat**

½ **cup dried lentils, sorted, rinsed**

1 **teaspoon ground cumin**

¼ **teaspoon salt**

3 **cloves garlic, finely chopped**

1 **can (15.25 oz) whole kernel corn, drained**

2 **cans (14 oz each) vegetable broth**

2 **medium tomatoes, chopped (1½ cups)**

1 **can (2¼ oz) sliced ripe olives, drained**

1 **cup crumbled feta cheese (4 oz)**

Pita bread, if desired

1 In 3- to 4-quart slow cooker, mix all ingredients except tomatoes, olives, cheese and pita bread.

2 Cover; cook on Low heat setting 3 to 4 hours.

3 Stir in tomatoes and olives. Increase heat setting to High; cover and cook 15 minutes longer. Sprinkle each serving with cheese. If desired, serve with toasted wedges of pita bread.

1 SERVING: Calories 200 (Calories from Fat 40); Total Fat 4.5g (Saturated Fat 2.5g; Trans Fat 0g); Cholesterol 15mg; Sodium 810mg; Total Carbohydrate 31g (Dietary Fiber 6g); Protein 8g **%Daily Value:** Vitamin A 10%; Vitamin C 4%; Calcium 10%; Iron 15% **Exchanges:** 1 Starch, 1 Other Carbohydrate, ½ Vegetable, ½ Medium-Fat Meat, ½ Fat **Carbohydrate Choices:** 2

If you've never tried the whole grain goodness of bulgur, this is a great recipe to start with. This nutritious food has a chewy, nutty texture that is a nice complement to the lentils.

Marinara Sauce with Spaghetti

Prep Time: 25 minutes • Start to Finish: 8 hours 25 minutes • **12 servings**

4 **cans (14.5 oz each) organic diced tomatoes with Italian herbs, undrained**

1 **can (6 oz) tomato paste**

1 **large onion, chopped (1 cup)**

8 **cloves garlic, finely chopped**

1 **tablespoon olive or vegetable oil**

2 **teaspoons sugar**

2 **teaspoons dried basil leaves**

1 **teaspoon dried oregano leaves**

1 **teaspoon salt**

1 **teaspoon pepper**

24 **oz uncooked spaghetti**

Shredded Parmesan cheese, if desired

1 Spray 3- to 4-quart slow cooker with cooking spray. In cooker, mix all ingredients except spaghetti and cheese.

2 Cover; cook on Low heat setting 8 to 10 hours.

3 Cook and drain spaghetti as directed on package. Serve sauce over spaghetti. Sprinkle with cheese.

1 SERVING: Calories 310 (Calories from Fat 25); Total Fat 2.5g (Saturated Fat 0g; Trans Fat 0g); Cholesterol 0mg; Sodium 840mg; Total Carbohydrate 61g (Dietary Fiber 5g); Protein 11g **%Daily Value:** Vitamin A 20%; Vitamin C 20%; Calcium 4%; Iron 20% **Exchanges:** 3½ Starch, ½ Other Carbohydrate, ½ Vegetable **Carbohydrate Choices:** 4

This all-purpose sauce is simple to prepare. Make it often and keep a few extra containers in the freezer. Ladle the cooked sauce into airtight freezer containers; cover and freeze up to 1 month.

Roasted Vegetable Stock

easy

Prep Time: **15 minutes** • Start to Finish: **7 hours 45 minutes** • **9 cups**

5 **carrots, peeled, cut in half crosswise**

2 **stalks celery, cut in half crosswise**

2 **small parsnips, peeled, cut in half crosswise**

3 **potatoes, peeled, halved**

1 **large onion, quartered**

4 **cloves garlic**

3 **tablespoons olive oil**

3 **tablespoons soy sauce**

5 **sprigs fresh parsley**

8 **small sprigs fresh thyme**

12 **whole peppercorns**

12 **cups water**

1 Heat oven to 450°F. In 15×10×1-inch pan, place carrots, celery, parsnips, potatoes, onion and garlic. Drizzle with oil; toss until well coated.

2 Roast uncovered 30 minutes, stirring once halfway through cooking time. (Vegetables will be browned, but may not be tender or fully cooked.)

3 In 6-quart slow cooker, place roasted vegetables and remaining ingredients.

4 Cover; cook on Low heat setting 7 to 9 hours or on High heat setting 2 hours 30 minutes to 3 hours 30 minutes hours.

5 Pour stock through fine mesh colander to strain out vegetables and herbs; discard vegetables and herbs.

1 SERVING: Calories 120 (Calories from Fat 40); Total Fat 4.5g (Saturated Fat 0.5g; Trans Fat 0g); Cholesterol 0mg; Sodium 350mg; Total Carbohydrate 17g (Dietary Fiber 2g); Protein 2g **%Daily Value:** Vitamin A 120%; Vitamin C 10%; Calcium 4%; Iron 4% **Exchanges:** 1 Starch, 1 Fat **Carbohydrate Choices:** 1

Use stock in 3 to 4 days, or for longer storage, pack stock in freezer containers, label and freeze. Be sure to pack the stock in containers with about the amount of stock you anticipate using in a recipe, for example, 2 cups. Freeze for up to 3 months. To use, thaw the stock overnight in the refrigerator.

Slow Cooker Zesty Black Bean Soup

Prep Time: 25 minutes • Start to Finish: 11 hours 35 minutes • **9 servings (1⅓ cups each)**

1 bag (16 oz) dried black beans (2 cups), sorted, rinsed

10 cups water

2 cartons (32 oz each) vegetable broth (8 cups)

2 cans (14.5 oz each) diced tomatoes with green chiles, undrained

2 medium carrots, coarsely chopped (1 cup)

2 medium onions, coarsely chopped (1 cup)

¼ cup chopped fresh cilantro

2 teaspoons finely chopped garlic

1 teaspoon salt

¼ teaspoon pepper

⅛ teaspoon ground red pepper (cayenne)

Sour cream, if desired

Chopped fresh cilantro, if desired

1 In 4-quart Dutch oven, heat beans and water to boiling. Reduce heat; simmer uncovered 10 minutes. Remove from heat; cover and let stand 1 hour.

2 Drain beans. In 6-quart slow cooker, place beans and remaining ingredients except sour cream and cilantro.

3 Cover; cook on Low heat setting 10 to 12 hours.

4 Serve soup topped with sour cream and cilantro.

1 SERVING: Calories 210 (Calories from Fat 5); Total Fat 0.5g (Saturated Fat 0g; Trans Fat 0g); Cholesterol 0mg; Sodium 1330mg; Total Carbohydrate 39g (Dietary Fiber 12g); Protein 12g **%Daily Value:** Vitamin A 60%; Vitamin C 15%; Calcium 8%; Iron 15% **Exchanges:** 2 Starch, 1½ Vegetable, ½ Very Lean Meat **Carbohydrate Choices:** 2½

Short on time? Soak the beans in cold water overnight rather than using the quick-soak method in the recipe.

Curried Carrot Soup

Prep Time: 15 minutes • Start to Finish: 7 hours 25 minutes • 6 servings (1 cup each)

SOUP

1⅔ cups chopped onions (about 3 medium)

1 tablespoon dried minced garlic

2 bags (1 lb each) frozen sliced carrots, thawed

1 to 2 tablespoons curry powder

⅛ teaspoon crushed red pepper flakes

¼ teaspoon salt

1 carton (32 oz) reduced-sodium vegetable broth (4 cups)

1 cup half-and-half

GARNISHES, IF DESIRED

Chopped dry-roasted peanuts

Chopped fresh cilantro or parsley

1 Spray 3½- to 4-quart slow cooker with cooking spray. In slow cooker, mix all soup ingredients except half-and-half.

2 Cover; cook on Low heat setting 7 to 9 hours.

3 Strain cooked vegetables from cooking liquid, reserving liquid. In blender or food processor, place vegetables. Cover; blend until smooth. Return vegetable puree to slow cooker. Stir in 1½ cups of the reserved liquid and the half-and-half.

4 Cover; cook on Low heat setting about 10 minutes longer or until warm. Garnish each serving with peanuts and cilantro.

1 SERVING: Calories 150 (Calories from Fat 50); Total Fat 6g (Saturated Fat 3g; Trans Fat 0g); Cholesterol 15mg; Sodium 580mg; Total Carbohydrate 20g (Dietary Fiber 6g); Protein 4g **%Daily Value:** Vitamin A 510%; Vitamin C 6%; Calcium 10%; Iron 6% **Exchanges:** ½ Other Carbohydrate, 2 Vegetable, 1½ Fat **Carbohydrate Choices:** 1

Adjust the amount of reserved liquid blended back into the soup to make a thicker or thinner soup, as you prefer. Cover and refrigerate the remaining reserved liquid. You may find that you will want to thin any leftover soup a little more when reheating it the next day. You can also use the flavorful reserved liquid for cooking rice, potatoes or other dishes.

Slow Cooker Winter Vegetable Stew

Prep Time: 20 minutes • Start to Finish: 8 hours 40 minutes • **8 servings**

2 **cans (14.5 oz each) organic diced tomatoes with Italian herbs, undrained**

4 **medium red potatoes, cut into ½-inch pieces**

4 **medium stalks celery, cut into ½-inch pieces (2 cups)**

3 **medium carrots, cut into ½-inch pieces (1½ cups)**

2 **medium parsnips, peeled, cut into ½-inch pieces**

2 **medium leeks, cut into ½-inch pieces**

1 **can (14 oz) vegetable broth**

½ **teaspoon salt**

½ **teaspoon dried thyme leaves**

½ **teaspoon dried rosemary leaves**

3 **tablespoons cornstarch**

3 **tablespoons cold water**

1 In 4- to 5-quart slow cooker, place all ingredients except cornstarch and water.

2 Cover; cook on Low heat setting 8 to 10 hours.

3 In small bowl, mix cornstarch and water; gradually stir into stew until blended. Increase heat setting to High; cover and cook about 20 minutes longer, stirring occasionally, until thickened.

1 SERVING: Calories 160 (Calories from Fat 0); Total Fat 0g (Saturated Fat 0g; Trans Fat 0g); Cholesterol 0mg; Sodium 620mg; Total Carbohydrate 36g (Dietary Fiber 6g); Protein 3g **%Daily Value:** Vitamin A 100%; Vitamin C 30%; Calcium 8%; Iron 15% **Exchanges:** ½ Starch, 1 Other Carbohydrate, 2 Vegetable Carbohydrate Choices: 2½

> **Parsnips, root vegetables that look like creamy white carrots, have a slightly sweet flavor. If you don't have any on hand, you can use carrots instead.**

Curried Sweet Potato and Lentil Stew

Prep Time: 15 minutes • **Start to Finish:** 5 hours 30 minutes • **6 servings**

3 cups cubes (1 inch) peeled dark-orange sweet potatoes

1 small onion, finely chopped (¼ cup)

1½ cups ready-to-eat baby-cut carrots

¾ cup dried lentils, sorted, rinsed

2 teaspoons olive or vegetable oil

1 tablespoon curry powder

1 teaspoon ground cumin

½ teaspoon salt

¼ teaspoon pepper

1 teaspoon finely chopped gingerroot

1 clove garlic, finely chopped

1 can (14 oz) vegetable broth

1½ cups frozen cut green beans, thawed

½ cup plain fat-free yogurt (from 2-lb container)

1 Spray 3- to 4-quart slow cooker with cooking spray. In slow cooker, mix sweet potatoes, onion, carrots and lentils.

2 In 8-inch skillet, heat oil over medium heat. Add curry powder, cumin, salt, pepper, gingerroot and garlic; cook 1 minute, stirring constantly. Stir in broth. Pour mixture into slow cooker; stir.

3 Cover; cook on Low heat setting 5 to 6 hours.

4 Stir in green beans. Increase heat setting to High; cover and cook about 15 minutes longer or until beans are crisp-tender. Serve topped with yogurt.

1 SERVING: Calories 190 (Calories from Fat 20); Total Fat 2g (Saturated Fat 0g; Trans Fat 0g); Cholesterol 0mg; Sodium 520mg; Total Carbohydrate 34g (Dietary Fiber 8g); Protein 9g **%Daily Value:** Vitamin A 320%; Vitamin C 10%; Calcium 10%; Iron 20% **Exchanges:** ½ Starch, 1 Other Carbohydrate, 2 Vegetable, ½ Very Lean Meat, ½ Fat **Carbohydrate Choices:** 2

Place the green beans in the refrigerator when beginning the recipe, and they will be thawed just in time to stir into the stew.

Slow Cooker Lentil Stew with Cornbread Dumplings

Prep Time: **15 minutes** • Start to Finish: **7 hours 50 minutes** • **8 servings (about 1 cup stew and 1 dumpling each)**

STEW

- 1 lb dried lentils (2 cups), sorted, rinsed
- 3 cups water
- 1 teaspoon ground cumin
- 1 teaspoon salt-free seasoning blend
- 3 medium carrots, thinly sliced (1½ cups)
- 1 medium yellow or red bell pepper, cut into 1-inch pieces
- 1 medium onion, chopped (½ cup)
- 1 can (14.5 oz) diced tomatoes with green chiles, undrained
- 1 can (14 oz) vegetable broth

DUMPLINGS

- ½ cup all-purpose flour
- ½ cup yellow cornmeal
- 1 teaspoon baking powder
- ¼ teaspoon salt
- ¼ cup fat-free (skim) milk
- 2 tablespoons canola oil
- 1 egg or 2 egg whites, slightly beaten

1 In 3½- to 4-quart slow cooker, mix all stew ingredients.

2 Cover; cook on Low heat setting 7 to 8 hours.

3 In medium bowl, mix flour, cornmeal, baking powder and ¼ teaspoon salt. Stir in milk, oil and egg just until moistened. Drop dough by spoonfuls onto hot lentil mixture. Increase heat setting to High. Cover; cook 25 to 35 minutes or until toothpick inserted in center of dumplings comes out clean.

1 SERVING: Calories 330 (Calories from Fat 45); Total Fat 5g (Saturated Fat 0.5g, Trans Fat 0g); Cholesterol 25mg; Sodium 650mg; Total Carbohydrate 52g (Dietary Fiber 12g); Protein 18g
% Daily Value: Vitamin A 70%; Vitamin C 30%; Calcium 20%; Iron 35% **Exchanges:** 3 Starch, 1 Vegetable, 1 Very Lean Meat, ½ Fat **Carbohydrate Choices:** 3½

Mediterranean Minestrone Casserole

Prep Time: 20 minutes • **Start to Finish:** 6 hours 40 minutes • **5 servings (1⅓ cups each)**

3 medium carrots, sliced (1½ cups)

1 medium onion, chopped (½ cup)

1 cup water

2 teaspoons sugar

1 teaspoon Italian seasoning

½ teaspoon salt

¼ teaspoon pepper

1 can (28 oz) organic diced tomatoes, undrained

1 can (15 oz) garbanzo beans, drained, rinsed

1 can (6 oz) Italian-style tomato paste

2 cloves garlic, finely chopped

1½ cups frozen cut green beans, thawed

1 cup uncooked elbow macaroni (3½ oz)

½ cup shredded Parmesan cheese (2 oz)

1 In 3- to 4-quart slow cooker, mix all ingredients except green beans, macaroni and cheese.

2 Cover; cook on Low heat setting 6 to 8 hours.

3 Stir in green beans and macaroni. Increase heat setting to High; cover and cook about 20 minutes longer or until beans and macaroni are tender. Sprinkle with cheese.

1 SERVING: Calories 350 (Calories from Fat 50); Total Fat 5g (Saturated Fat 2g; Trans Fat 0g); Cholesterol 10mg; Sodium 1180mg; Total Carbohydrate 59g (Dietary Fiber 10g); Protein 16g **%Daily Value:** Vitamin A 160%; Vitamin C 35%; Calcium 25%; Iron 30% **Exchanges:** ½ Starch, 3 Other Carbohydrate, 2 Vegetable, 1 Very Lean Meat, ½ Lean Meat, ½ Fat **Carbohydrate Choices:** 4

Looking to get a healthy dose of vegetables? This vegetarian main dish has carrots, onions, tomatoes and green beans, in addition to fiber-rich garbanzos.

Barley–Pine Nut Casserole

Prep Time: 15 minutes • **Start to Finish:** 6 hours 15 minutes • **5 servings**

1 cup uncooked pearl barley

1½ cups vegetable juice

½ teaspoon salt

¼ teaspoon pepper

2 medium stalks celery, sliced (1 cup)

1 medium bell pepper, chopped (1 cup)

1 medium onion, chopped (½ cup)

1 can (14 oz) vegetable broth

4 medium green onions, sliced (¼ cup)

¼ cup pine nuts, toasted*

1 In 3- to 4-quart slow cooker, mix all ingredients except green onions and nuts.

2 Cover; cook on Low heat setting 6 to 8 hours.

3 Before serving, stir in green onions and pine nuts.

*To toast pine nuts, bake uncovered in ungreased shallow pan in 350°F oven 6 to 10 minutes, stirring occasionally, until golden brown. Or cook in ungreased heavy skillet over medium-low heat 5 to 7 minutes, stirring frequently until browning begins, then stirring constantly until golden brown.

1 SERVING: Calories 230 (Calories from Fat 45); Total Fat 5g (Saturated Fat 1g; Trans Fat 0g); Cholesterol 0mg; Sodium 770mg; Total Carbohydrate 41g (Dietary Fiber 9g); Protein 6g **%Daily Value:** Vitamin A 30%; Vitamin C 35%; Calcium 4%; Iron 10% **Exchanges:** ½ Starch, 1½ Other Carbohydrate, 2 Vegetable, 1 Fat **Carbohydrate Choices:** 3

Barley is the perfect grain to cook in the slow cooker. The long, slow cooking makes the barley tender but not gummy. Serve this casserole with steamed edamame for a great dish with extra protein.

Creamy Split Pea Soup

Prep Time: 20 minutes • Start to Finish: 10 hours 50 minutes • 8 servings

1 **bag (16 oz) dried green split peas (2 cups), sorted, rinsed**

6 **cups water**

½ **cup dry sherry, if desired**

1 **large dark-orange sweet potato, peeled, chopped (2 cups)**

1 **large onion, chopped (1 cup)**

4 **cloves garlic, finely chopped**

1 **tablespoon salt**

3 **cups firmly packed chopped fresh spinach leaves**

1 **cup half-and-half**

2 **tablespoons chopped fresh dill weed**

Freshly ground pepper to taste

1 In 3½- to 4-quart slow cooker, mix split peas, water, sherry, sweet potato, onion, garlic and salt.

2 Cover; cook on Low heat setting 10 to 11 hours.

3 Stir in spinach, half-and-half and dill weed. Cover; cook on Low heat setting about 30 minutes longer or until spinach is wilted. Season with pepper.

1 SERVING: Calories 240 (Calories from Fat 35); Total Fat 4g (Saturated Fat 2.5g; Trans Fat 0g); Cholesterol 10mg; Sodium 920mg; Total Carbohydrate 37g (Dietary Fiber 16g); Protein 13g **%Daily Value:** Vitamin A 90%; Vitamin C 8%; Calcium 8%; Iron 15% **Exchanges:** 2 Starch, 2 Vegetable, ½ Very Lean Meat, ½ Fat **Carbohydrate Choices:** 2½

If you are looking for a meatless but not vegetarian recipe, use a 48-ounce can of chicken broth and 2 cups of water instead of 6 cups water.

Chipotle Four-Bean Chili with Lime

easy **lowfat**

Prep Time: 15 minutes • Start to Finish: 6 hours 15 minutes • **5 servings (about 1⅓ cups each)**

1 medium onion, finely chopped (½ cup)

2 cans (14.5 oz each) organic diced tomatoes, undrained

1 can (15.5 oz) red beans, drained, rinsed

1 can (15 oz) black beans, drained, rinsed

1 can (15 oz) garbanzo beans, drained, rinsed

1 can (15 oz) pinto beans, drained, rinsed

1 chipotle chile in adobo sauce (from 7-oz can), finely chopped

1 tablespoon dried minced garlic

2 teaspoons ground cumin

2 teaspoons chili powder

2 teaspoons packed brown sugar

½ teaspoon salt

2 tablespoons lime juice

1 In 5- to 6-quart slow cooker, mix all ingredients except lime juice.

2 Cover; cook on Low heat setting 6 to 8 hours or on High heat setting 2 to 3 hours.

3 Just before serving, stir in lime juice.

1 SERVING: Calories 590 (Calories from Fat 40); Total Fat 4.5g (Saturated Fat 0.5g; Trans Fat 0g); Cholesterol 0mg; Sodium 870mg; Total Carbohydrate 105g (Dietary Fiber 30g); Protein 33g **%Daily Value:** Vitamin A 25%; Vitamin C 30%; Calcium 20%; Iron 60% **Exchanges:** 6½ Starch, ½ Vegetable, 1½ Very Lean Meat **Carbohydrate Choices:** 7

Do you prefer one type of bean over others? This dish is colorful and flavorful with a variety of beans, but feel free to substitute one kind of bean for another if you have a preference.

Spicy Black Bean Barbecue Chili

Prep Time: **15 minutes** • Start to Finish: **11 hours 45 minutes** • **6 servings (1½ cups each)**

1 **bag (16 oz) dried black beans (2 cups), sorted, rinsed**

10 **cups water**

1 **tablespoon olive or vegetable oil**

1 **large onion, chopped (1 cup)**

6 **cloves garlic, finely chopped**

4 **cups water**

1 **can (14.5 oz) diced tomatoes with green chiles, undrained**

1 **cup hickory barbecue sauce**

1 **chipotle chile in adobo sauce, finely chopped, plus 1 teaspoon adobo sauce (from 11-oz can)**

2 **cups frozen soy-protein burger crumbles**

1 **medium green or red bell pepper, chopped (1 cup)**

¼ **cup chopped fresh cilantro**

1 In 4-quart Dutch oven, heat beans and 10 cups water to boiling. Reduce heat; simmer uncovered 10 minutes. Remove from heat. Cover; let stand 1 hour.

2 In 10-inch skillet, heat oil over medium-high heat. Add onion and garlic; cook about 8 minutes, stirring occasionally, until onion is tender and light golden brown.

3 Drain beans. Place beans in 3½- to 4-quart slow cooker. Add 4 cups water and onion mixture.

4 Cover; cook on Low heat setting 10 to 12 hours.

5 Stir in tomatoes, barbecue sauce, chile, adobo sauce and frozen soy-protein crumbles. Increase heat setting to High; cover and cook 30 minutes. Top individual servings with bell pepper and cilantro.

1 SERVING: Calories 420 (Calories from Fat 35); Total Fat 4g (Saturated Fat 0.5g; Trans Fat 0g); Cholesterol 0mg; Sodium 850mg; Total Carbohydrate 71g (Dietary Fiber 19g); Protein 26g **%Daily Value:** Vitamin A 10%; Vitamin C 25%; Calcium 15%; Iron 35% **Exchanges:** 2½ Starch, 1½ Other Carbohydrate, 2 Vegetable, 2 Very Lean Meat, ½ Fat **Carbohydrate Choices:** 5

For chili that is spicier, use 2 chipotle chiles and 2 teaspoons adobo sauce.

Vegetarian Chili with Spicy Tortilla Strips

Prep Time: 10 minutes • Start to Finish: 5 hours 10 minutes • **6 servings**

CHILI

1 **can (15 oz) dark red kidney beans, drained**

1 **can (15 to 16 oz) spicy chili beans, undrained**

1 **can (15 oz) pinquito beans, undrained**

1 **can (14.5 oz) chili-style chunky tomatoes, undrained**

1 **large onion, chopped (1 cup)**

2 **to 3 teaspoons chili powder**

⅛ **teaspoon ground red pepper (cayenne)**

SPICY TORTILLAS STRIPS

3 **corn tortillas (6 inch)**

1 **tablespoon vegetable oil**

   Dash ground red pepper (cayenne)

1 In 3½- to 4-quart slow cooker, mix chili ingredients.

2 Cover; cook on Low heat setting 5 to 6 hours.

3 Meanwhile, heat oven to 375°F. Brush both sides of tortillas with oil. Lightly sprinkle red pepper on one side of tortillas. Cut into ½-inch strips. Place in single layer on ungreased cookie sheet. Bake 10 to 12 minutes or until strips are crisp and edges are light brown.

4 Stir chili well. Top individual servings with tortilla strips.

1 SERVING: Calories 270 (Calories from Fat 35); Total Fat 4g (Saturated Fat 0.5g; Trans Fat 0g); Cholesterol 0mg; Sodium 810mg; Total Carbohydrate 45g (Dietary Fiber 12g); Protein 14g **%Daily Value:** Vitamin A 10%; Vitamin C 6%; Calcium 10%; Iron 20% **Exchanges:** 1½ Starch, 1½ Other Carbohydrate, 1½ Very Lean Meat, ½ Fat **Carbohydrate Choices:** 3

Pinquitos are small, tender, pink beans and are great in this chili—however, if you can't find them, just substitute pinto beans.

Veggie Joes

Prep Time: 10 minutes • **Start to Finish:** 4 hours 10 minutes • **16 servings**

4	cups frozen soy-protein burger crumbles (from two 12-oz packages)
1	medium onion, finely chopped (½ cup)
1½	cups ketchup
½	cup water
2	tablespoons packed brown sugar
2	tablespoons white vinegar
1	tablespoon yellow mustard
½	teaspoon pepper
¼	teaspoon salt
16	sandwich buns, split

1 Spray 3½- to 4-quart slow cooker with cooking spray. In slow cooker, mix all ingredients except buns.

2 Cover; cook on Low heat setting 4 to 6 hours. (If slow cooker has black liner, do not cook longer than 6 hours or mixture may burn around edge.)

3 To serve, fill each bun with ⅓ cup mixture.

1 SERVING: Calories 190 (Calories from Fat 20); Total Fat 2g (Saturated Fat 0g; Trans Fat 0g); Cholesterol 0mg; Sodium 640mg; Total Carbohydrate 32g (Dietary Fiber 2g); Protein 11g **%Daily Value:** Vitamin A 4%; Vitamin C 4%; Calcium 10%; Iron 15% **Exchanges:** 1½ Starch, ½ Other Carbohydrate, 1 Very Lean Meat **Carbohydrate Choices:** 2

This is a great recipe to make ahead for those nights you don't have time to cook. Make the recipe as directed. Freeze the desired portions in freezer containers up to 4 months.

Slow Cooker Tips

Slow cookers take the gold as a way to make easy, fix-ahead-and-forget recipes. For the most part, you can prepare the recipe, turn on the cooker and forget about it until dinnertime. For successful slow cooker meals, follow these guidelines:

- Spray the inside of your slow cooker with cooking spray for easy cleanup.

- Recipes using soy-protein crumbles absorb liquids, take less time to cook than traditional meat-based recipes (most recipes in this book cook in the slow cooker in less than 6 hours) and can begin to burn around the edges if cooked longer than the times given in the recipe. Follow the slow cooker recipes developed specifically for using soy-protein crumbles for best results.

- Root vegetables, like potatoes and carrots, take longer to cook, so cut them into smaller pieces and put them at the bottom of the cooker.

- Use dried herb leaves instead of ground because they keep their flavor better during long cook times.

- Ground red pepper (cayenne) and red pepper sauce tend to become bitter during long, slow cooking. Use small amounts and taste during the last hour of cooking to decide whether you need to add more.

- A Low setting is frequently used because longer cooking times fit well into workday schedules. Shorten the cooking time by using the directions for a High heat setting with the recipe you want to make. If there are no directions for a High heat setting, it means the recipe works best on a Low heat setting only.

- Don't peek! Removing the cover lets heat escape, adding 15 to 20 minutes to the cooking time, and for that reason, most slow cooker recipes don't require stirring. Can't wait to see inside? Try spinning the cover until the condensation and steam clears.

- Stir in fresh herbs during the last hour of cooking so they stay flavorful. Some herbs, like oregano and basil, lose flavor with an extended cooking time.

- Add tender vegetables, like fresh tomatoes, mushrooms and zucchini, during the last 30 minutes of cooking so they don't become overcooked and mushy.

- Frozen vegetables that have been thawed will keep their bright color and crisp-tender texture by adding them during the last 30 minutes of cooking.

- Adding liquids to a recipe because it looks dry when preparing it in a slow cooker is tempting, but should be avoided. Many ingredients will have liquid that comes out during the cooking process and will contribute to the overall moistness of the recipe.

- Dairy products, like milk, sour cream and cheese, tend to curdle. To help prevent curdling, add them during the last 30 minutes of cooking.

- Most cooked food can be held up to an hour on the Low heat setting without overcooking.

- For more texture and a little extra flavor, sprinkle slow cooker meals with chopped fresh herbs, grated cheese, crushed croutons or corn chips, chopped tomatoes or sliced green onions just before serving.

Slow Cooker Smoky Chipotle Soft Tacos

Prep Time: 20 minutes • Start to Finish: 4 hours 20 minutes • **18 tacos**

Cooking spray

1 **large onion, chopped (1 cup)**

1 **Anaheim chile, chopped (⅓ cup)**

6 **cups frozen soy-protein burger crumbles (from two 12-oz packages)**

¾ **cup chili sauce**

1½ **cups water**

½ **cup mole sauce (from 9-oz container)**

1 **tablespoon chopped chipotle chiles in adobo sauce (from 7-oz can)**

1 **teaspoon ground cumin**

¾ **teaspoon salt**

18 **flour tortillas for soft tacos & fajitas (6 inch; from two 8.2-oz packages)**

2 **cups shredded Cheddar cheese (8 oz)**

3 **medium tomatoes, chopped (1½ cups)**

1 Generously spray 8-inch skillet with cooking spray. Add onion and Anaheim chile; spray onion and chile with cooking spray. Cook over medium heat 4 to 5 minutes, stirring occasionally, until onion is crisp-tender.

2 Spray 3½- to 4-quart slow cooker with cooking spray. Mix onion mixture and remaining ingredients except tortillas, cheese and tomatoes.

3 Cover; cook on Low heat setting 4 to 5 hours. If slow cooker has black liner, do not cook longer than 5 hours or mixture may burn around edge.

4 To serve, spoon ⅓ cup burger mixture onto each tortilla; top with cheese and tomatoes. Roll up tortillas. Burger mixture will hold on Low heat setting up to 2 hours; stir occasionally.

1 TACO: Calories 250 (Calories from Fat 160); Total Fat 10g (Saturated Fat 3.5g; Trans Fat 0g); Cholesterol 15mg; Sodium 730mg; Total Carbohydrate 24g (Dietary Fiber 4g); Protein 15g **%Daily Value:** Vitamin A 15%; Vitamin C 10%; Calcium 15%; Iron 15% **Exchanges:** 1½ Starch, 1½ Lean Meat, 1 Fat **Carbohydrate Choices:** 1½

Carry out the Mexican theme of your menu with bowls of black beans, Spanish rice, tortilla chips and salsa.

Mole sauce is a rich, spicy and slightly sweet Mexican sauce. Look for it with the Mexican ingredients in your supermarket. If it's unavailable, enchilada sauce is a good substitute.

Beer-Glazed Brats and Beans

Prep Time: 15 minutes • Start to Finish: 3 hours 15 minutes • 8 servings

2 cans (28 oz each) vegetarian beans in sauce or baked beans

¼ teaspoon chili powder

2 tablespoons butter

1 large sweet onion, thinly sliced

8 vegetarian bratwurst

1 tablespoon packed brown sugar

1 teaspoon ground mustard

¼ cup barbecue sauce

¼ cup beer

8 hot dog buns, toasted

1 In 6-quart slow cooker, combine beans and chili powder.

2 In 10-inch skillet, melt butter over medium heat. Add onion; cook 6 to 8 minutes, stirring frequently, until onions are very tender. Using tongs or slotted spoon, remove onion from skillet; arrange in layer over beans. Do not stir into beans.

3 Arrange bratwurst over onion. In small bowl, mix brown sugar, mustard, barbecue sauce and beer. Pour over bratwurst; do not stir.

4 Cover; cook on Low heat setting 3 to 4 hours.

5 To serve, place bratwurst in each bun. Lift onion with tongs; arrange over bratwurst in buns. Serve beans as a side dish.

1 SERVING: Calories 540 (Calories from Fat 140); Total Fat 16g (Saturated Fat 5g; Trans Fat 0.5g); Cholesterol 55mg; Sodium 1530mg; Total Carbohydrate 72g (Dietary Fiber 9g); Protein 28g **%Daily Value:** Vitamin A 10%; Vitamin C 0%; Calcium 15%; Iron 25% **Exchanges:** 4½ Starch, ½ Vegetable, 2 Very Lean Meat, 2½ Fat **Carbohydrate Choices:** 5

Vegetarian brats vary by brand, but generally, most require very short cooking times and will dry or fall apart if overcooked. The slow cooker offers a great, gentle slow heat, but this recipe requires just 3 to 4 hours and is not one that can cook all day. Do not overcook this dish. You might also want to try different brands of brats so you can find the brand you prefer to use.

soups, stews & chilies

Tortellini Soup

Prep Time: 40 minutes • Start to Finish: 40 minutes • **5 servings**

2 tablespoons butter or margarine

1 medium stalk celery, chopped (½ cup)

1 medium carrot, chopped (½ cup)

1 small onion, chopped (¼ cup)

1 clove garlic, finely chopped

6 cups water

2 extra-large vegetarian vegetable bouillon cubes

2½ cups dried cheese-filled tortellini (10 oz)

1 tablespoon chopped fresh parsley

½ teaspoon ground nutmeg

¼ teaspoon pepper

Freshly grated Parmesan cheese, if desired

1 In 4-quart Dutch oven, melt butter over medium heat. Add celery, carrot, onion and garlic; cook, stirring frequently, until crisp-tender.

2 Stir in water and bouillon cubes. Heat to boiling. Reduce heat to low; stir in tortellini. Cover; simmer about 20 minutes, stirring occasionally, until tortellini are tender.

3 Stir in parsley, nutmeg and pepper. Sprinkle individual servings with cheese.

1 SERVING: Calories 280 (Calories from Fat 90); Total Fat 10g (Saturated Fat 6g; Trans Fat 0g); Cholesterol 50mg; Sodium 1030mg; Total Carbohydrate 37g (Dietary Fiber 2g); Protein 10g **%Daily Value:** Vitamin A 50%; Vitamin C 2%; Calcium 10%; Iron 8% **Exchanges:** 2½ Starch, ½ Vegetable, 1½ Fat **Carbohydrate Choices:** 2½

Next to the ever-popular chicken and beef bouillon cubes, you will now find vegetable bouillon cubes. These cubes are a convenient way to add great flavor in a flash! They're also a must for people who don't want to use any animal products.

Tomato-Lentil Soup

Prep Time: 15 minutes • **Start to Finish:** 50 minutes • **6 servings**

1 tablespoon olive or vegetable oil

1 large onion, finely chopped (1 cup)

1 medium stalk celery, cut into ½-inch pieces

2 cloves garlic, finely chopped

2 medium carrots, cut into ½-inch pieces (1 cup)

1 cup dried lentils (8 oz), sorted, rinsed

4 cups water

4 teaspoons vegetable bouillon granules

1 teaspoon dried thyme leaves

¼ teaspoon pepper

1 dried bay leaf

1 can (28 oz) diced tomatoes, undrained

1 In 3-quart saucepan, heat oil over medium-high heat. Add onion, celery and garlic; cook about 5 minutes, stirring occasionally, until softened.

2 Stir in remaining ingredients except tomatoes. Heat to boiling. Reduce heat; cover and simmer 15 to 20 minutes or until lentils and vegetables are tender.

3 Stir in tomatoes. Reduce heat; simmer uncovered about 15 minutes or until thoroughly heated. Remove bay leaf.

1 SERVING: Calories 180 (Calories from Fat 25); Total Fat 2.5g (Saturated Fat 0g; Trans Fat 0g); Cholesterol 0mg; Sodium 340mg; Total Carbohydrate 29g (Dietary Fiber 7g); Protein 9g **%Daily Value:** Vitamin A 90%; Vitamin C 20%; Calcium 6%; Iron 25% **Exchanges:** 1½ Starch, 1½ Vegetable, ½ Fat **Carbohydrate Choices:** 2

This soup is so easy because there's no need to soak lentils as you need to do with dried beans.

Tomato-Basil Soup

Prep Time: 45 minutes • Start to Finish: 45 minutes • 4 servings

2 tablespoons olive or vegetable oil

2 medium carrots, finely chopped (½ cup)

1 small onion, finely chopped (½ cup)

1 clove garlic, finely chopped

6 large ripe tomatoes, peeled, seeded and chopped (6 cups)

1 can (8 oz) tomato sauce

¼ cup thinly sliced fresh or 2 teaspoons dried basil leaves

½ teaspoon sugar

¼ teaspoon salt

Dash pepper

1 In 3-quart saucepan, heat oil over medium heat. Add carrots, onion and garlic; cook about 10 minutes, stirring occasionally, until tender but not browned.

2 Stir in tomatoes. Cook uncovered about 10 minutes, stirring occasionally, until thoroughly heated.

3 Stir in remaining ingredients. Cook uncovered about 10 minutes, stirring occasionally, until hot.

1 SERVING: Calories 170 (Calories from Fat 70); Total Fat 8g (Saturated Fat 1g; Trans Fat 0g); Cholesterol 0mg; Sodium 550mg; Total Carbohydrate 22g (Dietary Fiber 6g); Protein 4g **%Daily Value:** Vitamin A 170%; Vitamin C 50%; Calcium 4%; Iron 10% **Exchanges:** 4 Vegetable, 1 Fat **Carbohydrate Choices:** 1½

Three cans (14.5 oz each) diced tomatoes, undrained, can be substituted for the fresh tomatoes. Omit salt; increase sugar to 1 teaspoon.

Italian Bean Soup with Greens

Prep Time: 20 minutes • **Start to Finish:** 1 hour 10 minutes • **8 servings (about 1⅓ cups each)**

2 tablespoons olive oil

2 medium carrots, peeled, sliced (1 cup)

1 large onion, chopped (1 cup)

1 stalk celery, chopped (⅓ cup)

2 cloves garlic, finely chopped

2 cans (15 to 15.5 oz each) great northern or cannellini (white kidney) beans, drained, rinsed

1 can (28 oz) diced tomatoes, undrained

2 teaspoons dried basil leaves

1 teaspoon dried oregano leaves

½ teaspoon salt

¼ teaspoon pepper

4 cups vegetable broth

4 cups packed fresh spinach leaves

½ cup shredded Parmesan cheese (2 oz)

1 In 5-quart Dutch oven, heat oil over medium-high heat. Add carrots, onion, celery and garlic; cook about 5 minutes, stirring frequently, until onion is tender.

2 Stir in beans, tomatoes, basil, oregano, salt, pepper and broth. Cover; simmer 30 to 45 minutes or until vegetables are tender.

3 Increase heat to medium; stir in spinach. Cover; cook 3 to 5 minutes longer or until spinach is wilted. Ladle soup into bowls; top each with cheese.

1 SERVING: Calories 270 (Calories from Fat 50); Total Fat 6g (Saturated Fat 2g; Trans Fat 0g); Cholesterol 0mg; Sodium 990mg; Total Carbohydrate 39g (Dietary Fiber 9g); Protein 15g **%Daily Value:** Vitamin A 100%; Vitamin C 20%; Calcium 25%; Iron 30% **Exchanges:** 2 Starch, 1 Vegetable, 1 Medium-Fat Meat **Carbohydrate Choices:** 2½

Spinach will discolor if cooked in an aluminum saucepan and may also discolor the pan. For this recipe, use a Dutch oven that is made of stainless steel, is porcelain covered or is made of other nonreactive material.

Butternut Squash Soup

Prep Time: 30 minutes • Start to Finish: 45 minutes • **6 servings**

2 **tablespoons butter or margarine**

1 **medium onion, chopped (½ cup)**

1 **butternut squash (2 lb), peeled, seeded and cubed***

2 **cups vegetable broth (from 32-oz carton)**

½ **teaspoon dried marjoram leaves**

¼ **teaspoon black pepper**

⅛ **teaspoon ground red pepper (cayenne)**

1 **package (8 oz) cream cheese, cubed**

1 In 3-quart saucepan, melt butter over medium heat. Add onion; cook, stirring occasionally, until crisp-tender.

2 Add all remaining ingredients except cream cheese. Heat to boiling. Reduce heat; cover and simmer 12 to 15 minutes or until squash is tender.

3 In blender or food processor, place one-third each of the soup mixture and cream cheese. Cover; blend on high speed until smooth, scraping down sides of blender if needed. Repeat twice with remaining soup mixture and cream cheese. Return mixture to saucepan. Heat over medium heat, stirring with whisk, until blended and hot (do not boil). If thinner consistency is desired, add additional vegetable broth.

Slow-Cooker Directions: In 10-inch skillet, melt butter over medium heat. Add onion; cook, stirring occasionally, until crisp-tender. Spray 3½- to 4-quart slow cooker with cooking spray. In slow cooker, mix onion and remaining ingredients except cream cheese. Cover; cook on Low heat setting 6 to 8 hours. In blender or food processor, place one-third to one-half of the soup mixture at a time. Cover; blend on high speed until smooth. Return mixture to slow cooker. Stir in cream cheese with whisk. Cover; cook on Low heat setting about 30 minutes, stirring occasionally with whisk, until cheese is melted and soup is smooth.

*Squash will be easier to peel if you microwave it first. Pierce whole squash with knife in several places to allow steam to escape. Place on paper towel and microwave on High 4 to 6 minutes or until squash is hot and peel is firm but easy to cut. Cool slightly before peeling.

1 SERVING: Calories 240 (Calories from Fat 160); Total Fat 17g (Saturated Fat 10g; Trans Fat 0.5g); Cholesterol 50mg; Sodium 1220mg; Total Carbohydrate 15g (Dietary Fiber 2g); Protein 5g **%Daily Value:** Vitamin A 210%; Vitamin C 15%; Calcium 10%; Iron 8% **Exchanges:** 1 Starch, 3½ Fat **Carbohydrate Choices:** 1

Butternut Squash Soup with Maple-Pecan Apple Salsa: Make soup as directed. In small bowl, combine ½ cup diced unpeeled apple, ½ cup chopped toasted pecans, 2 tablespoons real maple syrup and ½ teaspoon ground cinnamon; stir well to coat. Top each bowl of soup with a spoonful of salsa.

Creamy Wild Rice Soup

Prep Time: 40 minutes • Start to Finish: 40 minutes • **5 servings**

½ **cup uncooked wild rice**

1¾ **cups water**

2 **tablespoons butter or margarine**

2 **medium stalks celery, sliced (1 cup)**

1 **medium carrot, coarsely shredded (½ cup)**

1 **medium onion, chopped (½ cup)**

1 **small green bell pepper, chopped (½ cup)**

3 **tablespoons all-purpose flour**

½ **teaspoon salt**

¼ **teaspoon pepper**

1 **can (14 oz) vegetable broth**

1 **cup half-and-half**

⅓ **cup slivered almonds, toasted**✳

¼ **cup chopped fresh parsley**

1 Cook wild rice in 1¼ cups of the water as directed on package.

2 In 3-quart saucepan, melt butter over medium heat. Add celery, carrot, onion and bell pepper; cook, stirring occasionally, until celery is tender.

3 Stir in flour, salt and pepper. Stir in wild rice, remaining ½ cup water and the broth. Heat to boiling. Reduce heat to low; cover and simmer 15 minutes, stirring occasionally.

4 Stir in remaining ingredients. Heat just until hot (do not boil).

✳*To toast almonds in microwave, place ½ teaspoon vegetable oil and the almonds in 1- or 2-cup microwavable measuring cup. Microwave uncovered on High 2 minutes 30 seconds to 3 minutes 30 seconds, stirring every 30 seconds, until light brown.*

1 SERVING: Calories 270 (Calories from Fat 140); Total Fat 15g (Saturated Fat 7g; Trans Fat 0g); Cholesterol 30mg; Sodium 660mg; Total Carbohydrate 26g (Dietary Fiber 3g); Protein 7g **%Daily Value:** Vitamin A 50%; Vitamin C 15%; Calcium 10%; Iron 8% **Exchanges:** 1½ Starch, ½ Vegetable, 3 Fat **Carbohydrate Choices:** 2

Wild rice isn't rice? No, it's an aquatic grass native to North America. The chewy texture of wild rice makes it a perfect meat substitute, but cooked white or brown rice can be used instead.

Tortilla Soup

Prep Time: 15 minutes • Start to Finish: 35 minutes • **4 servings**

3 **teaspoons vegetable oil**

4 **corn tortillas (5 or 6 inch),**
  cut into 2×½-inch strips

1 **medium onion, chopped (½ cup)**

2 **cans (14 oz each) vegetable broth**

1 **can (10 oz) diced tomatoes**
  with green chiles, undrained

1 **tablespoon lime juice**

1 **tablespoon chopped fresh**
  cilantro or parsley

1 In 2-quart nonstick saucepan, heat 2 teaspoons oil over medium-high heat. Add tortilla strips; cook 30 to 60 seconds, stirring occasionally, until crisp and light golden brown. Remove from saucepan; drain on paper towels.

2 In same saucepan, cook remaining 1 teaspoon oil and the onion over medium-high heat, stirring occasionally, until onion is tender.

3 Stir in broth and tomatoes. Heat to boiling. Reduce heat to low; simmer uncovered 20 minutes.

4 Stir in lime juice. Serve soup over tortilla strips; garnish with cilantro.

1 SERVING: Calories 110 (Calories from Fat 25); Total Fat 3g (Saturated Fat 0g; Trans Fat 0g); Cholesterol 0mg; Sodium 1010mg; Total Carbohydrate 19g (Dietary Fiber 3g); Protein 2g **%Daily Value:** Vitamin A 15%; Vitamin C 6%; Calcium 6%; Iron 4% **Exchanges:** 1 Starch, ½ Vegetable, ½ Fat **Carbohydrate Choices:** 1

Stale tortillas are never wasted by Mexican cooks and are used in many ways—you can use any you have for this recipe. Sliced and fried, tortillas add a distinctive flavor to this tomato soup.

Broccoli-Cheese Soup

Prep Time: 25 minutes • **Start to Finish:** 25 minutes • **5 servings**

1 tablespoon butter or margarine

1 medium onion, chopped (½ cup)

1 tablespoon all-purpose flour

1 teaspoon salt

3 cups original-flavored soymilk

2 teaspoons cornstarch

3 cups bite-size fresh broccoli florets or frozen broccoli florets (thawed)

1½ cups shredded Cheddar cheese (6 oz)

1 In 3-quart saucepan, melt butter over medium heat. Stir in onion, flour and salt. Cook 2 to 3 minutes, stirring constantly, until onion is soft.

2 In small bowl, mix soymilk and cornstarch with whisk until smooth. Gradually stir into onion mixture. Heat to boiling; boil 1 minute, stirring constantly, until bubbly and thickened.

3 Stir in broccoli. Cook 4 to 5 minutes, stirring frequently. Stir in cheese. Cook 2 to 4 minutes, stirring frequently, until cheese is melted.

1 SERVING: Calories 290 (Calories from Fat 140); Total Fat 16g (Saturated Fat 9g; Trans Fat 0g); Cholesterol 40mg; Sodium 790mg; Total Carbohydrate 19g (Dietary Fiber 4g); Protein 16g **%Daily Value:** Vitamin A 30%; Vitamin C 30%; Calcium 40%; Iron 15% **Exchanges:** 1 Starch, ½ Vegetable, 2 Medium-Fat Meat, 1 Fat **Carbohydrate Choices:** 1

Cauliflower-Cheese Soup: Use bite-size cauliflower pieces instead of the broccoli.

For a more intense Cheddar flavor, use sharp Cheddar. Want a fun garnish for this creamy soup? Throw on a handful of popcorn, but keep the bowl handy—folks will want to sneak more!

Chunky Vegetable Chowder

Prep Time: 20 minutes • Start to Finish: 30 minutes • 6 servings

1 tablespoon butter or margarine

1 medium green bell pepper, coarsely chopped (1 cup)

1 medium red bell pepper, coarsely chopped (1 cup)

8 medium green onions, sliced (½ cup)

3 cups water

¾ lb small red potatoes, cut into 1-inch pieces (2½ cups)

1 tablespoon chopped fresh or 1 teaspoon dried thyme leaves

½ teaspoon salt

1 cup half-and-half

⅛ teaspoon pepper

2 cans (14.75 oz each) cream style sweet corn

1 In 4-quart Dutch oven, melt butter over medium heat. Add bell peppers and onions; cook 3 minutes, stirring occasionally.

2 Stir in water, potatoes, thyme and salt. Heat to boiling. Reduce heat to low; cover and simmer about 10 minutes or until potatoes are tender.

3 Stir in remaining ingredients. Cook until hot (do not boil).

1 SERVING: Calories 230 (Calories from Fat 70); Total Fat 7g (Saturated Fat 4g; Trans Fat 0g); Cholesterol 20mg; Sodium 680mg; Total Carbohydrate 37g (Dietary Fiber 3g); Protein 5g **%Daily Value:** Vitamin A 25%; Vitamin C 50%; Calcium 6%; Iron 6% **Exchanges:** 1 Starch, 1 Other Carbohydrate, 1 Vegetable, 1½ Fat **Carbohydrate Choices:** 2½

Offer warm wedges of a cheesy focaccia on the side—they're great for dipping into the chowder!

Soybean-Squash Soup

Prep Time: 20 minutes • Start to Finish: 1 hour • **4 servings (about 1¼ cups each)**

2 tablespoons olive oil

1 large onion, chopped (1 cup)

2 cloves garlic, finely chopped

1 small butternut squash (about 1¼ lb), peeled, seeded and cubed (about 3 cups)

1 can (15 oz) black soybeans, drained, rinsed

1 can (14.5 oz) organic diced tomatoes, undrained

1 tablespoon ground cumin

½ teaspoon salt

¼ teaspoon pepper

¼ teaspoon crushed red pepper flakes

1 cup vegetable broth or water

1 In 5-quart Dutch oven, heat oil over medium-high heat. Add onion and garlic; cook 3 minutes, stirring frequently, until onion is tender.

2 Stir in remaining ingredients. Heat to boiling. Reduce heat; cover and simmer 40 minutes or until squash is tender.

1 SERVING: Calories 370 (Calories from Fat 150); Total Fat 17g (Saturated Fat 2.5g; Trans Fat 0g); Cholesterol 0mg; Sodium 770mg; Total Carbohydrate 34g (Dietary Fiber 10g); Protein 20g **%Daily Value:** Vitamin A 290%; Vitamin C 35%; Calcium 20%; Iron 45% **Exchanges:** 1½ Starch, 1½ Vegetable, 2 Very Lean Meat, 3 Fat **Carbohydrate Choices:** 2

Look for already peeled and cut-up butternut squash in specialty and club warehouse stores, particularly during the fall and winter months.

Yellow Split Pea and Potato Soup

Prep Time: 15 minutes • **Start to Finish:** 55 minutes • **6 servings**

SOUP

- 1 **tablespoon chili oil or vegetable oil**
- 1 **large red bell pepper, chopped (1½ cups)**
- 1 **large onion, chopped (1 cup)**
- 1 **large carrot, diced (1 cup)**
- 1 **teaspoon finely chopped gingerroot**
- 2 **cloves garlic, finely chopped**
- 1 **red jalapeño chile, seeded, finely chopped**
- 1½ **cups dried yellow split peas, sorted, rinsed**
- 2 **medium potatoes, peeled, cut into 1-inch cubes**
- 1 **tablespoon curry powder**
- ½ **teaspoon salt**
- 2 **cups vegetable broth**
- 1 **can (14 oz) coconut milk (not cream of coconut)**

CILANTRO-YOGURT SAUCE

- ⅓ **cup plain yogurt**
- 2 **tablespoons chopped fresh cilantro**
- ¼ **teaspoon grated lime peel**

1 In 3-quart saucepan, heat oil over medium-high heat. Cook bell pepper, onion, carrot, gingerroot, garlic and chile in oil, stirring occasionally, until onion is tender.

2 Stir in all remaining soup ingredients. Heat to boiling; reduce heat. Cover; simmer 25 to 35 minutes or until peas and potatoes are tender.

3 In small bowl, mix all sauce ingredients until blended. Ladle soup into 6 bowls; top each serving with sauce.

1 SERVING: Calories 400 (Calories from Fat 140); Total Fat 15g (Saturated Fat 11g; Trans Fat 0g); Cholesterol 0mg; Sodium 590mg; Total Carbohydrate 52g (Dietary Fiber 18g); Protein 15g **%Daily Value:** Vitamin A 80%; Vitamin C 70%; Calcium 8%; Iron 15% **Exchanges:** 2 Starch, 1 Other Carbohydrate, 1 Vegetable, 1 Very Lean Meat, 2½ Fat **Carbohydrate Choices:** 3½

> Save yourself some time by grabbing a jar of grated gingerroot from the produce section of the grocery store. It's a quick way to add zest to your meals!

Cajun Barley Stew

Prep Time: 15 minutes • Start to Finish: 35 minutes • 4 servings

2   teaspoons vegetable oil

1   large onion, chopped (1 cup)

1   medium stalk celery, chopped (½ cup)

½   cup uncooked quick-cooking barley

5   cups tomato juice

1   to 2 teaspoons Cajun or Creole seasoning

2   cans (15.5 oz each) great northern or navy beans, drained, rinsed

¼   cup chopped fresh parsley

1 In 12-inch skillet, heat oil over medium-high heat. Add onion and celery; cook, stirring occasionally, until crisp-tender.

2 Stir in remaining ingredients except parsley. Heat to boiling. Reduce heat to low; cover and simmer about 20 minutes or until barley is tender. Stir in parsley.

1 SERVING: Calories 500 (Calories from Fat 30); Total Fat 3.5g (Saturated Fat 0.5g; Trans Fat 0g); Cholesterol 0mg; Sodium 880mg; Total Carbohydrate 91g (Dietary Fiber 19g); Protein 26g **%Daily Value:** Vitamin A 35%; Vitamin C 50%; Calcium 25%; Iron 60% **Exchanges:** 5 Starch, 3 Vegetable, 1 Very Lean Meat **Carbohydrate Choices:** 6

Quick-cooking barley is a super time-saver— it cooks in less than half the time of regular barley. If Cajun or Creole seasoning isn't available, use 2 teaspoons chili powder, ½ teaspoon salt and ¼ teaspoon pepper.

Indian Lentil Stew

Prep Time: 55 minutes • Start to Finish: 55 minutes • **4 servings**

2 tablespoons butter or margarine

1 large onion, chopped (1 cup)

1 tablespoon curry powder

2 tablespoons all-purpose flour

1 can (14 oz) vegetable broth

¾ cup dried lentils (6 oz), sorted, rinsed

½ teaspoon salt

½ cup apple juice

3 cups 1-inch pieces peeled dark-orange sweet potatoes

1 cup frozen sweet peas

Sour cream or plain fat-free yogurt, if desired

Chutney, if desired

1 In 3-quart saucepan, melt butter over medium-high heat. Add onion and curry powder; cook 2 minutes, stirring occasionally. Stir in flour. Gradually add broth, stirring constantly, until thickened.

2 Stir in lentils and salt. Reduce heat to low; cover and simmer 20 minutes, stirring occasionally.

3 Stir in apple juice, sweet potatoes and peas. Heat to boiling. Reduce heat to low; cover and simmer 15 to 20 minutes, stirring occasionally, until vegetables are tender. Top individual servings with sour cream and chutney.

1 SERVING: Calories 330 (Calories from Fat 60); Total Fat 7g (Saturated Fat 4g; Trans Fat 0g); Cholesterol 15mg; Sodium 790mg; Total Carbohydrate 54g (Dietary Fiber 11g); Protein 13g **%Daily Value:** Vitamin A 320%; Vitamin C 20%; Calcium 8%; Iron 30% **Exchanges:** 3 Starch, 2 Vegetable, 1 Fat **Carbohydrate Choices:** 3½

Curry powder is made of many spices, most often including cardamom, chiles, cinnamon, fennel seed, fenugreek, cumin, turmeric, nutmeg, coriander and cloves. The apple juice in this easy stew adds a sweet note that perks up the curry flavor.

Bean and Vegetable Stew with Polenta

Prep Time: **1 hour 15 minutes** • Start to Finish: **1 hour 15 minutes** • **4 servings (1½ cups each)**

1 tablespoon olive or vegetable oil

1 medium yellow or green bell pepper, coarsely chopped (1 cup)

1 medium onion, coarsely chopped (½ cup)

2 teaspoons finely chopped garlic

2 medium carrots, cut into ¼-inch slices (1 cup)

2 cans (14.5 oz each) diced tomatoes with basil, undrained

1 can (15 oz) black-eyed peas, drained, rinsed

1 can (19 oz) cannellini (white kidney) beans, drained, rinsed

1 cup water

1 teaspoon Italian seasoning

½ teaspoon salt

¼ teaspoon pepper

1 roll (16 oz) refrigerated polenta

1 cup frozen cut green beans

1 In 4½- to 5-quart Dutch oven, heat oil over medium heat. Add bell pepper, onion and garlic; cook 5 to 6 minutes, stirring frequently, until onion is softened.

2 Stir in remaining ingredients except polenta and green beans. Heat to boiling. Reduce heat to medium-low; cover and cook 35 to 40 minutes, stirring occasionally, until carrots are tender and stew is hot.

3 Meanwhile, cook polenta as directed on package; keep warm.

4 Stir frozen green beans into stew. Cover; cook 5 to 6 minutes, stirring occasionally, until beans are hot. To serve, spoon stew over polenta.

1 SERVING: Calories 780 (Calories from Fat 40); Total Fat 4.5g (Saturated Fat 1g; Trans Fat 0g); Cholesterol 0mg; Sodium 2470mg; Total Carbohydrate 149g (Dietary Fiber 22g); Protein 34g **%Daily Value:** Vitamin A 130%; Vitamin C 80%; Calcium 20%; Iron 50% **Exchanges:** 9 Starch, 2½ Vegetable **Carbohydrate Choices:** 10

Any type of canned beans, instead of the cannellini beans, will work in this recipe. You may want to experiment with garbanzo beans, butter beans, great northern beans, red beans or kidney beans.

Southwestern Stew with Corn Dumplings

Prep Time: **15 minutes** • Start to Finish: **40 minutes** • **4 servings**

1   **tablespoon vegetable oil**

1   **large onion, chopped (1 cup)**

2   **cups cubed peeled sweet potatoes or butternut squash**

1   **cup drained whole kernel sweet corn (from 15.25-oz can)**

1   **can (15 oz) garbanzo beans, drained, rinsed**

1   **jar (16 oz) chunky-style salsa (2 cups)**

1   **cup water**

¼   **teaspoon ground cinnamon**

1   **pouch (6.5 oz) cornbread & muffin mix**

½   **cup fat-free (skim) milk**

1   **tablespoon vegetable oil**

1   **tablespoon roasted sunflower nuts, if desired**

1 Heat oven to 425°F. In ovenproof 4-quart Dutch oven, heat 1 tablespoon oil over medium-high heat. Add onion; cook about 5 minutes, stirring occasionally, until crisp-tender. Stir in sweet potatoes, corn, beans, salsa, water and cinnamon. Heat to boiling, stirring occasionally.

2 In medium bowl, mix muffin mix, milk and 1 tablespoon oil. Stir in nuts. Drop dough by 8 spoonfuls onto vegetable mixture.

3 Bake uncovered 20 to 25 minutes or until toothpick inserted in center of dumplings comes out clean.

1 SERVING: Calories 550 (Calories from Fat 100); Total Fat 12g (Saturated Fat 1.5g; Trans Fat 0g); Cholesterol 0mg; Sodium 1340mg; Total Carbohydrate 96g (Dietary Fiber 10g); Protein 16g **%Daily Value:** Vitamin A 220%; Vitamin C 10%; Calcium 10%; Iron 25% **Exchanges:** 4 Starch, 2 Other Carbohydrate, 1½ Vegetable, 2 Fat **Carbohydrate Choices:** 6½

> **A serving of this nutrition-packed meatless stew will give you plenty of vitamin A and iron. Another bonus: It's an excellent source of fiber.**

Cooking Legumes

Mild-flavored legumes are an excellent substitute for meat in recipes, and they easily combine with other flavors. Did you know beans, peanuts, lentils, soybeans and peas are considered to be legumes? Whether dried, canned or frozen, you can find a wide variety in supermarkets, whole food stores and food co-ops.

Storing Legumes

Uncooked (dried): Store up to 1 year in tightly covered containers, with labels and dates, at room temperature.

Cooked: Cover and refrigerate up to 3 days, or freeze in airtight containers up to 6 months.

Preparing Legumes for Cooking

Sort through beans or legumes before cooking to remove any shriveled, small or damaged beans and stones; rinse and drain.

Except for *black-eyed peas, lentils and split peas,* dried beans and legumes should be soaked before cooking to soften and plump them. They rehydrate to triple their size, so be sure to select a pot that's big enough. There are two methods for soaking beans:

Quick Soak: Place dried legumes in a large saucepan; add enough water to cover. Heat to boiling; boil 2 minutes. Remove from heat, cover and let stand for at least 1 hour. Drain, then cook in fresh cold water.

Long Soak: Place dried legumes in a large saucepan or bowl; add enough cold water to cover them. Let stand 8 to 24 hours. Drain, then cook in fresh cold water.

Cooking Legumes

1. Soak 1 cup dried beans using one of the methods described above in a 3- or 4-quart saucepan; add enough fresh cold water to cover.

2. Heat to boiling; boil uncovered 2 minutes.

3. Reduce heat to low. Cover and simmer (do not boil or legumes will burst), stirring occasionally, for the time indicated in the following chart, or until tender. Beans continue to dry with age, so you may need to add a little more water and cook them longer if beans have absorbed all the water but aren't quite tender. Very old beans may never soften completely.

TYPE OF BEAN OR LEGUME (1 CUP)	SIMMER TIME	YIELD IN CUPS
Adzuki Beans, Lentils	30 to 45	2 to 3 cups
Mung Beans, Split Peas	45 to 60 minutes	2 to 2¼
Black-Eyed Peas, Butter Beans, Cannellini Beans, Great Northern Beans, Lima Beans, Navy Beans, Pinto Beans	1 to 1½ hours	2 to 2½
Anasazi Beans, Black Beans, Fava Beans, Kidney Beans	1 to 2 hours	2
Garbanzo Beans	2 to 2½ hours	2
Soybeans	3 to 4 hours	2

Tomato-Vegetable Stew with Cheddar Cheese Dumplings

Prep Time: 20 minutes • Start to Finish: 1 hour 5 minutes • 6 servings (1 cup each)

STEW

- 2 tablespoons vegetable oil
- 2 large onions, coarsely chopped (3½ cups)
- 2 medium stalks celery, coarsely chopped (¾ cup)
- 2 cups frozen Italian green beans
- 1 can (28 oz) diced tomatoes, undrained
- 1¾ cups vegetable broth (from 32-oz carton)
- 1 teaspoon dried basil leaves
- ¼ teaspoon pepper

CHEDDAR CHEESE DUMPLINGS

- 1½ cups self-rising flour
- 2 teaspoons baking powder
- ½ teaspoon salt
- ½ teaspoon ground mustard
- ¼ cup cold butter or margarine
- ½ cup shredded sharp Cheddar cheese (2 oz)
- ⅔ cup milk

1 In 4½- to 5-quart Dutch oven, heat oil over medium-high heat. Add onions and celery; cook, stirring frequently, until tender.

2 Stir in remaining stew ingredients. Heat to boiling. Reduce heat to low; simmer uncovered 15 to 20 minutes or until beans are tender.

3 Meanwhile, in medium bowl, mix flour, baking powder, salt and mustard. Cut in butter, using pastry blender or fork, until mixture looks like coarse crumbs. Stir in cheese. Add milk; stir just until dry ingredients are moistened.

4 Drop dough by rounded tablespoonfuls onto simmering stew. Cover; cook over medium-low heat 20 to 25 minutes or until dumplings are firm when pressed.

1 SERVING: Calories 370 (Calories from Fat 150); Total Fat 17g (Saturated Fat 8g; Trans Fat 0g); Cholesterol 30mg; Sodium 1480mg; Total Carbohydrate 43g (Dietary Fiber 4g); Protein 10g **%Daily Value:** Vitamin A 30%; Vitamin C 25%; Calcium 35%; Iron 20% **Exchanges:** 2 Starch, ½ Other Carbohydrate, ½ Low-Fat Milk, 2½ Fat **Carbohydrate Choices:** 3

> **Resist the urge to stir too much!** Dumplings require very little mixing when the milk is added to the dry ingredients. If the dough is overmixed, the dumplings can become heavy and tough, so mix just until the dry ingredients are moistened.

Bean and Barley Chili with Cilantro–Sour Cream

Prep Time: 10 minutes • Start to Finish: 1 hour 10 minutes • 6 servings (about 1⅓ cups each)

2 tablespoons vegetable oil

1 large onion, chopped (1 cup)

2 cloves garlic, finely chopped

½ cup uncooked pearl barley

2 cans (14.5 oz each) diced tomatoes, undrained

2 cups water

2 tablespoons chili powder

1½ teaspoons ground cumin

Salt and pepper to taste

1 can (15 oz) black beans, drained, rinsed

1 can (15 oz) dark red kidney beans, drained, rinsed

¾ cup chunky-style salsa

CILANTRO–SOUR CREAM

½ cup sour cream

2 tablespoons finely chopped fresh cilantro

1 In 5-quart Dutch oven, heat oil over medium-high heat. Add onion and garlic; cook 5 minutes, stirring frequently, until tender. Stir in barley, tomatoes, water, chili powder, cumin, salt and pepper. Reduce heat; cover and simmer 30 minutes.

2 Stir in beans and salsa. Cook about 30 minutes longer or until barley is tender. Meanwhile, mix sour cream and cilantro until blended.

3 Serve chili topped with cilantro–sour cream.

1 SERVING: Calories 400 (Calories from Fat 90); Total Fat 10g (Saturated Fat 3g; Trans Fat 0g); Cholesterol 10mg; Sodium 640mg; Total Carbohydrate 61g (Dietary Fiber 17g); Protein 16g **%Daily Value:** Vitamin A 40%; Vitamin C 25%; Calcium 15%; Iron 30% **Exchanges:** 4 Starch, 1 Vegetable, 1½ Fat **Carbohydrate Choices:** 4

Do you like it spicy? If so, add ¼ teaspoon ground red pepper (cayenne) along with the chili powder and cumin; you can also use hot salsa.

Vegetable and Bean Chili

Prep Time: 40 minutes • Start to Finish: 40 minutes • **6 servings (1½ cups each)**

1 tablespoon olive or vegetable oil

2 medium onions, coarsely chopped (1 cup)

2 teaspoons finely chopped garlic

1 bag (16 oz) frozen broccoli, cauliflower and carrots

1 can (15.5 oz) red beans, drained, rinsed

1 can (15 oz) garbanzo beans, drained, rinsed

2 cans (14.5 oz each) diced tomatoes with green chiles, undrained

1 can (8 oz) tomato sauce

2 cups frozen whole kernel corn

2 tablespoons chili powder

1 tablespoon ground cumin

¾ teaspoon salt

⅛ teaspoon ground red pepper (cayenne)

1 In 4½- to 5-quart Dutch oven, heat oil over medium-high heat. Add onions and garlic; cook 4 to 5 minutes, stirring frequently, until onions are softened.

2 Stir in remaining ingredients. Heat to boiling. Reduce heat to medium-low; cover and cook 15 to 20 minutes, stirring occasionally, until chili is hot and vegetables are crisp-tender.

1 SERVING: Calories 320 (Calories from Fat 45); Total Fat 5g (Saturated Fat 0.5g; Trans Fat 0g); Cholesterol 0mg; Sodium 1100mg; Total Carbohydrate 55g (Dietary Fiber 13g); Protein 14g **%Daily Value:** Vitamin A 45%; Vitamin C 40%; Calcium 10%; Iron 30% **Exchanges:** 1 Starch, 2 Other Carbohydrate, 2 Vegetable, 1 Very Lean Meat, 1 Fat **Carbohydrate Choices:** 3½

Any combination of your favorite vegetables or canned beans will work well in this recipe. Try canned black beans, black-eyed peas or butter beans.

Home-Style Vegetable Chili

Prep Time: 30 minutes • Start to Finish: 30 minutes • **6 servings**

2 tablespoons vegetable oil

1 large onion, chopped (1 cup)

2 medium carrots, chopped (1 cup)

1 medium green bell pepper, chopped (1 cup)

1 pasilla chile, seeded, chopped (¾ cup), or 1 can (4.5 oz) chopped green chiles

1 cup water

1 tablespoon chili powder

1 teaspoon ground cumin

¾ teaspoon salt

2 cans (15 oz each) dark red kidney beans, drained, rinsed

2 cans (14.5 oz each) organic diced tomatoes, undrained

Shredded Cheddar cheese, if desired

1 In 3-quart saucepan, heat oil over medium-high heat. Add onion, carrots, bell pepper and chile; cook 3 to 5 minutes, stirring occasionally, until crisp-tender.

2 Stir in remaining ingredients except cheese. Heat to boiling. Reduce heat to medium-low; simmer uncovered 10 to 15 minutes, stirring occasionally, until vegetables are tender. Sprinkle individual servings with cheese.

1 SERVING: Calories 290 (Calories from Fat 50); Total Fat 6g (Saturated Fat 1g; Trans Fat 0g); Cholesterol 0mg; Sodium 640mg; Total Carbohydrate 46g (Dietary Fiber 12g); Protein 14g **%Daily Value:** Vitamin A 100%; Vitamin C 40%; Calcium 10%; Iron 25% **Exchanges:** 2½ Starch, 1½ Vegetable, ½ Very Lean Meat, 1 Fat **Carbohydrate Choices:** 3

Pasilla chiles are medium-hot in flavor and 6 to 8 inches long. When fresh, they are sometimes referred to as chilaca chiles. Canned green chiles can be used if pasilla chiles are not available, but the flavor might be slightly milder.

lowfat

Three-Alarm Spaghetti and Pinto Bean Chili

Prep Time: 35 minutes • **Start to Finish:** 35 minutes • **4 servings**

1 tablespoon vegetable oil

1 large onion, chopped (1 cup)

1 medium green bell pepper, chopped (1 cup)

3 cups water

½ cup taco sauce

2 teaspoons chili powder

½ teaspoon salt

¼ teaspoon ground cinnamon

2 cans (10 oz each) diced tomatoes and green chiles, undrained

4 oz uncooked spaghetti, broken into thirds (1½ cups)

1 can (15 oz) pinto beans, drained, rinsed

Sour cream, if desired

Jalapeño chiles, if desired

1 In 4-quart Dutch oven, heat oil over medium-high heat. Add onion and bell pepper; cook 3 to 5 minutes, stirring occasionally, until crisp-tender.

2 Stir in remaining ingredients except spaghetti, beans, sour cream and jalapeño chiles. Heat to boiling. Reduce heat to medium-low; simmer uncovered 5 minutes, stirring occasionally.

3 Stir in spaghetti and beans. Heat to boiling. Reduce heat to medium; cook uncovered 8 to 10 minutes, stirring occasionally, until spaghetti is tender. Garnish each serving with sour cream and jalapeño chiles.

1 SERVING: Calories 340 (Calories from Fat 45); Total Fat 5g (Saturated Fat 1g; Trans Fat 0g); Cholesterol 0mg; Sodium 1000mg; Total Carbohydrate 59g (Dietary Fiber 12g); Protein 14g **%Daily Value:** Vitamin A 25%; Vitamin C 40%; Calcium 10%; Iron 20% **Exchanges:** 3½ Starch, 2 Vegetable, ½ Fat **Carbohydrate Choices:** 4

This chili recipe is based on the well-known Cincinnati chili, which is chili served over spaghetti. To save time and energy, the spaghetti is cooked right along with this spicy chili.

White Bean Chili

Prep Time: 20 minutes • Start to Finish: 1 hour 20 minutes • 6 servings

¼ **cup butter or margarine**

1 **large onion, chopped (1 cup)**

1 **clove garlic, finely chopped**

¼ **cup chopped fresh or 1 teaspoon dried basil leaves**

3 **cups vegetable broth (from 32-oz carton)**

2 **tablespoons chopped fresh cilantro or parsley**

2 **teaspoons chili powder**

¼ **teaspoon ground cloves**

2 **cans (15.5 oz each) great northern beans, undrained**

1 **medium tomato, chopped (¾ cup)**

Corn tortilla chips, if desired

1 In 4-quart Dutch oven, melt butter over medium-high heat. Add onion and garlic; cook, stirring occasionally, until onion is tender. Stir in remaining ingredients except tomato and tortilla chips.

2 Heat to boiling. Reduce heat to low; cover and simmer 1 hour, stirring occasionally.

3 Serve chili topped with tomato and tortilla chips.

1 SERVING: Calories 240 (Calories from Fat 70); Total Fat 8g (Saturated Fat 1.5g; Trans Fat 1.5g); Cholesterol 0mg; Sodium 880mg; Total Carbohydrate 32g (Dietary Fiber 8g); Protein 11g **%Daily Value:** Vitamin A 20%; Vitamin C 2%; Calcium 10%; Iron 25% **Exchanges:** 1½ Starch, 1½ Vegetable, ½ Very Lean Meat, 1½ Fat **Carbohydrate Choices:** 2

White chili, a twist to traditional tomato-based chili, uses a vegetable broth as its base, rather than tomato.

Three-Bean Chili

Prep Time: 1 hour • Start to Finish: 1 hour 30 minutes • 8 servings (¾ cup rice and 1 cup chili each)

THREE-PEPPER SALSA

1 medium red onion, finely chopped

½ teaspoon salt

3 medium tomatoes, seeded, finely chopped (about 1¾ cups)

1 small yellow bell pepper, finely chopped (about ½ cup)

1 small poblano chile, seeded, finely chopped (about ⅓ cup)

1 small jalapeño chile, seeded, finely chopped

¼ cup chopped fresh cilantro

2 tablespoons fresh lime juice (½ large)

1 tablespoon olive oil

Salt and freshly ground black pepper to taste

GARLIC RICE

2 cups uncooked regular long-grain white rice

2 tablespoons vegetable oil

4 cloves garlic, cut into thin slices

3 cups water

1 teaspoon salt

CHILI

1 can (28 oz) organic diced tomatoes, undrained

1 can (15 oz) dark red kidney beans, drained, rinsed

1 can (15 oz) black beans, drained, rinsed

1 can (15 oz) chick peas (garbanzo beans), drained, rinsed

1 can (15 oz) tomato sauce

3 small bell peppers (any color), diced

1 Anaheim or jalapeño chile, seeded, chopped

2 tablespoons chili powder

½ teaspoon salt

¼ teaspoon pepper

SALSA-CREAM

1 container (8 oz) sour cream

⅓ cup Three-Pepper Salsa

1 In small bowl, rub onion and ½ teaspoon salt together with fingers. Add enough water to cover onion; pour onion and water into strainer to drain. Return onion to bowl. Repeat rinsing and draining several times to remove harshness. Drain well, removing all excess water. In medium bowl, mix onion and remaining salsa ingredients. Refrigerate until serving time.

2 In small bowl, place rice and enough water to cover. Let stand about 15 minutes. Pour rice and water into strainer to drain well. In 3-quart saucepan, heat vegetable oil over medium-high heat. Add garlic; cook and stir until light golden brown. Add rice; cook 3 minutes, stirring frequently. Add 3 cups water and 1 teaspoon salt. Heat to boiling over high heat. Reduce heat; cover and simmer 15 minutes. Before serving, remove garlic slices from rice with fork.

3 Meanwhile, in 4-quart Dutch oven, mix all chili ingredients. Heat to boiling. Reduce heat; cover and simmer 25 to 30 minutes, stirring occasionally, until bell peppers are tender.

4 In small bowl, mix salsa-cream ingredients.

5 To serve, spoon 1 cup rice on one side of each large shallow soup bowl. Spoon 1½ cups chili next to rice in each bowl. Top each with salsa-cream and, using slotted spoon, three-pepper salsa.

1 SERVING: Calories 750 (Calories from Fat 160); Total Fat 18g (Saturated Fat 6g; Trans Fat 0g); Cholesterol 20mg; Sodium 2000mg; Total Carbohydrate 122g (Dietary Fiber 18g); Protein 26g **%Daily Value:** Vitamin A 60%; Vitamin C 100%; Calcium 20%; Iron 50% **Exchanges:** 7½ Starch, ½ Other Carbohydrate, ½ Very Lean Meat, 2½ Fat **Carbohydrate Choices:** 8

Don't be intimidated by the long list of ingredients! Each ingredient adds to the specialness of this chili. And the extra flavors make this chili worth the effort.

Three-Bean Enchilada Chili

Prep Time: 35 minutes • Start to Finish: 35 minutes • **5 servings**

1 tablespoon vegetable oil

1 large onion, chopped (1 cup)

1 medium green bell pepper, chopped (1 cup)

1 can (28 oz) crushed tomatoes, undrained

1 can (15 oz) dark red kidney beans, drained, rinsed

1 can (15 oz) black beans, drained, rinsed

1 can (15 oz) pinto beans, drained, rinsed

1 can (10 oz) enchilada sauce (1¼ cups)

1 teaspoon dried oregano leaves

Tortilla chips, broken, if desired

Shredded Cheddar cheese, if desired

1 In 3-quart saucepan, heat oil over medium-high heat. Add onion and bell pepper; cook 5 minutes, stirring occasionally, until crisp-tender.

2 Stir in remaining ingredients except tortilla chips and cheese. Heat to boiling. Reduce heat to medium-low; simmer uncovered 10 to 15 minutes, stirring occasionally. Sprinkle individual servings with chips and cheese.

1 SERVING: Calories 390 (Calories from Fat 35); Total Fat 4g (Saturated Fat 0.5g; Trans Fat 0g); Cholesterol 0mg; Sodium 1300mg; Total Carbohydrate 68g (Dietary Fiber 21g); Protein 20g **%Daily Value:** Vitamin A 25%; Vitamin C 40%; Calcium 10%; Iron 30% **Exchanges:** 2½ Starch, 1½ Other Carbohydrate, 1 Vegetable, 1½ Very Lean Meat, ½ Fat **Carbohydrate Choices:** 4½

Pinto beans are two-tone kidney-shaped beans widely used in Central and South American cooking. They turn pink when cooked and are the most widely used bean in refried beans.

Ratatouille Chili

Prep Time: 25 minutes • Start to Finish: 25 minutes • **4 servings**

2	**tablespoons olive or vegetable oil**
1	**large eggplant (1 lb), cut into ½-inch cubes (4 cups)**
1	**large onion, chopped (1 cup)**
1	**medium green bell pepper, chopped (1 cup)**
1	**clove garlic, finely chopped**
½	**cup sliced zucchini**
3	**teaspoons chili powder**
1	**teaspoon chopped fresh or ¼ teaspoon dried basil leaves**
¼	**teaspoon salt**
1	**can (15.5 oz) great northern beans, drained, rinsed**
1	**can (14.5 oz) whole peeled tomatoes, undrained**
1	**can (8 oz) tomato sauce**

1 In 4-quart Dutch oven, heat oil over medium-high heat. Add eggplant, onion, bell pepper and garlic; cook, stirring occasionally, until vegetables are crisp-tender.

2 Stir in remaining ingredients, breaking up tomatoes. Heat to boiling; reduce heat. Simmer uncovered 10 minutes, stirring occasionally, until zucchini is tender.

1 SERVING: Calories 290 (Calories from Fat 70); Total Fat 8g (Saturated Fat 1g; Trans Fat 0g); Cholesterol 0mg; Sodium 830mg; Total Carbohydrate 43g (Dietary Fiber 14g); Protein 12g **%Daily Value:** Vitamin A 20%; Vitamin C 40%; Calcium 15%; Iron 30% **Exchanges:** 1 Other Carbohydrate, 6 Vegetable, 1½ Fat **Carbohydrate Choices:** 3

From the Provence region of France, the popular dish of ratatouille is often served as a side dish or appetizer. The flavors typical of this dish include eggplant, zucchini, tomatoes, olive oil and garlic, all of which are found in this savory chili version.

Chili Blanco

Prep Time: 30 minutes • **Start to Finish:** 30 minutes • **4 servings**

1 cup chopped onions (2 medium)

2 cloves garlic, finely chopped

2 cans (15.5 oz each) great northern beans, drained, rinsed

1 can (11 oz) white shoepeg corn, undrained

1 can (4.5 oz) chopped green chiles, undrained

1 extra-large vegetarian vegetable bouillon cube

2 teaspoons ground cumin

¼ teaspoon salt

¼ teaspoon pepper

2½ cups water

¼ cup chopped fresh cilantro

½ cup shredded Monterey Jack cheese (2 oz), if desired

½ cup broken tortilla chips, if desired

1 Spray 3-quart saucepan with cooking spray; heat over medium-high heat. Add onions and garlic; cook and stir 1 minute.

2 Stir in beans, corn, green chiles, bouillon cube, cumin, salt, pepper and water. Heat to boiling. Reduce heat to low; cover and simmer about 15 minutes, stirring occasionally, to blend flavors.

3 Remove from heat. Stir in cilantro. To serve, place 2 tablespoons cheese in each individual soup bowl. Spoon chili over cheese; top with tortilla chips.

1 SERVING: Calories 430 (Calories from Fat 15); Total Fat 1.5g (Saturated Fat 0g; Trans Fat 0g); Cholesterol 0mg; Sodium 800mg; Total Carbohydrate 79g (Dietary Fiber 16g); Protein 24g **%Daily Value:** Vitamin A 4%; Vitamin C 15%; Calcium 25%; Iron 50% **Exchanges:** 1 Starch, 3½ Other Carbohydrate, 2½ Vegetable, 2 Very Lean Meat **Carbohydrate Choices:** 5

If you crave a hot bite, use Monterey Jack cheese with jalapeño peppers! For fun, top with crushed colored tortilla chips.

Chili Verde

Prep Time: 45 minutes • Start to Finish: 45 minutes • **4 servings**

- 2 **small zucchini, cut into ½-inch pieces (2 cups)**
- 1 **large green bell pepper, cut into ½-inch pieces (1½ cups)**
- ½ **lb small red potatoes, cut into ½-inch pieces (1½ cups)**
- 2½ **cups water**
- ½ **cup salsa verde (from 12- to 16-oz jar)**
- 1 **can (15.5 oz) white or yellow hominy, drained, rinsed**
- 1 **extra-large vegetarian vegetable bouillon cube**
- 2 **teaspoons chili powder**
- ¼ **cup sour cream**

1 In 3-quart saucepan, mix all ingredients except sour cream. Heat to boiling over high heat. Reduce heat to low; cover and simmer 15 to 18 minutes, stirring occasionally, until potatoes are tender.

2 Top individual servings with 1 tablespoon sour cream.

1 SERVING: Calories 170 (Calories from Fat 40); Total Fat 4.5g (Saturated Fat 2g; Trans Fat 0g); Cholesterol 10mg; Sodium 600mg; Total Carbohydrate 29g (Dietary Fiber 5g); Protein 4g **%Daily Value:** Vitamin A 15%; Vitamin C 60%; Calcium 6%; Iron 10% **Exchanges:** ½ Starch, 1 Other Carbohydrate, 1½ Vegetable, 1 Fat **Carbohydrate Choices:** 2

This recipe was developed using salsa verde, meaning "green salsa" that's made with tomatillos and green chiles, versus tomato salsas that are made with jalapeños.

The Meatless Pantry

Going vegetarian or meatless? By keeping your pantry, refrigerator and freezer stocked with good choices, you can create great-tasting vegetarian meals or enjoy healthful meatless snacks anytime. Adjust this list based on your family's preferences, and add to it as you discover new meatless foods your family loves!

In the Cupboard

○ Baked snack chips
○ Canned and jarred sauces: chutney, mustards, pasta sauces, pesto, relishes, salsa
○ Canned tomato products: plain, seasoned
○ Canned vegetarian soups and broth
○ Canned vegetarian baked, chili-style and refried beans
○ Canned whole beans: black, butter, cannellini, great northern, kidney, navy, pinto
○ Dark chocolate, soy chocolate
○ Dried fruits: apricots, blueberries, cherries, cranberries, dates, mixed dried fruits, raisins
○ Dried legumes: beans, lentils, split peas, soy beans
○ Grains: barley, bulgur, oats, brown rice, kasha (roasted buckwheat groats), quinoa, wheat berries
○ Nuts: almonds, cashews, peanuts, pecans, soy nuts, sunflower nuts, walnuts
○ Pasta: wheat pasta or nonwheat pasta like lentil, lupini, mung bean, split pea, rice flour
○ Peanut butter and other nut butters
○ Popcorn
○ Prebaked pizza crusts and shells
○ Ready-to-eat fortified whole grain cereals
○ Shelf-stable soymilk
○ Shelf-stable tofu
○ Spices and herbs
○ Texturized soy protein (TSP) flakes and mixes (chili, sloppy joes, soup)
○ Wasabi peas
○ Whole grain crackers, pretzels and crispbread
○ Whole grain loaf breads, pita breads and rolls

In the Fridge

○ Bean dip
○ Cheese dips, salsa con queso
○ Cheeses and soy cheese
○ Flour and corn tortillas
○ Fresh edamame
○ Fresh fruits
○ Fresh herbs
○ Fresh vegetables
○ Fruit and vegetable juices
○ Hummus or baba ghanoush
○ Milk: dairy and soymilk
○ Miso
○ Olives
○ Refrigerated tofu
○ Smoothies: purchased ready-to-drink
○ Tempeh
○ Whipped topping (soy-based)
○ Yogurt and soy yogurt

In the Freezer

○ Cheese and vegetable pizzas
○ Edamame
○ Fruit and vegetable juice concentrates
○ Frozen fruits
○ Meat substitutes: soy-protein burgers, "chicken" patties and nuggets, hot dogs, sausages, vegetable burgers
○ Soy desserts (dairy free)
○ Vegetables
○ Whole grain flours

Vegetarian Substitutions

Here is a quick at-a-glance substitution guide for replacing meat, poultry, fish, seafood and animal products with a vegetarian option. Check the "Vegetarian Foods Glossary" on page 278 for more information on vegetarian ingredients.

FOR:	SUBSTITUTE:
Meat, poultry, fish or seafood	Cheese, eggs, legumes, mushrooms, nut butters (including almond, cashew, peanut, sesame, walnut), nuts, seeds, seitan, soy-protein products, tempeh, tofu
Meat, poultry, fish or seafood broth	Fruit juices, miso, vegetable broth and juices, wine, water
Cheese	Rice cheese, soy cheese
Eggs	Egg products, tofu
Milk	Nut milk, rice milk, soymilk
Honey	Agave nectar, barley malt syrup, brown rice syrup, real maple syrup
Gelatin	Agar-agar, arrowroot, unflavored gel product (from local natural food stores or online)

All About Soy

Soy products are everywhere! It's no wonder—the mild soy flavor makes them easily adaptable to other foods and flavors. Many soy products are great meat replacements because they are an excellent source of dietary protein, including all the amino acids. Soy has been a staple of Asian diets for thousands of years. Now one of our nation's largest crops, soybeans are being used in a myriad of ways with great enthusiasm. Read on for information on the benefits of soy and the variety of soy products.

Meat substitutes, or soy-protein products, have come a long way in taste, texture and variety. Look for products in these categories: breakfast, burgers, chicken, ground, hot dogs, pepperoni, sausages and entrées. Some soy-protein products may contain small amounts of cheese, dairy or egg products. Choose from frozen, canned and dried varieties.

Miso is a salty, rich condiment used commonly in Japanese cooking as a soup or to flavor other foods such as sauces, dressings and marinades.

Soy cheese is made from soymilk or tofu. It is available in many flavors including mozzarella, Cheddar and pepper Jack. Soy cheese can be purchased presliced, shredded or in blocks. Soy Parmesan, cream cheese and sour cream alternatives are also available.

Soy

Soy, unlike most plant foods, is a good source of high-quality protein. That makes soy a great substitute for animal protein. Most soy foods, like soymilk and tofu, are fortified with calcium as well. Diets low in saturated fat and cholesterol that include 25 grams of soy protein a day may reduce the risk of heart disease. Data on other potential benefits of soy are inconsistent, but studies continue to evaluate its roles in the diet.

Soy dairy-free frozen desserts often use soymilk to replace dairy products for products similar to ice cream.

Soymilk is made by pressing ground cooked soybeans. It is higher in protein than cow's milk. Because it's a nondairy product, it's a common substitute used by those with milk allergies. It is found in aseptic containers (nonrefrigerated) or in the dairy case. Flavored varieties, like vanilla and chocolate, are available.

Soy yogurt is made from cultured soymilk and is available in many flavors. Soy yogurt is lactose-free and cholesterol-free.

Whole soybeans are available raw, dried, as roasted nuts or nut butters and canned. Look for products in your supermarket, natural foods stores or online.

Dried soybeans are most commonly yellow soybeans but there are black and brown varieties as well. Use in place of dried beans, or soak to roast for snacks.

Edamame are soybeans harvested at a fresh green stage, before they are completely mature, and sold in their fuzzy green pods or shelled. Fresh edamame is available spring through fall in raw and ready-to-eat forms at co-ops, natural foods stores or large supermarkets. They're also available frozen in boxes or bags. Serve as a snack or add to main dishes or salads.

Roasted soybeans or soynuts are whole soybeans roasted in oil or dry roasted.

Soynut butter is made from roasted whole soybeans, soy oil and other ingredients. It contains significantly less fat than peanut butter.

Tempeh is made from fermented soybeans formed into chunky cakes that sometimes include grains. Tempeh has a firm, chewy texture with a mild smoky or nutty flavor. Look for cream-colored cakes with a few darker spots. As tempeh ages, the flavor becomes stronger and more spots appear. Do not use if it has many dark spots or smells like ammonia. It is sold raw, either flavored or unflavored, and ready to cook in the refrigerated or freezer case. Typically marinated, try it sautéed or grilled, or add it to soups, stews, casseroles and chili.

Soy crumbles, texturized soy protein (also known as TSP), is made from fat-free soy flour that has been compressed and processed into chunks, flakes or granules that require rehydration. It has a crumbled texture similar to ground beef and can replace it in some recipes. Chunk-size pieces also are available to replace stew meat.

Tofu is also known as soybean curd or bean curd. Soybeans are soaked, cooked, ground and then mixed with a curdling ingredient. The resulting curds are drained and pressed into cakes. Mildly flavored, it easily absorbs the flavors of the herbs, spices and foods it is cooked with. Look for tofu in the produce, dairy, deli or natural foods section of the supermarket in aseptic shelf-stable packages or water-packed in the refrigerator case of your supermarket or food co-op stores.

Extra-firm and firm tofu is solid and dense and works well for stir-frying, grilling, baking casseroles, deep-frying or any dish where you want to keep the shape of the tofu.

Soft tofu can be used in recipes like soup, chili and meat loaf, and in cream pie fillings and puddings.

Silken tofu has a creamy, custardlike texture that can be used in sauces, dips, beverages and desserts, and in any blended or pureed dishes.

Flavored tofu is packaged in a marinade to give it a specific flavor, and often the tofu is baked or broiled.

Reduced-fat or lite tofu, having a texture similar to soft tofu, is available for those watching fat grams. Use it in the same type of recipes as soft tofu.

Whipped toppings (soy based) are similar to other nondairy whipped toppings in a spray can, but are made with soy oil. Look for soy whipped toppings in the dairy case of your health food store or online.

Vegetarian Foods Glossary

With the growing interest in vegetarian foods, more new and unfamiliar ingredients are popping up in the supermarket, in articles about food and on restaurant menus. Here's the 411 on the most popular ingredients and foods you'll want to know about for meatless cooking:

Agar-Agar: A thickening agent made from dried sea vegetables. It is often used instead of unflavored gelatin, which is made from animal products.

Agave Nectar: Made from the sap of agave plants, it is a great substitute for honey. Vegans like it because it's completely plant based. Lighter varieties have a milder flavor; darker varieties have a more pronounced flavor.

Arrowroot: A powdery starch that comes from the tropical root of the same name. It's a substitute for cornstarch.

Barley Malt Syrup (Malted Barley Syrup): A dark, thick sweetener made from sprouted whole barley. It has a mild caramel flavor and is not as sweet as sugar or honey. It can be used instead of honey or molasses in most baked goods.

Brown Rice Syrup: A sweetener made from adding sprouted dried barley or barley enzymes to cooked rice and letting it ferment until it forms sugars. It has a mild flavor that's less sweet than sugar.

Egg Replacer: A cholesterol-free product made from starches and leavening ingredients that is similar to fresh eggs. This is different from cholesterol-free egg substitute products, which are made with egg whites.

Falafel: Spiced patties or balls made from chickpeas. It is a delicious meatless option on its own or in sandwiches (typically served in pitas), and is usually served with a flavorful sauce.

Flaxseed: Dark brown seeds that are used whole or ground into a powder (with a coffee grinder) to add to smoothies, baked goods or meat mixtures. Store it in the refrigerator to keep it from becoming rancid.

Kudzu: A powdery starch that comes from the root of the same name and can be used to thicken soups, sauces and puddings.

Meat Substitutes: Made from soybeans, they come in many different forms: burgers, sausages, crumbles, hot dogs, ready-made meal mixes (such as chili) and frozen dinners. For more information, see "All About Soy," pages 276 to 277.

Miso: A salty, thick, fermented paste made from aged soybeans and sometimes grains such as barley or rice. Ranging in color from yellow to red to brown, this paste is primarily used as a flavoring ingredient instead of chicken or beef granules.

Nori: Seaweed that has been dried in paper-thin sheets. Generally, it is used for wrapping sushi and rice balls.

Nutritional Yeast (Brewer's Yeast): This yeast has no leavening power and is used in making beer. Its flavor is a combination of meaty, cheesy and nutty. It can be added to foods in small amounts to boost B vitamin intake.

Seitan: A versatile meat substitute made by combining whole wheat flour and water. After the dough is mixed, it is repeatedly kneaded and rinsed while immersed in water to remove all of its starch. The resulting dough is then simmered in vegetable stock. You can make your own seitan or buy it in many forms.

Soy Products: See "All About Soy," pages 276 to 277.

Tahini: Also known as sesame seed paste, this Middle Eastern classic is made from ground raw or toasted sesame seed and is similar in texture to peanut butter. It's a key ingredient in hummus, a Middle Eastern dip of pureed garbanzo beans.

Tamari: A soybean product very similar in flavor to soy sauce, but more subtle and a little bit thicker.

Tofu: See "All About Soy," pages 276 to 277.

Vegetarian Vegetable Bouillon Cubes: Made from vegetables and used instead of chicken or beef bouillon cubes.

Metric Conversion Guide

Volume

U.S. UNITS	CANADIAN METRIC	AUSTRALIAN METRIC
¼ teaspoon	1 mL	1 ml
½ teaspoon	2 mL	2 ml
1 teaspoon	5 mL	5 ml
1 tablespoon	15 mL	20 ml
¼ cup	50 mL	60 ml
⅓ cup	75 mL	80 ml
½ cup	125 mL	125 ml
⅔ cup	150 mL	170 ml
¾ cup	175 mL	190 ml
1 cup	250 mL	250 ml
1 quart	1 liter	1 liter
1½ quarts	1.5 liters	1.5 liters
2 quarts	2 liters	2 liters
2½ quarts	2.5 liters	2.5 liters
3 quarts	3 liters	3 liters
4 quarts	4 liters	4 liters

Weight

U.S. UNITS	CANADIAN METRIC	AUSTRALIAN METRIC
1 ounce	30 grams	30 grams
2 ounces	55 grams	60 grams
3 ounces	85 grams	90 grams
4 ounces (¼ pound)	115 grams	125 grams
8 ounces (½ pound)	225 grams	225 grams
16 ounces (1 pound)	455 grams	500 grams
1 pound	455 grams	0.5 kilogram

Note: The recipes in this cookbook have not been developed or tested using metric measures. When converting recipes to metric, some variations in quality may be noted.

Measurements

INCHES	CENTIMETERS
1	2.5
2	5.0
3	7.5
4	10.0
5	12.5
6	15.0
7	17.5
8	20.5
9	23.0
10	25.5
11	28.0
12	30.5
13	33.0

Temperatures

FAHRENHEIT	CELSIUS
32°	0°
212°	100°
250°	120°
275°	140°
300°	150°
325°	160°
350°	180°
375°	190°
400°	200°
425°	220°
450°	230°
475°	240°
500°	260°

Index

Note: Page numbers in *italics* indicate illustrations.

Recipe Testing and Calculating Nutrition Information

RECIPE TESTING:

- Large eggs and 2% milk were used unless otherwise indicated.

- Fat-free, low-fat, low-sodium or lite products were not used unless indicated.

- No nonstick cookware and bakeware were used unless otherwise indicated. No dark-colored, black or insulated bakeware was used.

- When a pan is specified, a metal pan was used; a baking dish or pie plate means ovenproof glass was used.

- An electric hand mixer was used for mixing only when mixer speeds are specified.

CALCULATING NUTRITION:

- The first ingredient was used wherever a choice is given, such as ⅓ cup sour cream or plain yogurt.

- The first amount was used wherever a range is given, such as 3- to 3½-pound whole chicken.

- The first serving number was used wherever a range is given, such as 4 to 6 servings.

- "If desired" ingredients were not included.

- Only the amount of a marinade or frying oil that is absorbed was included.

RECOMMENDED INTAKE FOR A DAILY DIET OF 2,000 CALORIES AS SET BY THE FOOD AND DRUG ADMINISTRATION

Total Fat	Less than 65g
Saturated Fat	Less than 20g
Cholesterol	Less than 300mg
Sodium	Less than 2,400mg
Total Carbohydrate	300g
Dietary Fiber	25g

Complete your cookbook library with these *Betty Crocker* titles

Betty Crocker Baking for Today

Betty Crocker Basics

Betty Crocker's Best Bread Machine Cookbook

Betty Crocker The Big Book of Cupcakes

Betty Crocker The Big Book of Slow Cooker, Casseroles & More

Betty Crocker's Bisquick® Cookbook

Betty Crocker Bisquick® II Cookbook

Betty Crocker Bisquick® Impossibly Easy Pies

Betty Crocker Bisquick to the Rescue

Betty Crocker Christmas Cookbook

Betty Crocker's Cook Book for Boys and Girls

Betty Crocker's Cook It Quick

Betty Crocker Cookbook, 11th Edition
The **BIG RED** *Cookbook*®

Betty Crocker Cookbook, Bridal Edition

Betty Crocker's Cookie Book

Betty Crocker's Cooking Basics

Betty Crocker's Cooking for Two

Betty Crocker's Cooky Book, Facsimile Edition

Betty Crocker Country Cooking

Betty Crocker Decorating Cakes and Cupcakes

Betty Crocker's Diabetes Cookbook

Betty Crocker Easy Everyday Vegetarian

Betty Crocker's Easy Slow Cooker Dinners

Betty Crocker's Eat and Lose Weight

Betty Crocker's Entertaining Basics

Betty Crocker 4-Ingredient Dinners

Betty Crocker Fix-with-a-Mix Desserts

Betty Crocker Grilling Made Easy

Betty Crocker Healthy Heart Cookbook

Betty Crocker's Indian Home Cooking

Betty Crocker's Italian Cooking

Betty Crocker's Kids Cook!

Betty Crocker's Living with Cancer Cookbook

Betty Crocker Low-Carb Lifestyle Cookbook

Betty Crocker's Low-Fat, Low-Cholesterol Cooking Today

Betty Crocker Money Saving Meals

Betty Crocker More Slow Cooker Recipes

Betty Crocker's New Cake Decorating

Betty Crocker One-Dish Meals

Betty Crocker's Picture Cook Book, Facsimile Edition

Betty Crocker's Quick & Easy Cookbook

Betty Crocker's Slow Cooker Cookbook

Betty Crocker 300 Calorie Cookbook

Betty Crocker's Ultimate Cake Mix Cookbook

Betty Crocker's Vegetarian Cooking

Betty Crocker Why It Works